The Evolution of an Ordinary Leader

K.C. Hildreth

Dedication

To my wife. Your love and support make everything possible.

Acknowledgments

Special thanks to my clients, friends and family. I am very grateful for your unswerving encouragement and support.

The Journey

I see,
I see now

What was always there,
always there

But obscured by limitations
I placed before myself.

It was only as I walked,
each step, one foot

In front of the other,
one step after another

That the masks began to fall away,
the ideas of intellect

Meant to hide, to protect
dissolved

Dissolved in my heart
and I finally could see again.

I saw myself.
I saw the other.

I saw the truth
and dropped the illusion.

I saw the truth
and the illusion dropped.

Neha H. Vyas

"Do not follow where the path may lead. Go instead where there is no path and leave a trail."
Ralph Waldo Emerson

"Leaders instill in their people a hope for success and a belief in themselves. Positive leaders empower people to accomplish their goals."
Unknown

"Leadership and learning are indispensable to each other."
John F. Kennedy

Other books by K.C. Hildreth

Supercharge Your Startup!

Creating a Powerful Vision and Business Plan in 5 Easy Steps

Living Into Your Highest Potential

3 Key Steps to Personal Growth

Fund Your Dreams!

Proven Tools for Pitching Investors

The Power of You

Understanding and Unleashing the Incredible Potential Within

Contents

Introduction

I write this introduction on the day before my 52nd birthday. It seems like only yesterday that I was turning 18 and wondering what I would be doing at the ripe old age of 35! I had no idea that even at age 35 I would just be *starting* my journey of learning and development…a process that continues to this day.

This book is the culmination of over 50 years of work, learning and a personal search for happiness and productivity. My 'career' is almost bizarre in it's sheer variety. Since 1985, when I graduated from college, I have worked on Wall Street and Capitol Hill, founded or co-founded 8 different companies, completed 4 advanced degrees, and worked as a consultant to Fortune 50 companies. Over the most recent 10 years I have spent thousands of hours coaching leaders and executives on personal and professional development. During this time I've read hundreds of books on subjects ranging from physics and biology to psychology, spirituality and community development.

As I meandered through my professional life I have worked for privately held companies, charity groups and large multination organizations, and have held positions from 'assistant water-boy' to CTO and CEO. My industry experience includes areas as diverse as banking and telecommunications, as well as technology, hospitality and entertainment. Lest you think I am bragging, I am not: For the longest time I actually felt quite insecure about being 'a jack of all trades', with little mastery in any one thing.

Only in the past few years did I realize that my path has turned out to be quite purposeful. By experiencing so many different industries, roles, company cultures and situations I have been afforded a "50,000 foot view" of the social world we call 'work'. I have observed great leaders, and suffered through abysmal cultures. I have experimented with my own leadership style, and worked with others on theirs. The resulting insights are what make up this book.

The bottom line is this: I have come to believe that our human societies are reaching a plateau of productivity that can only be surpassed if we take a completely new look at the way we relate to 'work', both in how we see ourselves and how we interact with others. Fear-and-pressure based management is simply not working anymore, and it is incumbent upon all of us to look deeply inside ourselves to find a better way.

This book is a story of an executive who goes on a personal search for meaning and leadership excellence. His process is the combination of my own 50 years of self-exploration and the experiences of countless others that I have both worked with and coached. The material is dense by design. I am trying to convey to you that which took me (and others) literally tens of thousands of hours to understand, so be patient if you find yourself a bit bored by, say, a dialogue on the nature of quantum biology. Just keep pushing through until you find something that resonates.

I chose a man as the main character because I had to choose a gender and was more able to relate to the male experience. I do not doubt that a woman will read this differently than I might, and I believe that will add value to the discussion. After coaching many female executives, I have found that women generally 'get' these ideas somewhat more easily and at a level that is more 'heart' than 'brain' centered. No matter what your gender, however, the concepts are universal and as old as time. Even so, do not simply believe what I have written. Each person must find his or her own truth, and this is a version of my own. I encourage you to challenge, to seek, and to *think*.

Some of the topics in this story might feel controversial or unbelievable. For example, I debated quite a bit about including references to God. On the one hand I did not want to alienate those who find God irrelevant, and yet neither did I want to offend those who have a very strict notion about who, or what, God is. I myself came from a place of agnosticism. But as I began to ponder the deeper nature of things, the question begged an answer. I have come to believe that there is a God, but I absolutely do not want to foist that position upon you.

Overall, my deepest wish is for you to read this book with an open mind, consider what it says, and perhaps learn something from it. If it prompts further exploration, I will feel that my purpose has been achieved. If it triggers in you something deeper, perhaps a renewed sense of meaning or happiness, then my joy will be complete.

I wrote this as a service project...to share what I had learned over the past 50 years of inefficient exploration in the hope that you might save yourself the time. I believe that if you can go deeply inside yourself and find your Truth, you (and our society) can reach unimaginable levels of happiness and productivity. This book is meant to help you in that quest.

Sincerely,
K.C.
September 2015

Chapter One

As Michael Benson walked out into the hospital parking lot, he could not help but shake his head at the irony of it all. Just that morning he had been thinking that things couldn't possibly get worse. And now his Dad. What in the world have I done to deserve this, he thought, not without a twinge of embarrassment at his self-centeredness. His father had told him so casually. As if he were going to take a trip, or buy a car. "I am going to die within 3 months, and there is nothing I can do about it." My God. Michael didn't even know his father was ill! How in the world could he have kept something so important so quiet!?

The thoughts were swirling around in Michael's head. Part of him wanted to yell at his father, to tell him that it was not fair that he was doing this to him. Another part felt bad for his Dad because he knew that he was, in his own terms, "the rock", and that he bore the progression of this illness alone. Michael's Mom had passed away many years since, and he assumed that his fath er was okay alone. What did I miss? Michael thought. He had visited once every month or so, played golf with his Dad a couple of times a year, but he had not really seen anything special. Sure, his Dad sometimes grunted when he got out of the car… but that was part of aging, right?

On top of a vague feeling of guilt came another wave of thoughts centered around one question: "How am I supposed to deal with all of this?" Just the day before Michael's wife had told him she was unhappy and was considering a divorce, and the CEO had come down on him for missing his numbers during the semi-annual performance review. Michael knew the implications: Get his life in order or find himself alone, jobless, and drowning in legal bills. How cynical is *that*, Michael thought. And now his Dad is dying. More thoughts flashing: "Well at least I will have an inheritance…maybe I can quit my job and be happy". Then panic "Dad spent a lot of money recently, what if there is nothing left?" Then remorse "How can I think like this? This is *horrible*!" His mind seemed to be spinning out of control.

Michael loved his wife dearly, but knew this was coming. A few months earlier she had shocked Michael by screaming during an argument. She *never* screamed. Maria Fletcher Benson was the most composed woman he knew…and yet the guttural, impotent wail that came out was something almost other-worldly. He knew then that this was serious. And it was what she said just before the scream that really chilled him. She said "You are turning into your father!" When Michael heard this he simply reverted to his standard approach to emotional conflict: He walked out. Isn't this ironic, he thought. My wife thinks I am turning into Dad, and now my Dad is dying. If she divorces me and my Dad is dead…boy will she feel guilty, thought the victim within him.

Not that she wasn't right to be angry. Michael's Dad, Roy Benson, was not, nor had he ever been, a loving man. He was successful and powerful and tough and fair and all that, but warm and kind were words he would never use to describe him. If Maria thinks that I am becoming my Dad, Michael thought, well, I'd be pissed too. And in his heart of hearts he knew there was truth to this. Michael had been leaving early, working late and going into the office on weekends. When he did come home he spent a good portion of his time either trying to catch up on emails or checking his iPhone surreptitiously under the table. In many ways he was only "home" when he was asleep…a fitful 6 hours a day.

His two kids, Thomas and Lisa, hardly knew him anymore. Lisa had broken his heart a few weeks earlier when she asked "Daddy, what if I brought my schoolwork to your office? That way we could both work and I could see you more!" She had said it with such problem-solving innocence that he could not help but to flash back to his own childhood when his father seemed to drift in and out of the house like an apparition. An obligatory pat on the head, a scotch and soda, a distracted dinner, and into the office. How Michael had wanted to go into his father's office and sit on his lap…even if just for a moment. But that was unthinkable.

Have I re-created this?, Michael thought as he got into his car. Am I turning into my father? "Oh God, what if Maria is right?", he said to himself in a shrill, panicky voice. We are never intimate anymore. I have not kissed her in…I don't even know since when. We have sex maybe once a month, and that is purely by plan. I don't share anything anymore. We sit and exchange pleasantries like we are two people sitting on a bus. I know more about my co-workers than I do about her. Is this how my Dad was?

Michael thought back and realized that he never did see his mom and dad kiss. Affection was a nicety in his childhood house. It was simply inefficient and un-businesslike. He had always known that some families had loving relationships, but he had never experienced that himself. The only emotion he had ever seen was anger, and that was expressed in an almost unbelievable rage followed by eerie silence. It got to the point that Michael really didn't know how to cope with the uncertainty of it all. He felt so alone…it was a God-send that he had brothers and sisters. They at least could commiserate on their mutual loneliness. Now it was as if he had created the very thing he found so painful.

But what do they expect me to do?!, Michael angrily thought. I have a CEO who is in my office *every fucking day* asking me how I am doing. I have a board that wants results and employees who want bonuses. *Every bloody quarter* I have to sweat my numbers so that the "The Street" will issue a favorable opinion on our stock. Everybody either wants something from me or is bitching at me. "I can't take this!!" he screamed and pounded the steering wheel. Fantasies of changing his name, running away and spending the rest of his life in an island beach bar started to run through his head.

So, Dad, you found a way to not let me do what I wanted…again, he thought. Now that you are dying I have to stick with it all, grin and bear it, be the good son. He remembered his Dad's admonition 20 years earlier. "Son, you are supposed to hate your job. That is what hobbies are for" he had said. Michael had wanted to be an archaeologist, but his dad had put his foot down and said that if he was going to go to college, then it had to be business. Nothing "frivolous" like a "social science meant for the undirected children of un-ambitious parents". So Michael had relegated himself to reading National Geographic and watching nature shows. *What a bastard*, Michael thought. My life is turning to shit, and he gets to check out with a quick "I am dying son" and a slap on the shoulder. *What about me? Did you think about me?!* No wonder Mom checked out when she did. She could not take the silent judgment, the endless love-less lonely nights. "Life is a forced march", he used to say.

"You trained me well, Pops!" Michael said as he started his car.

Chapter Two

Pulling into his office parking lot Michael reflexively looked to see if his CEO was there. For some reason it seemed like it mattered, whether or not Armand was in the building or not. Armand Vicoste was a CEO that liked to manage directly, and his "direction" was very stressful for Michael. It wasn't that he feared the man, he simply felt more comfortable when he wasn't there. And in this case, mercifully, Armand's car was not in its designated spot.

As Michael walked up the stairs he kept flashing back to what his father had told him this morning. It seemed like his mind was trying to digest something inedible, something so foreign that it did not go through the normal cognitive pathways. His father was dying. And *I am going to work?* Michael thought. A flash of unfairness hit him again. What type of world is this? I am expected to be at work and perform to a high standard as if none of this is going on.

Sure, Armand will be sympathetic, Michael knew that. He will ask me how things are going and if he can do anything. Then he will pause uncomfortably and ask about the most recent production and sales numbers. It never failed. It seemed like personal issues in the office were a distraction, sort of like having mud on your shoes in an otherwise clean house. *So unfortunate to be human*, thought Michael sarcastically. Well, I guess my Dad was right. We are not supposed to like our jobs. "Another day another dollar" was his refrain.

Michael swung around his desk and flipped open his laptop. As the computer re-awakened with its familiar whirring and clicking, Michael began to clean up the chaos that was his desk. *God knows I could use an assistant*, Michael thought, as he put reimbursement requests, purchase orders, post-its, project plans and sales forecasts into their respective piles.

As he worked, he slowly became aware that there was a strange silence in the direction of his computer. Glancing at the screen he saw what he always half expected to see...a partially populated desktop and a frozen cursor. "Damn it", Michael cursed under his breath, "sometimes I want to throw this piece of shit out of the window." And the urge was real. He felt an overpowering desire to put his laptop over his head and throw it through the window. The rage that bubbled up inside frightened Michael...yet somehow felt strangely satisfying. *Boy, would that create a stir*, Michael sarcastically thought to himself. *Shake this fucking place up a bit.*

The truth was that Michael secretly loathed the people in the office. Ever since he had become the SVP in charge of operations and sales it seemed like people were becoming more unreal. Some, mainly his former peers, were openly jealous and incredulous that he had gotten the role. Others, like his direct reports, either kissed his ass openly or pretended to be loyal while at the same time talking shit behind his back. And now his boss, Armand, spent a good portion of his day crawling up Michael's ass. *There is not a single person I would call "a friend" in this crazy joint*, Michael sadly thought.

But there is Yoda, Michael remembered as he grabbed his laptop and headed down the hall. Chris Falling, aka "Yoda", was the head of the internal IT group and was as close to a friend as Michael had at the company. Michael liked Chris because of his intelligence, attitude and the fact that he was always willing to have an interesting conversation. Yoda had also taken an interesting and non-traditional path, which intrigued Michael. Christopher Lee Falling had graduated from MIT at age 16 with a degree in Software Technology. By age 20 he had gotten a doctorate in Systems Design at the University of Chicago, had designed and written most of the kernel for a major release of desktop software, and to top it all off he had started a small company that sold software objects to web-designers. It was rumored that he had an IQ of 160, but Yoda always demurred when needled about that.

This was not the most interesting thing about Yoda, however. Strangely, after all this success, he had decided to check out and become an internal systems manager for Michael's company. When Michael asked him why, after all this success, he was here (not saying what he thought: *Doing this shitty work*), he replied in his cryptic faux Yoda voice, "Have not the constitution for stressful work, Yoda does"…and left it at that.

And nobody had the guts to push him any further, because the entire company knew what a jewel they had in this guy. The in-house software developers practically followed Yoda around like acolytes waiting for a blessing. Whenever they had a seemingly intractable problem with their code they would stop by his office and, invariably, Yoda would not only solve the problem but sketch out a larger solution that would completely revolutionize what they were doing. They paid him the highest respect when they would exclaim, "You don't understand dude! He *is* Yoda! *He really is.* Or maybe Neo…at least Morpheus!"

For Michael, Yoda was a good conversationalist. Michael loved to read "Scientific American" and "Popular Science", and talking to Chris Falling was like talking to a walking science library. Given that his laptop crashed every other day, Michael got a lot of time to catch up on the latest Science news. *I guess there is at least one upside to crappy software*, Michael laughed to himself.

"What's up, Yoda?", Michael asked as he rounded the corner to Chris's office.

Chris did not look up from the disassembled server on his desk. "My blood pressure, dude," he mumbled.

"Well, then I am going to add another few points to that number," Michael said as he tossed his laptop onto Chris's desk.

Chris grunted. He was getting familiar with Michael's "software issues". "Can't you take this over to Rajiv?" he protested. "I'm in the middle of something."

"No, " Michael replied (there were times when pulling rank had its privileges). "I want you to work on it. Besides, you are so much fun to talk to!" Michael smiled his warmest "boss smile".

Chris sighed and grabbed that laptop, flipped it over, removed the battery and began his normal system boot override routine.

"What's new in your life?" he asked distractedly.

"You don't want to know," Michael sighed.

"That bad?" Chris continued.

"Well, personal life is complete shit. Work life is complete crap. I guess that leaves nothing but shit and crap," Michael replied as he sat down in the Hermann Miller chair across from Chris's desk.

"Armand is all over my ass to make the numbers this quarter, and my team just can't seem to work any harder. I'm not sure if they can't or they won't, but we just keep hitting this ceiling and can't seem to break through." Michael said as he pushed his hands in the air. "I have talented people…it's just that we have this burst of performance and then seem to "top out" at some point. I don't know how we are going to keep growing the numbers unless we acquire another company. I'm at my wit's end!"

Chris sat back in his chair and smiled his "Yoda smile", which made him look more like a bearded walrus than the Star-Wars character. "An energy problem, you have," he said cryptically.

"Oh God, please don't talk in Yoda-speak about this. I may have to fly across this room and go Jedi on your ass" Michael said half jokingly. "I am way too stressed out today."

Chris nodded. "I get it," he said. "But I'm serious. This sounds like an energy issue more than anything."

"Ok, I'll bite. What do you mean?"

"Well, think of it this way. There is enough energy in this space…"

with his hands he drew in the air a box about 1 meter in size, "...to power the entire world for one year."

Michael leaned forward a bit. "Yeah, I get that there's a lot of energy in atoms. But why does this matter for me?"

"Well," Chris smiled, "Our challenge as human beings has always been accessing that energy, right? I mean, we've spent a great deal of our existence trying to figure out how to pull this energy out of things. Early humans, and all animals for that matter, did this through eating. Eating is really just taking energy from the sun in a form that living beings can use."

"I don't follow," Michael said.

"Yeah, the way it works is that energy from the sun in the form of electrons and photons - they are interchangeable you know - hits the leaves of plants and is converted, using molecules from the air and soil, into carbohydrates, proteins, enzymes and fibers that animals can ingest. As humans, we either eat the plants directly or we eat the animal that ate the plant. Either way, we have just 'eaten the sun'!" Chris said as he opened his arms and looked up in the air.

"One of the things that differentiates man from animals, however, is our ability to access energy in more and different ways" Chris continued. "For instance, when man first discovered fire, we were essentially releasing the energy locked up in wood, oil, gas or other 'burnable' substances. Then, through the scientific method, we learned how to release chemical energy and even later nuclear energy. They're all ways to access energy that already exist inside of atoms. We have continued to learn better and more efficient ways to get at that energy."

Yoda was on a roll, and Michael was getting interested...though he could not quite see the point.

"And so you are probably thinking 'so what?'" Chris said reading Michael's mind.

"Well, the point is that there has never been an 'energy shortage', but simply a lack of understanding around how to gain access to the energy that already is! It's like we have a cherry tree in front of us but no ladder to get at the cherries. And I don't necessarily mean energy in the sense of simple electricity or gas or nuclear or whatever. I mean energy in the broadest sense...the energy to create and modify matter." Chris said as he picked up Michael's now-fixed laptop.

"Whoa, whoa, whoa!" Michael exclaimed. "Now you have really lost me. Energy creating matter? You've been watching way too much Star-Trek, my friend!"

Chris laughed. "Not in the way you're thinking, but yes energy creates matter." "OK," Chris pushed his chair back and got up to the whiteboard behind his desk, "let's do a quick nuclear and quantum physics refresher."

At times like this Michael had the feeling he was being taunted. A 'refresher'?! He felt like he was in a dream where he had missed the classes all semester and was heading into the final.

Chris laughed even harder. "Don't get freaked out! I promise, this is easy to understand. First, let's look at how we as humans figured out how to get more and more energy out of things. It really has to do with our ability to see smaller and smaller things. At our level of perception, for instance, we can only sense what we can see, feel, smell, etc, with our eyes, hands, noses, right? Well, at that level, we could experiment with all sorts of things like wood, coal, and oil and see that it had energy, that it could produce fire.

"But as we developed methods to see smaller and smaller things, through microscopes and such, we were able to 'drill down' and see that there were things called cells, then molecules, then atoms, then sub-atomic particles like electrons and quarks and bosons and...well that's as far as physicists have gotten to date. The super-colliders that cost billions of dollars are all dedicated to seeing what is smaller than the smallest things we know so far. The scientists using these colliders are like little kids with their toys: They just keep smashing them into smaller and smaller pieces so they can see what's in there. Are you following me so far?"

"I think so. Why does everyone claim quantum physics is so complicated then?" Michael asked.

"Great question." Chris responded. "That's because at a certain level of 'smallness', at the level of the atom in this case, things start to look really, really strange. The classical Newtonian world of gravity, momentum, motion, etc., that makes our surroundings seem rational does not apply to this world. It seems that the 'sub atomic' world (the level of the atom and lower) behaves by a set of rules that are completely out of whack with our understanding of the way things are. And this, my friend, has thrown the entire scientific establishment into a conundrum."

"But isn't this all normal science? The same thing physicists have been doing since Copernicus and Newton?" Michael asked.

Chris gave a knowing smile. "It should be," he said, "but there is a crisis in Camelot. You see, for 300 years, exactly since Copernicus and Newton, scientists believed that the universe was predictable and machinelike…sort of like a clock. According to this theory, everything in the universe was an object and each object acted upon other objects with measurable, calculable and predictable force. The result, in this view, is an incredibly complex machine that can be understood *completely* if only we could gather enough information to see how each of the parts works. It's called 'reductionist thinking' because if we can reduce the whole into the sum of its parts, and understand each part, then we can understand and, more importantly, control, the "machine" to our advantage."

"And this has worked quite well hasn't it?" Michael exclaimed. "I mean, look at the advances that man has made over those 300 years!"

"Absolutely!" Chris continued. "But now scientists are faced with the same dilemma they faced those many years ago. From the years 1500 to 1700, these 'new scientists' found themselves often at odds with the prevailing thinking of the church. The classic example is Copernicus and the motion of the planets around the sun. Until that time, the church maintained that the earth was the center of the universe. The new information was threatening to them."

Chris sat back down and sighed. "Ironically, but not surprisingly, this same conflict is being played out today between scientists because the old 'universe as machine' argument is not playing out at the sub-atomic level. Now we have tension between the 'classical physicists' and the 'new physics' – a tension which hasn't been resolved yet. Personally, I believe it's all part of the ongoing evolution of scientific thought."

"Okay, okay, this is all interesting," said Michael, looking at his watch, "but what about quantum or 'new' physics is so different and, more importantly, how does this connect to my 'issue with energy'?"

"Yes, I guess I should get back on track here," Chris said looking around. "We are at work after all?!

"Well, here's the deal. What's happening at the smallest level of existence, or at least the smallest that we know of today, is nothing short of freaky. First, if you were to put yourself at the size of an atom and look around, you would see nothing but shimmering energy. Atoms, to our eyes, are 99.999% space. The only reason we can feel material objects is because they are vibrating so fast that they act like solid masses, like a propeller on an airplane.

"Second, particles at this level are both matter (solid) and light (wavelike). It is not that they are either matter or light…they are both. They exist in a kind of 'dual state' until they solidify into something we would recognize, which I will talk about in a second.

"The third freaky thing is that particles that have been in contact with each other, *stay in contact with each other when separated.* As an example, take two baseballs in our classical world. If I put them together very tightly and turned one, the other would turn in the opposite way, right? Then if I separated them and turned one, nothing would happen because they are separate, right? Well at the sub-atomic level *they stay connected.* No matter how far apart they are, if I were to turn one particle,

26

the other would turn as well. This cannot be explained using classical physics. Something is keeping these particles connected, and the communication between them is faster than the speed of light…which is theoretically impossible according to the old models."

"Hmm, so that means that something at the 'ground level' is keeping everything in contact," Michael finished.

"Precisely, and that's led to theories that there's some kind of field, some call it the 'Zero Point Field', that underlies and connects everything in the universe instantaneously. This field is theorized to be the pure energetic source of everything and brings all matter into existence."

"But how does matter come into existence, then, if everything is energy?" Michael was getting excited because this was all making sense. Following along with Yoda was an accomplishment in and by itself!

"And that's the last, and by far, the most revolutionary and potentially threatening thing we have talked about. You see, not only is the base level universe made up of pure energy, which then transmutes into both light and matter (Einstein's equation was brilliant because it was so simple: $E(Energy) = M(Matter)$ times C (Light) squared), but it also contains information, which is theoretically stored in the Zero Point Field."

"OK, now I'm lost again. Information? What does that mean?" Michael said in mock frustration.

"Information in the universe," Chris continued, "simply means that there is some 'in-forming' going on. Think about it this way: During the moments after the big bang, there was nothing but a soup of energy, but very quickly elementary particles began to form. They then became atoms, then molecules, then compounds then rocks, then planets, etcetera, until we come to where we are today…complex life. So, along the way there has to have been some sort of guide, some information to indicate what things should form to be. Call it a blue-print, a 'law', whatever. Things did not form randomly! Even classical physicists have said that if the universal laws were any different by even a hair the universe would fly apart. We would not exist."

"No way. You are not talking about God are you? You? Yoda the scientist?" Michael needled.

Chris put his hands up in mock protest. "No, I'm not there yet. Not writing it off, but very much still believing that we can understand all this. Let me tell you about the strangest aspect of all of this."

"OK, but we really have to wrap this up. My team meeting starts in a half hour and I have to prepare," Michael persisted.

"OK, so hold on to your hat. Quantum theorists have discovered that at the 'ground state', matter exists as pure energy (both light and matter) *until it is measured*. According to the mathematics, a particle is both there and not there, in one place and in another, existing only as a *probability until someone observes it*. When it is observed (measured), then it collapses to a definite place in space. Until then it exists only as a possibility."

"So the whole universe is just a possibility waiting to happen?" Michael laughed. "That does not seem like the place I live in!" he said as he banged his knuckles on the desk.

"No, I know," Chris insisted, "but according to this theory, our universe is real because we are here to observe it. Because we are conscious of it, we've collapsed the universe into being. If we follow this logic, we literally make the universe what it is, and this is driving classical scientists to distraction because it means that things are NOT separate and distinct. It means that everything is connected and that we can actually change the physical world through thought, through being aware."

"C'mon! Is this new-age mumbo jumbo? 'We are what we think'," Michael mocked with a waving of his hands.

"Hey man, I am just telling you what's going on," Chris protested. "You can read the studies yourself. This stuff is actually being proven at Princeton and other universities through random-number work. According to these studies, and there are many of them, our thoughts have actual energy that goes outside of our heads and subtly changes the world around us. The implications are staggering. This new way of thinking starts to explain remote viewing, mind reading, and a host of other 'wacky' things that are well documented through history. And that's precisely why traditional, classical scientists are doing battle with these new theories. The problem is the data is real…so there is a kind of 'I can't hear you' going on in the scientific community," Chris said with his hands over his ears. "Just like when science was talking to the Church 300 years ago. History repeats itself!"

"Wow. Wow. My mind is blown, my friend. Very interesting. But I only have 5 more minutes, Yoda, and I still don't get how this applies to me and getting more energy out of my team," Michael insisted.

"Okay, one last piece that will hopefully tie all of this together. As humans we take in energy through food and then move throughout their day applying that energy, right?" Chris asked.

"Yep, got it," Michael replied.

"Well, what I'm saying is that there is no limit to this process: If we try hard enough, we can access unlimited amounts of energy and, because we are all connected, we can choose to apply that energy to a common cause with almost unlimited possibility," Chris said definitively.

"I disagree on two fronts," Michael retorted. "First, I believe our energy is limited. We can only access so much because we can only eat so much. And second, the reality is that we are separate. We can only do what we can do. Sure, cooperation is possible, but it is merely the sum of the parts."

"Thinks the universe is so simple, does he," Chris replied in his best Yoda voice. "On your first point: Dude, haven't you ever heard of people who have survived in the Arctic for weeks with no food or shelter? Or guys who have survived in a little boat for months? Or the old lady who lifts the car off her husband's chest? Or the team that comes back against all odds? If you take the 'limited energy' point of view, these things should not be possible. But they are. We say those people and teams have incredible 'spirit' and accept that it happens. But this is *real energy*, man!" Chris laughed. "And we can access it!"

"On your second point, we are not separate on *any* level. At the gross physical level, as humans moving around, we are constantly exchanging matter. Every time you smell something you are literally taking in the particles of that odor and making them part of you."

Michael grimaced at the thought of his company's bathroom.

"And what are 'you' anyways?" Chris continued. "The body that makes up 'you' has more bacterial cells than human cells. And those bacterial cells are constantly communicating with each other. So 'you' are more than just your own cells!"

"In addition," Chris said, getting up and pacing, "our very thoughts and emotions intertwine us with each other. If you smile at the grocery clerk you may create a good mood in him, and he may go home and be kind to his kids, who then may help someone, and on and on it goes. Or if you have an idea or thought and tell someone else, you can change her whole life! If you express love or hate to another person, you are subtly changing the whole world, one moment at a time…just like in the quantum world. Everything, *every-thing*, is inextricably connected! We are not separate!

"So to finish," Chris sat down with a thud, "your energy problem is that you have not figured out how to draw the power you need from what is essentially an unlimited system. I like to think of each person on this planet as a living 'nuclear reactor' that can, if they choose, apply an unlimited amount of energy in any direction. And because we are all connected, we can come together and increase the power through our aligned thoughts, because thoughts are the most powerful creators we have."

Michael sat, stunned, as he took in the visual of his team being a huge reactor of potential. "But how do I access this creative energy?" Michael asked, both exasperated and thrilled.

"To the initial question, he returns!" Chris smiled. "Look dude, that is the issue that virtually every leader in this world has faced. All I know is that from a scientific perspective there is almost no limit to the energy we can access…it's just figuring out how to get at it. If it helps, a little guy named Gandhi simply walked around in a bed-sheet telling people what he thought and got 100 million people to change an entire country. Can't be all that hard!"

Michael laughed. "Yeah", he said, "but so did Hitler."

Chapter Three

Michael came back to his desk and sat down with a sigh. The weekly team meeting was exhausting, as usual. Although he had only been in his role for 6 months, the exciting newness had worn off long ago. Being 42 and having had ten different jobs in his career to-date, he was long past the time of idealism and excitement in new roles. The pattern had recreated itself many times. A new job, a burst of excitement and hope, and then the inevitable spiral into overwork, stress, and disillusionment.

It was true that every new promotion or job did bring a satisfaction, a feeling of growth and accomplishment. And this new role was no different. It just seemed to be shorter lived each time, as if his experience was telling him 'don't focus too long on the excitement, because this inevitably is going to be more of the same.' It was precisely this merry-go-round that triggered escape fantasies in Michael. He dreamt that if he could somehow do something drastically different – like work for himself, or become an hourly worker, or *anything* else – he might end this feeling of entrapment, this notion that he was on a treadmill of unending and escalating stress.

He knew that he didn't really hate the people he worked with, he just hated the situation. His team was smart, competent and they cared, but the challenges of management seemed to nag at him no matter how good his people were. Each person presented a host of issues that he had to deal with, no matter how productive they were. The high performers, for example, needed constant coddling and re-assurance.

Michael laughed to himself because it seemed that they were the ones most worried about their jobs and their roles.

Then there were the 'sliders' who knew just what they needed to do to get the job done. No more, no less. They needed constant prodding and direct intervention to do anything that pushed the bar even a little higher. And the underperformers, who were largely bored with their lives and simply wanted inspiration. The complainers, the gossipers, the superficial ass-kissers, and, exhaustingl y, the eager achievers who wanted to learn as much as possible before looking for their next lateral-but-slightly-higher move.

The challenge with management, he had always thought, was not establishing vision, mission, goals and strategy but the maddening variability of human wants, needs and personalities. Getting Yoda's 'infinite energy' to be expressed in one direction would be easy if people weren't so damn difficult to understand, if they were all alike and just did what they were told.

But then again, he knew that wasn't right either. Here he was, criticizing his team for their 'humanness', when he himself could not separate the feelings he had inside himself. The stress of his home life, the news of his father's illness, and the frustration with the upcoming quarterly numbers – all of this he tried to separate and compartmentalize but couldn't. As hard as he tried, the thoughts and feelings popped up and disappeared like those infuriating whack-a-mole games. If I can't control my own issues, he thought, then how in hell can I ask others to do it?

Yet it seemed like the cultures of most businesses today, reflecting a current that also runs through the country, was that we as people should bring our brains and bodies to work, but leave our emotions and spirits behind. Or, more accurately, bring our positive emotions and spirits to work, but leave everything negative or painful at home. This was separation of himself that Michael felt so acutely: That he was supposed to be one person at home, and another at work, and that his own 'wholeness' was something to be realized when he had a week off and took his kids to Disneyland. "*How the hell did I get here?*" he asked himself.

His mind immediately flashed back to business school, and the hope and promise of new horizons. He was 3 years out of college and had worked in a number of odd roles from executive assistant to paralegal to a brief stint as the co-founder of a small company that sold office supplies door-to-door. His father, having an ever-watchful eye over Michael's career, told him in his oh-so-caring way that "if you don't get your shit together and get a real job, I'm going to cut you off." Michael was humiliated, both because he did not like to be told what to do but also because he had been intermittently dependent on his father for supplemental income.

So, he had enrolled in an upper-middle-tier business school, to assuage his father, certainly, but mainly to buy some time and figure out what he wanted with his life. And business school had been fun, really. The material was interesting and the salaries of graduates were enticing. The course work revolved around the business classics: finance, accounting, strategy, marketing, quantitative analysis and everyone's favorite blow-off, organizational behavior. Michael had to laugh at the irony that the biggest blow-off course turned out to be the most important, and one that probably should have been half of the entire curriculum.

Upon graduating he undertook a series of predictable, unremarkable roles in consulting, business development, a stint in marketing, a brief role as a COO in a dot-com, then to his current employer as the director of operations, VP, then SVP. Ask any business school grad about their path and you were likely to get a similar answer, he thought sarcastically. Sure, there were a lucky, inspired few who took 'the road less travelled', but by and large everyone he knew had taken a different version of the same path.

Not that he was unhappy or thought he had made the wrong decisions. He had actually done quite well in his roles. He was pretty sure his dad would approve, even though he seemed constitutionally incapable of saying so. Michael had a beautiful house, wonderful kids, enough for college and almost enough for retirement – all that a 'good man' can be expected to achieve at his age. So why did he feel so frustrated and stressed? What made this job seem so endless and intolerable?

He knew part of it was just the Sisyphean chore of pushing teams to achieve higher and higher revenues with less and less of a budget. That seemed to be the common denominator in every job he had ever had: an ongoing drive to increase profits. But he also felt that there had to be more. There seemed to be something missing from this work-life that could never be filled by hitting goals…something intangible that he was longing to achieve.

Over his career, Michael had been part of or led almost every program designed to 'increase productivity and employee well-being'. He had worked with consultants, taken on new operating methods, done off-sites and team building. Michael had tried process improvement, personality assessments and performance workshops, ad infinitum. His office bookshelf was lined with books like *Execution*, *Hope is not a Strategy*, *The Fifth Discipline*, on and on. Yet he still seemed to hit performance ceilings and always, always had to manage employee satisfaction. All this talk about 'accessing energy' was well and good in concept, but Michael had tried just about everything known to the business world and simply could not fathom how to do any more.

He leaned back, looked out the window and exhaled a whispered and decidedly secular question: "God…how can I learn to be successful and happy in this life?"

At that moment his phone flashed with an incoming call. The receptionist buzzed through. "Michael, it's your Dad on 402…do you want to take it?"

Michael looked up in the air and said, with a sarcastic tone, "Really?"

"Sorry, I didn't catch that…what did you say?" his assistant asked, confused.

"Nothing, nothing. Yes, put him through," Michael replied.

There was a brief pause, and then he heard his father's familiar rasping breath. The years of smoking had taken a toll on him, as was evidenced by his recent announcement. "Hey Dad," Michael said with more melancholy than he had intended.

"Hi Son," Roy Benson responded in an uncharacteristically subdued tone. "You kind of left in a hurry earlier today, so I wanted to make sure everything was OK."

His father, always making sure everything is buttoned up, Michael thought. No emotion, just pure analysis and execution. Making sure everything is taken care of in an efficient manner.

"Dad, why didn't you tell me about this earlier?" Michael asked. "I'm, …well, I'm still in a state of disbelief. I don't even know what to think or say."

Sighing his father gave an answer Michael had heard many times in the 'conversations' between he and his mother. "Well, son, I really didn't want to worry you. I thought I'd take care of this on my own, but it got out of hand."

"But Dad, *terminal lung cancer*? That doesn't just materialize out of thin air!" Michael almost shouted. "How long have you been keeping this from me?"

"Well, Son, truth be told I haven't been feeling great for a long time. I only went to see the Doctor about a month ago and found out it was too late. It's stage 5, Son. I'm not going to beat this", his father said with a finality that made Michael's stomach drop.

"But, but, isn't there *anything*? Can't we do *anything*?" Michael could feel the tears welling up but quickly pushed them back. Men did not cry in this family. "Why, Dad, why didn't you tell me?" he pleaded.

"I don't know, Son. I was brought up in a different time. I was taught to deal with challenges head-on, alone…to 'suck it up' and manage without complaint. And I guess that's what I did. Please don't take this personally. Remember, I'm the one who's dying."

So there it was. 'The martyr's jab', as Michael and his sister called it.

The message was 'suck it up', but there was also an undertone of 'poor me'. Michael felt bad for thinking these things, but it's so perfect...even as he dies he's playing the role of tough-loner-and-victim.

"Dad, I get that you're dying and I am sorry for being so selfish, but please understand that my head is swimming here. I found out this morning that you have months to live, that you aren't going to try to save yourself, and basically you're asking me to just accept it and move on. Pardon me, but I just don't think of things the way you do!"

"Ok, ok, I'm sorry son," his father softened. "I think we both are struggling here. I really don't want to spend my last months on earth fighting with you. God knows we spent enough time doing that. I guess I just want to reach out and talk to you, to maybe get to know you a bit more. Make up for lost time."

Michael's head was spinning. In truth, he had used anger to block out the news he heard this morning and had gone about his day as if nothing happened. But this did happen. His father was dying, and he was going to have to manage this with everything else. The sense of exhaustion and confusion was overwhelming.

"Dad," he answered, "I get it. I'm sorry. I just have a lot going on right now that I can't seem to get my head around. This news, your, well, your...dying, is tough for me to digest right now. Can we talk about this more later, when I've had a chance to internalize this a bit? I don't mean to blow you off, I really just...well, my head is a bit under water right now."

"I get it Son," his father responded. "Over the next few days I am going to take care of some of the details around my final months, so give me a ring or stop by when you can. And talk to your sister, she's pretty broken up."

Shit, Michael had forgotten about his sister. Sandy, short for Sandra, never really handled things like this very well. High strung and highly emotional, she usually wasn't terribly helpful in these situations. When their mother passed, Sandy didn't stop crying for weeks.

"Yeah Dad, I get it. I'll talk to her. And I'll be in touch. You...well, you take care of yourself, OK?" Michael asked impotently.

"Will do Son. You too," his father said, hanging up.

Michael put his head in his hands and took a deep breath. He could not see how his life could get any more miserable, he thought selfishly. His father, sister, wife, employees, his boss, his workload, his kids...it was all closing in on him. He clenched his fists and softly pounded them into his temples. *Life is too much.* He wasn't sure if he could do this, keep going on. He felt like he wanted to jump out of his own body, to leave this life and its crappy trials. "It's just not *fair,*" he wanted to scream.

And what's the point anyway? Is this what it comes down to...work and then die? He was busting his ass trying to meet an ever-moving goal so he could put his kids through school and finance a life that his wife clearly hated and...and...then what? To die in some God-forsaken hospital wishing that things had been different?

He wondered if his Dad had those same thoughts. He must have. His father's life was all work, retirement, and then endless rounds of golf. *"God, is THAT how life is supposed to turn out?"* Michael asked himself. Roy Benson barely knew his own kids...what in the world could be going through his head right now? Did he feel anything when his own parents passed? There was so much Michael didn't understand, so much he wanted to ask.

Chapter Four

A week went by before Michael called his Dad. He felt guilty about it, but in truth, he was just avoiding dealing with the situation. He had called his sister the night after he had spoken to his father, and the conversation had been exactly what he expected, a flood of emotion that bordered on hysteria. He told his wife, who was caring and attentive, but he also noticed the distance that she maintained. It was as if she knew what she had to do, but was not completely present while doing it.

So Michael did what he normally did under these circumstances: He checked out. He became emotionally distant, avoided challenging people and conversations, put his head down and did his work. Just like his Dad used to do. But he knew he couldn't avoid dealing with the situation forever. His guilt wouldn't let him. So he called his Dad and set up a time to visit after a long delayed doctor's appointment. "Might as well be efficient," he thought.

Michael winced as he got in the car…he had scheduled time to see this doctor months ago because his back was absolutely killing him. The pain was the worst when he got out of bed or into his car. He thought it might be the chair he was using at work, but couldn't be sure. A co-worker had seen him getting up slowly and recommended he see his brother, a top-rated back pain specialist.

Michael had done research on the doctor and found he had quite an extraordinary background. Yale undergraduate, Harvard Medical School, interned at Johns-Hopkins, author of 30 different studies, overall quite an impressive resume. And most intriguing, Michael thought, was what his co-worker had said about his 'unorthodox style'. Michael had probed for more information, but the co-worker had just said, "trust me, check him out." And so he did…although he had to book his appointment months out, as the doc was quite busy.

As Michael followed the disembodied voice of his GPS and quietly dreaded the sterility of the medical center he'd soon be visiting, the reality of his Dad's illness struck him again. God, how he hated medical facilities. The smell, the lack of color, the anxiety, and the omnipresent potential for news that could either alter or end a life. He shivered as he thought about living the end of his life in these places.

The GPS indicated he was getting closer to his destination, but this didn't look like any medical center neighborhood he had visited previously. The buildings were quite beautiful…almost residential, in a turn of the century sort of way. This was in stark contrast to the hermetically sealed cinder block campus where his father learned his fate. For a brief moment Michael thought how nice it would be to actually *live* here.

He parked his car and headed around front, entering through what would have been a front porch in 1911, the year indicated on the bronze historical society plaque. The lobby was beautiful and comfortable… much more like a Four Seasons entryway than a doctor's waiting room. A receptionist greeted Michael from a low desk on one side of the room, asked him if he wanted coffee, and showed him the various reading materials. This was some Doctor's office, Michael thought…nothing like what he had pictured.

Michael took a moment to fill out the requisite paperwork, and then the doctor (who was on time!) personally came out to greet him. He introduced himself as Steve Holtzman, not *Dr.* Holtzman, but *Steve!* The informality was new…and refreshing. Michael also guessed that Steve was in his mid 40's, which was surprising given the depth and accomplishment of his background.

Steve escorted Michael into a room toward the back of the building that had two comfortable wing-backed chairs and a small examination table. Like the entryway, the room was very comfortable and welcoming. Steve sat down in one chair and motioned for Michael to sit in the other. "What can I help you with Michael?" Steve started with a smile.

"Well," Michael replied, "I've been having lower back pain, primarily when I wake up, but also when I've been sitting for a long time. It's getting quite bad and starting to interfere with my concentration."

"I'm sorry to hear that Michael. I hope I can help. I know from experience how distracting this type of pain can be. Do you mind if I ask you a series of questions, and then we can do an examination?" Steve asked.

"Sure...fire away," Michael replied.

The young doctor then went through a long list of questions, the purpose of which Michael could not fathom. Questions about his personal life, stress level, work situation, family history, diet, relationships and, most strangely, questions delving into the way he grew up and how he thought about things.

"Did I make a wrong turn and end up in a psychiatrist's office?" Michael joked.

Steve laughed and said, "Well, I have a different way of approaching things...does it bother you?"

"No," Michael replied, "I guess I just don't understand what this has to do with my back!"

Steve smiled. "I probably should have explained a bit more in the beginning, but since you were referred by Frank I presumed you already knew. You see, I view the body as a system, which includes the brain. So, I feel it's important for me to understand as much as I can about you before I move toward any diagnosis. Does that make sense?"

Michael thought about it. It did make sense but seemed extreme given that this seemed to be a simple muscular-skeletal issue. "I think so, but I just haven't really had a doctor before who took such an interest in my life," Michael admitted. "I guess I'm not used to it."

The doctor smiled and said, "I'll explain more later, but you'll see that it makes a lot of sense for both of us. Now, time to take a look."

Over the next half hour Steve had him go through a series of movements, stretches and postures, asking him all the while to explain the location and severity of any pain. Then he had Michael lie down while he probed the lower spine and surrounding muscles. To finish, the doctor asked him to step into the next room and get a quick X-ray.

"The next room?" Michael asked. "Aren't you going to send me to a different specialist for X-rays, MRI's and everything else?"

"No," the Doctor replied. "I like to keep things simple and less expensive. I don't think you need much more than an X-ray to give me an idea as to what's going on here."

This was like no medical visit Michael had ever experienced. Courteous, caring, fast, efficient, thorough...this was almost like a well-run small business, but with *heart*, he thought. He understood now why Frank said that Dr. Holzman...Steve, he corrected himself...was unorthodox.

When he returned to the examination room, Steve was already coming down the hall with the X-rays in hand. "Incredible," Michael said to himself.

Steve came in, sat down and began writing out something on a pad of paper. Michael assumed it was a prescription for pain medication or a referral to another specialist. "OK Doc, give it to me straight. Surgery, meds, what's the deal?" Michael half-joked.

"Michael, there's nothing wrong with you," Steve said as he handed Michael the slip of paper. "I'm referring you to a psychologist."

Michael was stunned. "Huh? But...but I have pain in my back, not my head."

"Well, there's not really a huge difference there. I am not a psychologist myself, but I strongly suspect you're holding some kind of anger or hurt in your lower back. Something unresolved," Steve said with a certainty that made Michael cringe inside.

"Whoa, whoa, whoa!" Michael almost shouted. "What do you mean 'holding anger in my back'!? I thought you were supposed to do something to fix my back...not psychoanalyze me!" A small part of Michael noticed that his voice was becoming shrill in a self-righteous sort of way.

"Okay, okay, let's take a step back." Steve said soothingly. "I think I need to explain some things to you before we proceed. I've come to understand some truths about the human body that most medical doctors are either unaware of or unwilling to accept."

"First," Steve started, "the human mind and body are not separate things. Your brain, muscles, and organs – every single cell in your body in fact – are part of a highly complex system that operates both independently and interdependently."

"Let's take, for example, a human cell. At the moment of conception and cell division, each cell looks exactly like another. In fact, every cell has the capability, and the necessary instructions, to be just about any specialized cell in the human body. One cell may become a toe cell, while another may become a brain cell. But in the beginning, they all look the same. Do you follow?"

"Yes, I think so, but then how do they know what to become?" Michael asked, as he wondered how he ended up in this ongoing science class, first with Yoda, and now with his doctor.

"That's a great question, and it's the key to what I'm about to say. You see, it seems that every living thing has a known form, or something it's supposed to be. This form is pure information and is, in a way, the 'guide' for your body. This is how each cell in your body, and your body as a whole, has the ability to figure out what it's supposed to grow into or become. As an example, a zebra embryo has the information in it that guides it to become the 'zebra' form, and so while there may be various permutations of stripes and height and weight among zebras, it still adheres to the form of a zebra."

"Okaaay..." Michael said, still not understanding *how* these cells and organisms know.

Steve continued, "We used to think that each cell was told this by the 'genes' of the cell and the DNA contained within those genes. Now, however, we understand that the DNA is somewhat passive, sort of like a blueprint that contains all the potential permutations and possibilities for the cell but not the instructions themselves. So, any individual cell really *does* have the capability to be a toe cell or a brain cell, it just needs to be told what it's supposed to become. The question is, again, *where does it get its instructions?*"

"I'm dying here…how does it?" Michael joked.

"From a provable, scientific perspective…we still don't know," the doctor replied.

"Anticlimactic!" Michael jibed.

Steve smiled. "But we *can* theorize, and I believe I understand what's happening. It seems that somewhere in the experience we call 'the universe' there is information. And this information contains instructions that cause things to have form, including all life. Some biologists and physicists are calling this a 'morphic field'."

"I have heard this before. I think I get it," Michael offered.

"Great," Steve went on. "Each cell in the human body seems to have the ability, with antennae-like structures on the surface of the cell, to communicate with both its own and the surrounding world's energetic fields. A cell can open and close pores on its skin, taking in or excreting chemicals as it senses the surrounding energetic vibrations. If the body is under duress, the cell responds instantaneously by either shutting off its skin or opening pores only to compounds necessary to respond to the situation. Scientists for a long time thought this was a purely chemical response to adrenaline or other compounds in the body, but chemical exchange is far too slow of a process for it to be the cause. There's some way that all cells are giving and receiving instructions at the speed of light. For our purposes, it's instant."

"So you're telling me that cells are sending and receiving a sort of 'radio signal' from and to…well from and to *what?*" Michael asked.

"So here's what I believe is the sea-change in medicine as we know it. Each cell is not only communicating with every other cell, but it's getting and giving instructions from the brain, from the surroundings, from the universe…to and from *everything.* Cells are completely connected to every experience, action, and chemical that exists in our world. In this way our bodies are highly interconnected, vibrating entities that feel and communicate with the world in a complex and interrelated way. You are a massive operating system composed of trillions of cells, all operating in parallel, and communicating instantly with every aspect of the universe." Steve finished.

"Wow. Very interesting, and makes sense because of a conversation I just had with a colleague about quantum physics." Michael said. "But how do we *know* this? I mean, how can you, as a Medical Doctor, be saying this?"

The Doctor laughed again. "Well the medical profession, at least here in the west, is still not on-board with this. Medicine in the U.S., especially until recently, has been composed of two things: drugs (chemical intervention) and surgery (physical intervention). Both these things tend to deny the 'whole' of the organism and treat the human body as a collection of parts."

"Reductionism." Michael offered.

"Yes," Steve nodded. "Surgery seeks to take out or modify the body part, while drugs seek to modify a particular cellular operation to achieve a desired outcome. Because the body is a highly complex, interrelated system, simply bathing a cell in certain chemicals or removing whole body parts have a cascading effect, what we call 'side-effects'. I heard a biologist describe it as having a series of switches and dials that are all connected somehow but we don't exactly know how. Every time we flip one switch or turn one dial, we end up turning twelve others. Sometimes to disastrous effect."

"So how are we supposed to heal?" Michael asked.

"Well, that's the basic conundrum of the medical profession. The body has the ability to heal itself because each cell knows what its ideal 'form' is supposed to be. From this view, disease (or dis-ease) is merely the cell losing connection with what it's supposed to be. In this framing, cancer is a group of rogue cells that have lost touch with their morphic field. A virus can now be seen as an invader that succeeds in convincing certain cells not to respond or to respond inappropriately. Clogged arteries even become a mismanagement of products put into our bodies. Put simply, the body becomes 'ill at ease' and stops functioning properly."

"But that's what medicine seeks to cure, right? This 'body revolt'?" Michael pressed.

"Yes," Steve responded, "but through our standard reductionist method, we're mainly trying to *force* the body back into alignment. We're trying to fix the symptom, not provide a cure…and this is where the medical world is divided. There's a lot of money in providing temporary solutions, so the inertia has kept our profession stagnant for nearly a hundred years."

"Well, if it's not working, then how do you suggest doing it?" Michael was becoming exasperated again.

"By looking at what has driven the cell to lose touch in the first place!" Steve said, standing up. Grabbing a marker for his whiteboard he drew a circle, "Let's imagine, for instance, a cancer cell."

"Appropriate", Michael said.

"Right…your Dad. So your Dad is a long time smoker who exposes himself to toxic chemicals on a daily basis for years. The cells then turn 'rogue' due to this exposure, right?" Steve asked.

"Got it." Michael replied.

"But why is it that some people are more susceptible than others? Why are some people able to cure themselves and others not? We used to think it was genetics, but it turns out it's more complicated than that. If a cell is constantly communicating with the mind, other cells, and the outside world, then it's 'going rogue' is caused by the thoughts, experiences, dietary habits, memories, and basically the entire experience of that person. Although a specific toxin can certainly cause an increase in the probability that something will happen to a cell, it's really the physical, mental, emotional 'soup' that determines what *will* ultimately happen."

"Thus, 'holistic medicine'", Michael finished for him.

Steve sat back and said, "You got it. It's merely looking at the big picture, a large portion of which is your mind. Let me give you a couple of examples that you may find interesting. First, many doctors, to the chagrin of the pharmaceutical industry, have found that 'the placebo effect' works. It's been proven over and over again that the mind can and does alter the body's physical processes. Why? Because the mind issues instructions to the cells to do certain things, and they respond!"

"Second, heart transplant surgeons have noticed that the recipients of new hearts sometimes take on thought characteristics and/or memories of the heart donors."

"Get out of here!" Michael interjected incredulously.

"It's true," Steve insisted. "There's a book called 'The Heart's Code' in which the author, a heart surgeon, details specific, gripping examples of this. One example is the little girl who received the heart of another little girl who had been murdered. The recipient went into counseling after surgery, which is normal, and began to speak of vivid dreams of being murdered. Over time, the little girl began to draw highly detailed scenes of the murder including, with the help of a sketch artist, the murderer himself. The psychologist brought the pictures to the police and, with the help of other physical evidence found on the man matching the description, they were able to convict the murderer. Read the book...this is just one of many stories."

"Whoa, that's creepy." Michael shivered.

"But what's most interesting," Steve continued, "is that our cells clearly store information about our experiences that can be shared with other, unrelated cells. Which leads to a third example: The fact that people who are in close proximity have an effect on each other's physical state. The obvious example of this is the synchronization of the monthly cycles of women, but other experiments have shown that our heartbeats and brain-waves synchronize, our stress hormones change, our skin responses alter, all in response to other living beings. And, I should add, 'proximity' does not have to be physical. Studies have shown that people, when 'entrained' with each other tend to stay connected over vast distances. Mothers feel shocks when their children are hurt, a twin 'knows' that her brother has passed. This isn't science fiction, this is real!"

"I have to admit I'm fairly stunned by all of this. I knew about the placebo effect and all that, but I really did not understand the interrelation, the complexity of our bodies and minds. Geez, what does this mean for me, for medicine, for everything?" Michael asked as he sat back.

"For you, not much, except I encourage you to see your thoughts and emotions as a larger part of your physical health. For medicine, well, we're evolving. I'm seen as 'unorthodox' because I believe that the larger view is important, not only for our health, but also to the way we relate to each other as human beings. This hypothesis forces us to consider that anger, fear, hatred, selfishness, and meanness are all *public health issues* because through these 'low mind states' we create a disease-promoting cocktail. Each of our cells can read and resonate with these states of mind, and I see it as my job to draw that connection." Steve finished.

"And thus you are referring my angry soup of cells to a psychologist!" Michael said sarcastically.

"I didn't mean it that way," Steve laughed, "I just know from experience that many physical symptoms that can't obviously be traced to a cause are likely driven by 'contextual energy'…mental, emotional, situational. And resolving that simply isn't in my bailiwick."

"So, no prescription for Vicoden and muscle relaxants?" Michael asked hopefully.

The doctor gave one loud belly laugh. "Nope," he said, "But I think a little love, compassion and emotional healing might do you one better."

Chapter Five

As Michael drove to his father's house, he reflected upon the two con-versations he had just had. It's always interesting, Michael thought, how certain information seems to come in waves. First his discussion with Yoda...well more of a learning session...then his talk with Steve. Michael sensed a theme and, as he had always done when learning some-thing new, spent some time debriefing himself so he might more fully understand what he was hearing.

There was definitely something here about energy, that energy permeates all things and, in fact, makes up all matter. He also got the concept that humans have been learning, over time, how to access this already-existing energy and, through creative choice, apply that energy to the world around them. But what was this notion about information? Both Yoda and Dr. Steve (calling him 'Steve' was too weird) talked about some sort of pre-existing information that gave things form. This part was more challenging because if there's indeed information imbedded in the universe, and this information has somehow guided or shaped the form of everything (in-formed things, so to speak), then it logically follows that someone, or something, might be a source of that informa-tion. If there weren't information behind form, then the universe would have developed in a completely random way, wouldn't it? The universe just seemed too consistent, ordered and balanced for this to be the case!

Which led Michael to ruminate life's role in all this. If thoughts and actions are essentially the application of energy, and if everything is composed of highly interconnected energy fields, like both Yoda and the Doc said, then wouldn't what all conscious beings do and think continually modify how everything works? Given what he had heard about mind-body and mind-matter interaction, the answer seemed to be 'yes'.

So...if there is both static information in the universe, like *laws* or *guides*, and conscious choice, which is the *directed application of energy* within those guides, then the universe is kind of an act of ongoing creation. We are both *subject to* the laws of the universe but also, through choice, able to create our own universe. Michael smiled to himself. *"I think I'm getting this,"* he said to himself.

The one notion that was pointedly *not* discussed, the 'Gorilla in the room' so to speak, was the question of God. Michael was certainly not overly religious – his parents had raised him Methodist but he was not devout, nor even necessarily a believer – but he did sometimes wonder about it. After all, the universe is an incredibly complex and balanced place with, as he had learned, information, energy, light, fields, all matter of things that seemed to operate both in a pre-determined yet fluid way. How in God's name ('pun intended,' he thought) could all that be organized without some entity at the helm?

This last question came to him just as he was pulling into his father's driveway. Interesting as all this was, he knew enough about himself to be aware of his propensity to escape reality through complex philosophical daydreams. He still had vivid memories of his father coming into his bedroom and snapping, "I told you to clean up your God-damn room, and here you sit staring at the wall. Get to it, or I will give you something to daydream about." Michael never understood what he meant by that, but knew that his father thought daydreaming was an undesirable trait in a person and that, somehow, people who did it were not necessarily lovable.

Michael sighed. "Well," he mumbled to himself, something he seemed to be doing more and more, "here goes."

As he walked up to the door, he could see his father inside bent over the sink. He seemed to be doing dishes. It struck Michael as funny, in an odd sort of way, how someone with only 3 months to live, could be concerned with doing something as rote and mundane as the dishes. But then again, what else is he going to do but live his life as he usually did?

He pulled open the door and said, "Hey Dad!" in as cheery a tone as he could muster. Immediately he was flooded with memories of growing up in this house. It was the *feeling* of the place, the mix of emotions and sensations that he remembered as a child. They were not pleasant or unpleasant, yet somehow vaguely historical. Like he had walked into a museum that contained invisible artifacts of his childhood experience, on display for no one but him.

His father turned around and attempted a smile, "Hello Son," he said. Michael was shocked at how bad his father looked. It was like someone had flipped some hidden switch that caused his father to age at an accelerated speed. In just one week he looked like he had lost 20 pounds in weight and 5 inches in height.

"How're you doing, Pops? You look good," Michael lied.

"Give me a god-damned break," his father barked, partly in jest and partly in judgment (the versatile 'god-damned' being his favorite adjective-adverb). "I look like shit."

Michael laughed. He always liked his father's cutting sense of humor, though not necessarily his callousness. "Well, that's understandable Dad," Michael weakly acknowledged.

"Yeah, the old man is going to kick the bucket. I guess I'm doing pretty good, all things considered. Have you spoken to your sister? I heard from her a couple of days ago and she could not stop crying. I don't know where she got her temperament. Your mother was always so composed," his father said, shaking his head.

"Well, Dad, we can't all be like you and Mom. She's doing her best," Michael felt like he needed to defend his sister, or himself, he wasn't quite sure which.

"Oh, cut the crap. You both have done well for yourselves. We did pretty well as parents, I think."

Here we go again, Michael thought. "Dad, I did not come here to fight. I'm sorry, it's just that things in my life are challenging right now and I don't know how to handle everything. I feel a bit adrift."

"Maria?" his father probed.

"Partly," Michael replied, knowing that his Dad never really approved of his choices. "But more a combination of everything," he paused. "Dad, how did you manage it all? I mean, how did you deal with everything...family, work, all of the obligations, all of the stress?"

Roy Benson laughed. "Son, I don't believe you ever met my shrink. His name is Johnny Walker and he's been with me since I was 20," his father replied.

"Scotch? That was your answer?" Michael asked incredulously.

His father sat down and motioned for his son to have a seat. Instinctively, Roy patted the breast pocket of his 1960's-era short-sleeved shirt for a pack of cigarettes. It had been 10 years since he quit, and yet he still did this after meals or when he was about to begin a conversation. "It's about to kill me and I still can't stop thinking about having a smoke," he grunted.

"Son," he continued, "we just didn't think about things the way you kids do today. And I guess we didn't think about things the way our parents did either. You see, your grandparents came up during the depression, the *real* depression," his father did not think that the 'great recession' of 2008-10 constituted much of a challenge, "and they saw a great deal of suffering. There was twenty-five percent unemployment. Fathers were leaving their wives to find jobs or to escape the burden of their children. Whole families broken up and distributed among relatives. Your grandparents were happy to have *any* work...if it put food on the table then life was good. My Dad worked two jobs, and my Mom cleaned houses when she could. I remember nights when there was very little food on the table and my Dad hadn't been home for more than a couple of hours a night, but we were happy to have what we did." His father was lost in reflection.

"So, when it came time for me to find a job," he said, sighing, "I wanted stability, consistency and most of all *money*. I wanted a career that would allow me to live as my parents couldn't: with predictability, savings, and an easier life for my kids. And I think a lot of people wanted that. We all went to work for large companies, and those companies became our stability, our structure and our future."

Michael had never heard his father reflect like this before. "But it wasn't all roses, was it? I mean, I remember some tough conversations between you and Mom," Michael said, with what was, to him, extreme understatement. He remembered a great deal of fighting, slamming doors, and sulking.

"Of course it wasn't, god-dammit," his father shouted. "But we sucked it up. We did what we needed to do. This is something I've never gotten about you kids. You complain about how awful it was growing up, how much you wish you could do something you 'love', but you don't seem to be willing to power through anything. You take the jobs of older workers and then complain that you hate what you're doing. Where is the appreciation, the gratitude, for having any job at all!?"

"Whoa, whoa, Dad," Michael soothed. He did not want this to turn into a fight. "We're *all* just looking to improve on the past, right? I mean you wanted a better life than your parents, and we want a 'better' life than you had, and my kids will want a better life than me. Kind of like a continuing evolution, right? I mean, that is how we got to the modern society we have now, right?"

"I will grant you that," his father nodded. "But where does it end? Where is it going? What more could you possibly want? You have a nice home, good kids, a fine wife, money in the bank, food on the table… what are you looking for?"

This was a question that Michael had been asking himself as well. What is this dissatisfaction inside? What is this need for *more*? And more of *what?*

"I don't know Dad. I really don't. It's kind of like Maslow and his hierarchy of needs. I think we're looking for our true purpose in life... well, I am. For peace. For happiness. For a sense of worth in what we are doing. And I think this is even more true for the latest generations entering the workforce. Money and titles are great, but they also seem so *empty.* I have had so many jobs, so many titles. I'm the leader of a group of over 200 people, I make a great living, yet I seem to be constantly under stress and wishing I were someplace else." Michael stood up and threw his hands into the air. "It's maddening! I should be happy. I should be content. But I'm *not.*"

"I think you need to see my counselor," his father half-joked. "Dr. Walker has always been good to me during these times. Takes the edge off, as they used to say."

Michael sighed. "I don't know if we do it that way anymore, Dad. I wish it were that easy. I have a feeling I have to get through this with a clear mind."

"Suit yourself," his father replied. "But just remember, son, gratitude is not a bad thing. I think it's okay to want more, but try to be thankful for what you do have. That's something that I always kept in mind, especially during tough times. Because the reality is this: You are much better off than any generation in history. Many people on earth would give their left-arms, literally, for what you have. Progress and 'evolution' are important, but without gratitude for the present, you will end up like a hamster on a wheel."

Michael sat back down and looked at his hands. His dad was right. He could cultivate more gratitude. But what about this feeling that there must be more? More of what? He didn't want to just let go of this; he felt like it was important.

"Thanks Dad. I really needed that. But I didn't come here to vent to you," Michael said, slightly chagrined.

"Why, because I'm the one who's going to croak?" his Dad winked.

Michael didn't remember this much humor in his father. It was refreshing but slightly unnerving.

"Oh God, Dad, don't talk like that. Seriously, though, how are you doing?"

"I'm doing OK. I think a part of me knew this was coming. I didn't go to the Doctor or tell anyone because I just wanted to enjoy my life. I didn't want to worry about it, or worry anyone else," his father admitted.

"Just sucking it up?" Michael jabbed.

His Dad looked away and said, "Yeah, I guess so." He looked back and raised his upturned hands, "Can't teach an old dog new tricks!"

Michael laughed because this was one of his Dad's favorite 'isms'. The family used to call them 'Royisms'. It was his father's way of both explaining his behavior and justifying his conservative propensities. Change simply wasn't in his father's make-up. He was what he was and he made no excuses...which was somehow refreshing given the fluidity of his own generation.

"Well Dad, I want you to know that you don't have to do this alone. I am here, and I want to go through this with you. I know you want to be tough, to look like the provider until the end, but please let me be a part of this." Michael had never been more earnest than he was now. He didn't know why, but he got the feeling that this was very important. "I really mean it, Dad."

"Okay, okay!" his father said, visibly uncomfortable. "The door's open."

"Thanks Dad. I have to check in with work now." His father always understood getting back to work. "But you take care of yourself, you hear?" Michael patted his Dad's knee and headed for the door. He knew his Dad was never going to admit that he was in pain, and Michael wanted to spare him the discomfort of having to talk about it. Or was it his own discomfort he was avoiding? He couldn't tell.

"I will call you tomorrow, OK?" and he headed out the door.

Chapter Six

Although he hadn't told his father the complete truth about going back to the office, Michael did sit in the car for an hour answering emails on his iPhone. Why was he so uncomfortable being around his Dad when things got mushy? He felt like he was being propelled out of the door by some strange force field, something designed to keep people from getting too close to each other. Or was it just his own 'force field'? So many things were swimming around in his head. Anger at his Dad's unwillingness to be vulnerable and to reach out; frustration with his job and his team; even a reluctance to go home, for God's sake. Why was he sitting here doing emails when he had a family to go home to? What is this?"

Michael threw the iPhone in the seat next to him and snarled, "Fucking thing." Why did he have such a problem being grateful for what he had? Everything was a distraction, like he was trying to get away from his own life. Whenever he felt at peace he would quickly grab his iPhone to see if he was missing something. He was a hamster on a wheel!

And this whole thing about gratitude had hit a nerve. He had heard this before from his Dad, the 'you don't know how good you have it' refrain. But this was taking on a different quality. It was almost as if this statement reached inside of him and hit something very raw and very real. Michael knew he had a lot to be grateful for, but it seemed like events always conspired to make him feel like he was moving away from peace and gratitude rather than toward it.

Was this some sort of trend in modern life? Were things getting better...or worse? Michael was reminded often of the book *Shantaram*, in which one of the characters speaks of the nature of the universe as moving from simplicity to complexity and that everything in existence is constantly unfolding in the direction of a higher awareness. At the time, this had made so much sense to Michael. The universe had begun as a single point, but in a flash moved from that one point to a highly complex existence that is still unfolding. Life on earth began as a pool of single celled creatures but has evolved into highly complex, sentient and adaptive life forms. Simplicity to complexity.

Even in culture he recognized this pattern. Early humans were concerned simply with survival, then they formed clans, cities, nations and organizations in order to pursue more complex goals. With these social organizations came an increasing awareness around 'human rights' and the importance of caring for our fellow man. Examples are everywhere: Just 200 years ago slavery was commonplace and accepted, women were not allowed to participate in government, and 'the environment' was not even discussed. Heck, when Michael was a boy he could remember people just throwing trash out the windows of their cars. It was not until the 'crying Indian' of the 1970's did people start to wonder if trashing the environment was perhaps not in our best interests. Now we take it for granted.

As he sat in his car, though, Michael could not see where higher awareness could possibly go from here. Sure, things were getting more complex technically...man was becoming ridiculously good at manipulating atoms for his own needs. But was this really 'evolving', in any positive sense of the word? He had more toys and tools and distractions than he could count, yet he felt more distant from happiness, people, serenity and peace than he had ever been. How could this possibly be called 'development' if we moved forward technically but were always left with a vague sense that we were moving further and further away from the simple, more meaningful things?

Again, the book *Shantaram* came to mind. In one scene, the main character, an Australian, is traveling to a small, very poor, rural town in India. When he arrives late in the evening, one family takes him in and gives him a bedroll and space in the community sleeping area. As he was drifting off, he noticed that the entire clan had gathered around his mat and lightly placed their hands on him. His startled look prompted the mother to say, "We want to make sure you feel loved, because we know you are so very far away from your family." At the time Michael had almost wept at the touching nature of the scene, how one family with nothing physically to offer could so completely offer everything.

For Michael, this scene stood in stark contrast to the reality of his world. He and his family had every major convenience but almost none of the closeness and connection that seemed to exist in simpler times. He had a job that paid him a great deal of money, relatively, but he worked in a pressured, joyless environment. His relationship with his friends seemed to revolve around alcohol and physical fun, but with very little in the way of true communion. He didn't really know his neighbors well and his "community" seemed to consist of the occasional, obligatory visit to the local church. Was this really a 'movement toward increasing awareness'? It certainly was more complex, but did not seem very 'aware' at all!

Michael started the car and thought about what the doctor had said. Maybe anger was driving some of this pain. He did sense, as he sat there, that *something* in the way he was experiencing his life was acting on his physical state. His whole body seemed to tense when he thought about his life. He found himself clenching his fists and bearing down as if he were in battle with some unseen enemy. Maybe not anger but *frustration*...frustration with the way things *are* versus the way he thought they *should be*.

Michael dialed the number of the psychologist. He felt ashamed and defeated at the prospect of reaching out, and he knew why. For the longest time Michael had wanted to see in himself the image of his

Dad: a self-reliant, self-made man who could figure things out without help from some touchy feely shrink being paid to make him cry. But he also knew that he was reaching a breaking point and that the only thing worse than the thought of seeing a psychiatrist was the thought that he was going to have to make sense of this by himself. And being in his mid 40's and somewhat out of shape, he wasn't completely sure his body could handle that.

With an appointment set at two weeks from today, Michael hung up the phone and figured that he'd at least have some time to change his mind. Maybe after two weeks things would resolve and he could avoid this humiliation. But then again, he thought as he pulled into his office parking lot and saw his CEO's car, that's a fairly low-probability event.

Chapter Seven

Over the next two weeks Michael experienced what he could only term a 'shit storm'. Virtually everything that could go wrong did. Not only did it look like his group was going to miss their numbers this quarter, but he found out his largest customer was shopping for a new provider and his top salesperson was leaving for what he called 'a better opportunity'. At one point Armand came into his office and suggested, with barely contained rage, that they both might want to get their C.V.s in order.

To top this all off, Michael was feeling extremely guilty about his father. He hadn't seen his dad since his last visit and had only spoken to him once or twice over the phone. Maria had been very understanding in spite of what Michael knew was a simmering resentment. She had done her best to bring his father meals and a bit of company. But Michael knew this couldn't go on and that at some point he was going to have to spend time with his dad. Was he avoiding this? He felt like he had good reason to be at work. After all, how was he going to hold onto his job if he wasn't there? His team needed him more than ever!

Still, he had a nagging feeling that he was using work as a distraction…something to take his mind off of his own belief that he was failing as a son, a husband, a brother, a boss, and well, in every aspect of his life. He wasn't sure what he was supposed to be doing, but he did know that whatever he was doing was not working. Virtually every relationship in his life had become distant, full of conflict, or dependent.

His direct reports seemed needier and more difficult than ever, his wife could barely contain her frustration, he felt like he didn't even know his kids, and now he was avoiding contact with his dying father. The fantasy of escape began to well up in him again.

It was with all this in mind that he headed out the door for his appointment with the shrink, Dr. Louise Hartnett. As he left the building he could think of a million other things he could and should be doing with this time, but something was pulling him to do this. "Man," he mumbled to himself, "is she going to get an earful today."

Michael walked into Dr. Hartnett's office and was surprised to see no receptionist, just a tastefully decorated anteroom complete with a running waterfall, fish tank and soft music and lighting. He had to admit to himself that it was very relaxing here as he fought the urge to take a nap. At exactly 3:00, the time of the scheduled appointment, Dr. Hartnett came out to greet Michael. As he stood to introduce himself, he could not help but notice the warmth and radiance of her smile. She seemed to almost glow with kindness and serenity. He didn't know what he was expecting, but what he was seeing and feeling put him a bit off balance.

"You must be Michael," she said as she clasped his hand in both of hers.

"Mmm hmm," he nodded dumbly, smiling like he was a little boy. Then it occurred to him what he was feeling. She was like an extremely loving and nurturing mother. She reminded Michael of his own grandmother before she passed. Unbounded love and kindness. Warmth enveloped Michael in a wave. Perfect peace.

"Why don't you come into my space so we can get to know each other," she said as she led him to an adjoining room. The room was nothing like he expected, as there was no desk, therapist's couch, or any other of the accouterments that his mind's eye associated with a psychologist's office. It actually looked more like a well-decorated conference room, without the table but with lots of plants and paintings and warm tones.

It felt very homey, but also very purposeful.

Dr. Hartnett had placed two very functional but comfortable looking chairs in such a way that anyone seated would be sitting face-to-face with their knees almost touching. "Was he supposed to sit *there*? *That* close to her?" he wondered with discomfort.

Sensing this, Dr. Hartnett smiled and said reassuringly, "Don't be alarmed, you'll get used to it fairly quickly. It seems we have developed a discomfort with physical closeness in our culture and time, but I've found that it goes away very quickly. I believe," she mused, "that it's in our *nature* to be close, don't you?"

"Gee, I don't know," Michael replied, "I guess I never thought about it before. But you're the doctor and I'm the patient, so I guess I'm following along here!" Michael said with a shrug. He was getting an unnerving feeling inside, but he was also determined to follow through.

"I'd like to correct you on that point, if I might," Dr. Hartnett said as she motioned Michael to sit in one of the chairs. Wow, this *is* close he thought as he sat down with his knees less than an inch away from hers. "You see," she continued, "I don't view you as being my 'patient', or 'client', or anything of the sort. I view you as simply being another person on this planet that I'm blessed to be able to talk to. I see you as special and as bringing me as much as I can bring you. So you aren't the object of study or analysis, but more an equal who has come to share his life with me…and for that I'm grateful and will try my best to be of service."

Michael pondered this for a moment. He had always assumed that doctors treated paying clients as objects to be studied or problems to be fixed. "Okay," Michael replied, "so you aren't here to fix me or make me better?"

Louise Hartnett threw her head back and beamed with a positively huge smile. "No," she said as she shook her head and looked at Michael with what he felt was *affection*. "No, Michael. You are perfect just the way you are. Whatever is happening inside of you is merely a prodding, a questioning that you yourself have a desire to heal. I'm merely an instrument for your healing. You brought me into your life to help you, and I accept my role in that.

"In the past, many of us in the 'healing professions' took science to be, not only a method of learning and analysis, but also a way of *being*, which was a mistaken notion on our part. What I mean is that we went from using science as a method of examining the world we saw 'outside of us', which is very helpful and powerful to a point, to believing that we were somehow separate from each other, that one person could analyze another as a separate entity. And this simply isn't true."

Michael reflected again on his conversation with Yoda and the idea that everything is connected to everything else, the antithesis of the 'mechanistic universe' theory. "So you don't think we are separate and independent beings?" he asked.

"No, I think we're interconnected in every way. I cannot 'analyze you' as a separate being because *my* issues, *my* way of being is influencing and affecting *your* issues and way of being in every moment. All the sciences are finding this out. The observer affects the observed in every moment. The only thing I can do is use whatever skills and abilities I have to help you understand and heal yourself. *You*, Michael, are the agent of change. This situation, indeed *every* situation, is a vehicle for you to learn how to be joyful, happy and at peace with yourself. And by the way," she finished, "call me Louise. Dr. Hartnett is far too formal and 'separating'," she winked.

"Wow, this *is* different than what I expected," Michael said with a smile. "Then how do we proceed? I want to be joyful and happy and all that stuff! How do I do it?"

Louise smiled her motherly smile and said, "Well, let's take some baby steps first. Why don't you tell me a bit about yourself, why you're here, how you experience things, that kind of thing. Really, whatever's on your mind."

"Okay," Michael started, "but I guess I'd also like to say that I really don't go in for a lot of emotional stuff. I'm a very analytical person and can rationally think through things fairly easily. I don't think I've cried in 30 years. Well, I got weepy during Titanic, but thank god nobody saw that. Anyway, I hope this works for you."

"Yes, it works for me just fine," Louise nodded. "In fact, if I were a money-focused person I would be quite happy with that because the 'non-emotional' route takes a lot longer! I could count on you being a client for quite some time! Would you perhaps, as a start, be willing to say that you would be *open* to dealing with your emotions? You don't have to promise anything, just be open to the idea that you have emotions and may at some point express them. Are you willing to do that?"

"Sure," Michael responded. "I *know* I have emotions, I just don't express them much."

Louise leaned forward and looked Michael directly in the eye and said, "Emotions are the gateway to understanding ourselves and to healing the issues that cause us discomfort or unhappiness. By denying our emotions, we deny not only our 'bad' feelings, but our 'good' feelings as well. We can try to banish anger and sadness and pain, but in our attempt we also banish joy and truth and love. Emotions are simply energetic signposts that tell us whether we are aligned or misaligned."

"Misaligned with what?" Michael asked.

"The love that already exists within us," Louise answered while rolling her hands outward from her heart. "Painful emotions merely tell us that we are 'looking for love in all the wrong places', as the song goes. And if we deny or suppress them it's like a reservoir of energy that builds up inside of us and eventually bleeds into our lives. We cannot suppress our emotions forever...they *will* express themselves. Just as you can't seal a boiling pot because it will explode. Our curriculum as human beings is to learn the most productive ways to acknowledge and express our emotions so that we can move into a greater and greater place of peace. If it's easier for you, it's sort of like acknowledging the energy within us and allowing a pathway for its release. Does that help you?"

Michael had an immediate sinking feeling as he followed this thought to its logical conclusion: he was going to have to acknowledge and express emotion. For some people, like his wife, this wasn't a big issue. Crying was a part of her ongoing method of expression. But for Michael this was a huge challenge. He had grown up in a family that rarely hugged, kissed or did anything remotely affectionate. The last time he cried, when he was 6, his father had slapped him and called him a 'whiney little girl'. So for most of his life he had simply shut off his feelings, except when he was very angry or very happy...which was strange because shouting or cheering seemed acceptable while other methods of expression were not.

He sighed and said, "Yes, I get it. I can't promise this is going to be easy for me or will happen anytime soon, but I am open to expressing my emotions."

"Great! I think that is a fantastic start!" Louise seemed truly excited. "And I have some processes that may even help you along in that. I will also set the intention to give you information in a clear, straight-forward way, in a way you might call 'analytical'. I can see you are intelligent and thoughtful, so I won't beat around the bush if I'm trying to make a point. I'll explain the concepts directly and then we can go from there. Does that work for you?"

"Ah yes," Michael laughed. "*This* I get. I am definitely a thinker and open to feedback, so give it to me straight, Doc!"

"Louise", she admonished with a smile. "Ok then Michael, why don't you just start telling me what's on your mind and we'll see where it takes us. We still have over an hour, so relax and just talk."

And so, over the next hour Michael just talked...about his situation at work, his frustration with his boss and team, his wife, his father, everything. Words came tumbling out in a chaotic mess, almost as if he were vomiting up everything running through his mind over the past year. At first he was self-conscious about talking so much, but Louise was so receptive and interested, that after a few minutes he found he didn't want to stop. It felt so good releasing this mental commentary. He felt lighter and lighter as the hour progressed.

As he went along, Louise was so present, so absolutely focused on what he was saying, that he became convinced that she really did want to understand him, to hear about what was going on in his life. It was as if a part of him had been trapped for years in an agonizing and silent 'internal dungeon', and this person had just cracked the door to the cell. He smelled the air of freedom, and wanted more.

When Michael became self-conscious or seemed to run out of steam, Louise would ask a question that was both open-ended and provocative, immediately prompting a cascade of memories and thoughts that kept Michael talking. She seemed to have an endless repertoire: 'When was the first time you felt this way?', 'What does the word 'frustration' mean to you?', 'What is the physical feeling you have when you think about this?'. None of the questions seemed to be seeking an answer, yet they were so clearly on-point that Michael couldn't help but continue sharing.

By the end of the session he felt exhausted yet strangely light, as he sometimes felt after a long hike, setting down his backpack. The hour had been a journey through most of his life. He was starting to see strings that attached his childhood to his teen years to his present situation. It was as if he had flown at 10,000 feet over his life and seen the patterns and lines and barriers for the first time. Everything made so much more sense to him suddenly. His life was *not random*.

Louise sat quietly while Michael reflected, and then softly said, "Michael, I want to thank you for being open with me here. I really hear your frustration with the way life is unfolding for you right now, and I can hear your pain about some of the things that have happened in the past. This is a tremendous first step, and I believe you're grasping the key to your own happiness. Let's pick up here in our next session, because I think you may have more to say the next time we see each other."

Michael agreed with her and was secretly grateful the time was up because he felt physically wiped out. As he walked out the door Louise lightly touched his arm and said, "Michael, you may want to splash some cold water on your face or wash your hands. Sometimes when we start to release emotional energy like this we can become 'ungrounded'," she said with a smile. "Water can help get you back to reality so that you can drive, work, all of that."

"Yeah, I do feel a little loopy," Michael shook his head. "I'll be careful."

"OK, see you next week?" Louise asked as she opened her date-book.

Michael set up a series of weekly appointments going forward for two months. Normally he would have felt pressured by Louise's assumption that he was continuing, but the combination of the way he felt and his recent awareness that there was more to unravel, made the decision to keep going natural and obvious. He felt this was very important, even though he couldn't say exactly why.

As he headed to his car Michael was definitely unmoored. He felt tired, elated, relieved, somewhat confused…a cacophony of thoughts and feelings spun in his head like a free-flying carousel. The image that came to mind was an old bottle of Yoo-Hoo that had been shaken to get the sediment off the bottom. Everything was flying around inside him. He wasn't sure what he had been expecting, he thought as headed back to work, but his visit to Louise had certainly been impactful.

Chapter Eight

Louise was right. The days following his first session were filled with so many memories and reflections that he found it difficult to work. Michael began to remember things that he had thought had very little meaning, but in seeing them in the context of his entire life, they somehow became seminal. When he was five or six, he remembered being excited to show his father a drawing. Michael had burst into the door of his father's office with pride and anticipation, only to have his dad turn around and snap, "Get out of here, I told you not to bother me while I'm working." What struck Michael as powerful was not the memory itself as much as the realization that he still had *feelings* that went along with the memory.

At the time Michael remembered being at first shocked, then hurt, then angry. The first two feelings had come so close together that they were almost one: The unexpected response and then the pain of…of… not being loved. It seemed so silly today, Michael thought, but it was so *real* then. Michael remembered sitting in his room replaying the hurt over and over in his head until it became a running story, a reason why his father didn't really love him. And the scary part for Michael was the realization that this feeling was still with him, especially the anger. He had felt this simmering resentment at work, at home, and in virtually every aspect of his life. It sat below the surface waiting to be triggered.

Michael couldn't put his finger on it but there seemed to be something important here, information that could perhaps explain his current situation. If this anger was still present, then clearly there were other strings that led from his childhood to today. It was starting to become apparent to Michael that life was not a discreet set of circumstances…that there were currents of thought and feeling that have been persistent and present his entire life. And in a rush, they seemed to be coming forward all at once. "What have I gotten myself into?" he said to nobody in particular.

Another strange thing was happening. Thoughts of his father kept popping into his head unbidden, like some Freudian drama being created by his mind. He would be in a meeting, or driving home, or talking to a client and suddenly his father's voice or face would appear. Or he would remember something very specific about his Dad while doing something random, like laundry. It was getting a bit ridiculous, like he had some bizarre ghost of his living father living inside his head. More fodder for Louise, he thought, as he dove into the reports that lay on his desk.

At that moment the phone buzzed and his assistant's disembodied voice came on the line. "Michael, your sister's on the phone, and she doesn't sound good. I think it's important. Can I put her through?"

"Yes," Michael answered, not without a hint of dread in his voice. His sister had a tendency to get emotional and hysterical over even the smallest things, and he usually had to step in and put things back together. *That anger again…there it is!* He thought. *What is that?*

Amanda wasn't over-reacting this time. Michael's father had been rushed to the hospital unconscious and his sister was in shock. She had gone over to visit her father and found him on the floor with a very weak pulse. Michael grabbed his jacket and headed for the door. He glanced back at the unfinished reports sitting on his desk and thought that he should probably tell Armand they were going to be late. In a staccato burst of thoughts and feelings, he felt guilt for not getting his work done, then self-judgment for caring about that when his Dad was dying, then anger at Armand for being such an uncaring prick, then

74

frustration with his team for not getting *their* reports done on time, and finally bitterness at the unfairness of his life and this situation. He knew all these thoughts were not rational (or were they?), but they were real and he couldn't deny them. At least he couldn't deny them *anymore*.

God-awful hospitals again, Michael thought to himself as took the stairs to his father's floor. He could not imagine how people could work in these places with the smells and illness and death all around. Either they had a predisposition to be caretakers or saw themselves as part of some higher ideal, he mused as he approached the nurses' station.

"I'm looking for Roy Benson, can you direct me to his room?" he asked, out of breath. He briefly thought about how bizarre and ironic it would be if he died of a coronary right here as his father fights cancer. He really had to get back in shape…too many of his friends and colleagues had already begun to have health issues associated with work, stress and general neglect. *That* was something he definitely didn't need right now.

He was about to enter his Dad's room when he almost bumped into a staff doctor coming out. Michael could see his father in the background sitting up and watching one of his silly courtroom dramas on TV. He loved the right versus wrong debates. Strange how the most mundane habits persist even as life ebbs away.

"Oh, hello. I assume you're Michael Benson," the doctor stated. He seemed young for a doctor, but Michael thought *everyone* looked too young nowadays. Another aspect of growing old.

"Yeah." Michael responded. "How is he?"

"Well, his personal physician, Dr. Peterson I understand, is on the way over, but I can tell you that your father is in a weakened state due to the rapid progression of his illness and its effects on his body, mind and spirit. It's a common story…he feels terrible and becomes depressed, which affects his appetite, which then in turn affects his energy level. He starts to lose his desire to keep going, which feeds his depression. In short, he loses Spirit. Once the human desire to live is gone, the entire organism begins to collapse. Your father's moving through just such a collapse."

"So, there's nothing we can do?" Michael asked, incredulously. "Are we just giving up?"

"All we can really do is make him comfortable, get him some nourishment, and try to keep his spirits up. I know it's hard to hear this Mr. Benson, but your father is dying and there isn't much we can do about that. We must work within our capabilities and the reality of the situation." The young doctor finished. Michael could tell he was doing his best to be compassionate, but professionally, the doctor was done with the case.

Anger again. Unbidden and reflexive. Michael took a deep breath. "I understand, Doc. Thank you for your help. I'll talk to Dr. Peterson about what we might be able to do."

Michael turned and walked into his father's room with his best 'how are you doing, you old rascal' smiles.

"So what have you gotten yourself into this time?" Michael said in a half-hearted attempt to be funny. If he thought his Dad looked bad the last time he saw him, this time was even worse. His father was aging dramatically before his eyes.

"Damn, Son, hell if I know," his father responded, turning off the television. "I wasn't feeling particularly well this morning, so I started making some coffee and walked out into the living room…only to wake up here. I guess I passed out."

"Geez Dad, you need to take it easy on yourself. You scared Amanda half to death," Michael was trying to be light-hearted but it came out more awkward than anything else.

"Son, I'm dying. And honestly I'm ready. I've been 15 years now without your mother, and I just don't see the point anymore. The doctor said we could try to fight this, go through chemo, the whole nine yards…but I simply don't want the pain. Bob Sampson went through that shit for 8 months before he croaked, and honestly I wouldn't wish that on my worst enemy. This life has been good for me, and it's my time, Son." His father looked into Michael's eyes with both determination and sorrow. His Dad was nothing if not decisive. Michael knew there was no point discussing this.

"OK, Dad. I get it," Michael smiled and put his hand on his Dad's shoulder. He felt a surge of tenderness toward his father. "And I'm sorry I haven't been around much lately. Work's been – and this is certainly no excuse – a bit difficult lately. I feel bad. I really want to spend more time with you over the next few months."

His father smiled and shook his head. "Work is important, Son. Don't screw anything up on account of me. I've been there, and I know you have to live your life. Seriously, spend what time you can with me but don't compromise your life."

Michael felt that now-familiar burst of anger again. Why didn't his Dad want to be with him? He has a couple of months to live and he wants me to *work*? The coldness of his house growing up seemed to return in a wave. The lack of love, the underlying anger, the judgment. Can't we just heal this and act like a loving family?

Michael looked directly into his father's eyes. "No, Dad. No! I feel like I have lived the past 40 years not really knowing who you are or what you think. I want to talk to you, to listen to you. We can't just push this out Dad, there aren't many tomorrows." It seemed strange to tell his father all this given he was the one with limited time, but this was important. Michael felt like he was giving that hurt little boy a voice, saying what needed to be said.

His father looked at him with a combination of surprise and respect. Roy Benson wasn't used to his kids pushing him, and it showed. He relented, "Okay, okay. Whatever you want. It's your life. If you want to waste it talking to a dying old man, then who am I to argue?" Roy said with mock sarcasm. Michael could tell however, that a small part of his Dad was pleased.

Roy Benson paused, slightly uncomfortable. He wasn't used to having real conversations. And neither was Michael. The whole family operated under the unstated assumption that meaningful dialogue was unnecessary and all communication should be kept at a level that required no real truth-telling. This would go on until the pain reached a crescendo and then burst forth in screaming, insults, slamming doors and days of sulking.

Now Michael and his father sat staring at each other having no idea where to start. "So," his father said, "how do you want to do this? You want to ask me some questions?" The underlying tone was clear to Michael: *This was your idea, so you lead.*

"Okay, Dad," Michael sighed. He wanted to start at a relatively superficial level so as not to make his father uncomfortable. This was a minefield…his Dad had a history of shutting down when anything of depth came up. "Let's start with your career. Why did you choose the defense industry? What led you into management?" Michael always wondered why his Dad chose what he did, because he seemed so unhappy most of the time.

"Well," Roy Benson crossed his arms and leaned back, "I guess I just thought it was the thing to do. My Dad came home from the war in '46 and went back to his job at Douglas as a welder, so I decided to follow him into that industry. As a soldier he was a hero to me, and it seemed the most patriotic thing I could do aside from enlisting…and he would have none of that. Dad was very clear that he wanted me to go to college, get into a big business, and become an executive. I think the war took a toll on him, and he didn't want me to go down that path.

"And honestly, the defense industry made a lot of sense. With Korea, Vietnam and the Cold War, there was no shortage of business. It was fairly easy to be successful. Most of the production capacity of the world had been knocked out during the Second World War, so U.S. industry, including defense, was the center of the new global economy. From 1945 until the mid 1970's, a vast majority of the world's consumer goods were manufactured *here*, which seems hard to believe looking at the economy today. So, management in this environment was a 'no-brainer' as you would say. I got a college degree, started at Boeing, and rose through the ranks. As I told you before, Son, I was just grateful to have a job and I was willing to work hard."

Michael was becoming interested. He knew about the booming post-war U.S. economy from his history classes, but was seeing it from his father's perspective for the first time. "So what was it like working in that environment? I mean, everyone paints the 50's as being so rosy and the 60's as being a time of conflict. Did you see that?"

"Not really. I was in my own world. You kids came along in the late 60's when I was just starting out in my career. I was focused on trying to make a buck, get ahead, do what I was told. Remember, Son, there was a great deal of expectation back then. People in the corporate world didn't question things. We *worked*. Many of the men in our teams came out of the war and so were tough, structure-oriented individuals. I developed a style of management that was consistent with that. Tough, heads-down, execution oriented. We didn't talk about how we felt or whether or not we were happy. It was irrelevant."

"But how did you cope with stress? I mean, what was your outlet?" Michael was on thin-ice here. As a child he had witnessed his father's deep reservoir of anger. The tie being ripped off, the scotch on the rocks, the universal 'daddy's had a hard day, dear'.

Roy Benson looked sharply at his son. "We dealt with it. We did our part, just like the guys in the war did. This is just what people did...they sacrificed and dealt with it." The implied criticism hung in the air.

"I get that, Dad," Michael backed off. "But weren't things changing? I mean the late 60's were a time of social revolution. Didn't that show up in careers, in management?"

"Not really," his father settled. "The 'peace and free love' crap was a social oddity for us. Sure, we had guys who started growing their hair longer, especially in the 70's, but generally everyone was too busy making money to bring that stuff into work. The hippies didn't work in organizations anyways. They weren't interested in working for 'the man'. Nor were they wanted for that matter."

Roy seemed lost in thought. "Sure, as managers we started to hear theories around human motivation and performance, but they were largely relegated to academics like Deming. I can see how those theories might've been influenced by certain social movements, but we largely stuck to our own methods."

"What were those methods?" Michael asked. "How did you manage people, teams?" He was becoming curious, because he himself was reaching some impasses as a manager and wondered how his father got people to perform.

"Hmm….good question. We didn't really talk about it as something discreet. I guess we just made assumptions about how people worked. For instance, we assumed people wanted things and were willing to work to get them. Things like money, power, titles and, to some extent, accolades. And for the most part they were. And we also assumed that people didn't want to lose their jobs, and so were willing to do a certain amount of work to stay employed. Sort of a 'carrot and stick' approach," he said with a grin.

"But," he continued, "I started to notice that the 'stick' approach didn't work terribly well as the 80's and 90's came about because the economy was too good. People had no fear around being unemployed so we couldn't really control them. Everyone wanted more money, more titles, more of everything. The 'carrots' kept getting bigger and bigger, until it was unsustainable. Then all of these management theories started being tested. Team building, trust building, theory X vs. theory Y, all that crap. But I don't really think anything changed all that much…people still mainly wanted money. And I think that's probably true today."

Michael reflected on what his father was saying. "But what about self-actualization? Maslow's hierarchy? I mean, people have to want more than money, right?"

His father shook his head, "Frankly, Son, I didn't give a shit about that. Sure, I believe that we all want to be 'self actualized' and all, but I also believe that companies are built for one thing: shareholder profit. Employees come to a company under a specific agreement…to work for the shareholder and to get paid for that work. Every employee has one job: to execute. I had a little sign on the wall that I would show to each employee on their first day of work. It said:

You will:

Come to work on time every day

Execute flawlessly

Commit to making the company successful

Conduct yourself with propriety and respect

I will:

Pay you well

And that was that. Self-actualization was *their* problem, not mine."

Michael tilted his head incredulously. "But it's just not that easy today, Dad. If you did that today your team would quit. Sure, all of that is important, especially the execution part, but people won't stand for that anymore."

"And that's why this economy is all fucked up. It all started in the 70's with the 'me generation' and look where it's led us. The 80's were an orgy of greed, then the 90's and corporate excess, and just the past 10 years with the internet boom, bust and then the financial meltdown… all the result of people trying to 'get theirs' and get out. There's no loyalty anymore. Nobody cares about how long they've been at a company or how the company performs. They just want what's good for them. That's why I retired, Son. I just didn't get it anymore."

Roy Benson was getting himself worked up into one of his diatribes, and Michael was getting nervous. Was this good for his health? But he was also strangely interested because as he himself was advancing in age and management level, he could see what his father was talking about. It was almost impossible to please anyone anymore.

"Right before I retired, we had a kid come in," his father continued, "some kind of computer specialist. He couldn't have been more than 25 years old. Do you know that he wanted a salary that was higher than *mine, and* stock in the company, *and* perks that nobody in our company ever got?! Utterly preposterous…and, he *got it.* That did it for me. I had to assume I was just getting old."

Michael had heard this story before, and at the time, he hadn't had much sympathy. As his father used to say, "The market is the market." But now, as he himself was regularly asked to review candidates, he could relate. Thankfully the downturn had made interviewees less demanding, but he had experienced the frustration of wanting to hire talented people and not being able to meet *their* requirements.

"But, Dad," Michael interjected, "isn't this like we talked about before? Kids are just trying to do better than their parents, just like you and I. Really, we're training them to do this, aren't we? We teach them that money is all-important, that status is something to be proud of, and that their value is tied to what they do. So is it a surprise that they want these things, that they demand more?"

"Sure," his father snapped, "but where's the respect? Where's the humility? We tried to teach you kids to be successful but also be humble, didn't we?"

Michael didn't want to go down this path. Certainly his parents had demanded respect, but they didn't offer it. Growing up, he knew that his place was to say 'yes, sir' without hesitation, without opinion or any other expression. Michael's parents saw respect as a one-way street. He couldn't begrudge kids today if they demanded respect in return.

"Well," Michael responded tentatively, "you did teach us respect, but you also taught us to respect ourselves." He thought he might try another angle. "And I think kids today are just trying to ask for what they believe they deserve. I understand how it comes across, believe me, but I do think that this is an evolutionary process of finding balance between being respectful and respecting one's self. Maybe it's like Hegel's dialectic, it swings back and forth until we find a nice balance." Michael glanced at his father, wondering how he would take this. Compromise was not his Dad's greatest strength.

"Hummpf," his Dad growled. "I guess I am too old for this shit. Gray areas don't suit me too well."

"Well, let's not go into it then," Michael wanted to change the subject. He didn't want his last conversations with his Dad to be ongoing arguments. He had had enough of that growing up.

"When are they going to let you out of this place? Hospitals give me the creeps," he offered up as an olive branch. He knew his Dad hated hospitals as much as he did.

"I don't know. I'm waiting to talk to Doc Peterson. I'm not sure what they're going to do with me here anyway. I'm not going to do chemo and I told them I want to spend as much time at home as I can."

"Well, Dad," Michael stood, "do you want me to wait around and take you home?"

"Nah, you go ahead, Son. I'm sure you have enough going on. Your sister's coming back from lunch in a few minutes and can take me back. How's work going, anyway?"

Michael shook his head, "Don't ask, Dad. We're going to miss our quarterly numbers, I'm losing people and customers, and my boss is being a shit. Nothing changes except the bar gets a little higher each time. You know how it is."

"God, yeah," his father laughed. "Better you than me. That shit almost killed me as I got older. Then again, maybe it did." Michael couldn't help but notice that his Dad's ironic sense of humor hit a little too close to home this time. Something in the man seemed defeated.

"Okay, Dad," Michael reached to give his father an awkward hug, "I'll see you in a few days...I promise. I can't do much about the work situation anyway, and I really do want to spend more time with you. Take care of yourself, you hear?" Michael seemed to be saying that a lot lately. Why is it we always want people to take care of *themselves*?

As he headed out the door, Michael saw the TV jump back to life. A feeling of profound sadness passed through him. "Is this what we have come to?" he silently asked himself. "Dying alone in front of Judge Judy?"

Chapter Nine

On his way out the door, Michael bumped into his sister who looked visibly shaken by the morning's events. Seeing her, Michael had a flashback to his mother's death 10 years ago. What struck him now, as it did back then, was just how different each person deals with tragedy and death. His sister Amanda was an emotional griever who would cry her eyes out, flail dramatically, and then move into a place of acceptance. Michael was like his father, the 'strong and analytical type', who would go inside himself and try to think his way through it.

His relatives were all over the map, from uncles that used morbid humor to aunts who reverted to maternal roles. Some weep silently, some rage at God and the world. It was never predictable how someone would act. Michael reasoned that this was probably true about people generally. If his experience in management had taught him anything, it was that people were, almost maddeningly, infinitely variable in their actions and reactions. Everyone had a unique perspective and unique reactions, which was both a blessing and a curse. It seemed like more of a curse lately, but that was the bitch of life.

As he walked back into his office he glanced at his calendar, then his watch. "Shit, Maria is going to kill me," he said, as he spun and headed back for the door. Michael had forgotten he had his son's parent-teacher conference in 15 min. He was barely going to make it, he thought, as he took the back way out. Armand could not see him leaving again. His personal life was beginning to seriously impede on his work life, and

Armand was certainly not going to let this continue. With gallows humor, he thought about what deep, perfect irony it would be if his Dad died while his wife filed for divorce and he lost his job. With a strange martyr's glee, he thought about how bad people would have to feel then.

"Snap out of it," he mumbled as he headed for his still-warm car. "You can do this."

Michael pulled into the school parking lot 10 minutes late for his meeting with Mr. Busci, his son's teacher. His son loved this teacher, which was rare for a 9-year-old boy who generally hated school. Thomas was a great kid, but the classroom was not his favorite place.

As he walked toward the school's main entrance, he felt his iPhone buzz in his pocket. He glanced at the screen and saw a text from his wife saying that she wasn't going to be able to make the meeting because she was helping Amanda get his father back to the house. Michael got the feeling again that Maria was trying to avoid him, and he wasn't completely sure why. He knew she was unhappy generally, but thought maybe everything had blown over. His gut was telling him otherwise.

Whatever the reasons, he did not have time for this merry-go-round of conversation. She knew that he was overwhelmed, and she was just going to have to deal with it for a while. Michael was doing the best he could, and just couldn't see a way out. She was being unreasonable to think that he was somehow responsible for all of this. Sometimes life's a bitch and you have to deal with it.

"Focus," Michael said as he rounded the corner to his son's classroom. He wanted this hour to be about Thomas, not his worries. He had had enough of his own mental churnings and was getting tired of them.

He walked up to Room 4C, his son's 3rd grade classroom. He peeked in and saw that Mr. Busci was still meeting with his previous appointment and felt relieved that his being late wouldn't be noticed. Michael had a thing about being late. He felt it showed disrespect for another's time, especially when it happened to him. His direct reports knew of the holy wrath they would incur if they made an appointment and failed to show up on time.

As he stood in the hallway, he reflected on how *small* everything seemed in an elementary school. Today, Michael would have to kneel if he wanted to drink out of the drinking fountain and the desks seemed made for a race of midgets. When he was in third grade everything seemed so big and new. It brought back the feelings he had as a kid, the slow realization that adults wanted him to be and act a certain way, that learning meant structure, that fun was not necessarily what school was supposed to be about. Michael remembered with sadness the year that school ceased being *fun*.

Michael snapped out of his reverie as he saw the parents coming out the door. Mr. Busci was behind them smiling and saying how much he enjoyed meeting them and how they had a wonderful, amazing, and truly special little girl. And then, to Michael's amazement, he *hugged* them each in turn. Michael had never seen a teacher hug anyone, and felt a wave of dread as Mr. Busci turned and smiled at him.

Awkwardly, Michael smiled and said, "Hello, Mr. Busci. I'm Michael Benson, Thomas's dad," while simultaneously reaching out his hand in order to head off any physical embrace.

"Michael!" the teacher exclaimed as he shook hands, "please call me Leo. Mr. Busci is for my little prodigies!" Although he didn't hug Michael, Leo shook his hand vigorously and placed his other hand on Michael's shoulder. Although he was still a bit uncomfortable, at least there was no body-to-body contact, Michael thought.

Leo continued to hold Michael's hand as he guided them to the desk at the front of the room. Thankfully, Leo had placed three full-sized chairs in a triangle off to one side, to which he motioned. "I'm sorry, but my wife won't be able to make it tonight," Michael said motioning to the empty chair. "Family emergency."

The teacher leaned forward with concern. "That's fine, of course, but I do hope everything is alright."

"Yes, yes," Michael lied with a dismissive wave. "Everything's fine. We're just working around some scheduling conflicts regarding my father. He's been ill lately and…" Michael couldn't put his finger on it, but he felt an urge to tell this man everything, to let all the pent up frustration come spilling out. Leo just seemed so kind and open and concerned. It was slightly unnerving.

"…Well, just family stuff. We'll get through it. But this meeting is about Thomas," Michael said, quickly changing the subject. "How is he doing?"

Taking his cue, Leo reached around and grabbed a folder from his desk. "Let's take a look," he said thumbing through the folder. "OK, so let me say first of all that your boy is a wonderful, amazing kid and I love him dearly. He has such a great sense of humor and is really quite funny. I see so much potential in him and want you to know how much I care about that little boy."

Michael let out a little chuckle and said "I bet you say that about all the kids…just before you tell their parents that they're failing!"

In a flash Leo turned serious. Not angry, but very intense in an almost emotional way. "Michael, I *do* say that to every parent because I believe, deeply and completely, that every child is a genuine gift. Every one of these children, including *yours*, is a bundle of light with the potential to do incredibly beautiful things. I feel so privileged to be allowed to teach them…I can't express enough my deep gratitude for being in their presence."

Michael was a bit taken aback. "I'm sorry Leo, I was just joking. I didn't mean to question your belief in them. I just, well, I just get used to hearing that Thomas is not living up to his potential and was waiting for the other shoe to drop." What Michael didn't say was that he had become cynical from years of work reviews. Feedback started with 'You're a great guy who's doing wonderful work,' and ended with the 10 things he was doing wrong.

Leo softened and smiled. "I understand, and I didn't mean to jump like that. It's just that I have a particular issue with seeing children as limited rather than filled with potential. Our system of education seems to promote this, the idea that we need to talk about what each child is *not* doing, rather than what he or she has the potential to become. I feel like it's our responsibility as teachers and parents to look at each child as an enormous, stupendous bundle of potential waiting to be released," Leo said throwing his arms wide with a big smile on his face.

"So," Michael smiled back, "I guess the question is, then, how is Thomas doing in 'releasing his potential'?"

"Ahhh…now that's the question I want to hear!" Leo laughed. "And the truth is," Leo continued more seriously, "that Thomas has not yet made 'the choice', so he's still struggling in a number of areas. But I have faith in him. I think he'll make the choice soon, and it will be a glorious moment when he does!"

"O-kay," Michael said, "I'll bite. What choice are you talking about?"

Leo leaned forward and in a near whisper said, "The choice to believe in his own unique and divine gifts."

Michael was not sure he understood what Leo was saying, and his face must have expressed this because Leo continued, "Michael, every human being on this planet comes into the world with a gift of some kind, a gift that, when realized, releases a tremendous wave of creative potential that changes lives, worlds…indeed universes…and results in unbounded happiness and serenity. *Each of us has this*, and part of the purpose of our lives is to find this gift, this 'purpose of self' that will allow us to create an even greater version of ourselves. We're here to remember and nurture our greatness Michael, but we can only do this through *choice*.

"Now, unfortunately, our educational system isn't set up to encourage this choice. We as teachers are not trained for it, nor are our classrooms or curricula organized to promote it. Our system is built on teaching *content*, not *self-realization*. We sit kids in neat rows, spout knowledge at them, tell them how important it is to follow rules, want them to take tests to prove their competency, and then we churn them to the next level. Factory learning," Leo made a bicycling motion with his hands.

"But what we forget is that children must make a choice about themselves in order to learn and to realize their own potential. They have to *choose to see the possibility in their own growth* instead of relying on what parents, teachers and society tell them they are 'supposed' to do. Unfortunately, we as adults believe that we can force, or at least assume, the choice…which creates a fear-based culture of learning because kids come to believe that the love they receive is conditional upon them doing what they are supposed to be doing: being good little children who sit in rows and parrot back the information we cram into their heads.

"What we *don't* seem to see is the dysfunctional nature of the results," Leo continued, "because the kids who do well in this system, the ones who are 'traditionally intelligent', that is, their genetics are suited for a particular style of learning, move forward in their lives dependent on accolades for self-fulfillment. They need grades, money, titles, all the things that our traditional system of education has taught them are important.

"But the non-traditional learners, the kids who learn by experience, or by body motion (kinesthetically), or through stories…I could go on and on because I actually believe this is *most* children…must learn to navigate this system in a state of uncertainty about themselves. They are faced with the choice of either abandoning their own uniqueness and moving through their lives in mediocrity or 'checking out' of the whole system and renouncing the love they think they can never adequately earn.

"And what gets me really riled up," Leo was standing now, "is that this is a false choice!" he practically shouted. "Because there is a third choice: the choice to believe in his or her own unique and divine potential and to seek to cultivate that potential. *That's* what teaching should be about. That's what I try to do."

Leo sat back down with a thud. "Sorry, Michael, I get a bit worked up about this stuff because when it works, the results are truly amazing. I've seen kids with seemingly no interest or aptitude, kids whose previous teachers had labeled them as 'challenges', tap into this current of potential and do incredible and amazing things! Dancing, painting, mathematics! Fixers, storytellers, craftsmen! Emotional savants, analytical geniuses! Each one of the children on this planet - and adults, mind you - have something beautiful and amazing to offer!

"Our job," he pointed to himself and to Michael, "is to create an environment that encourages this choice. It's easiest to do when they're at Thomas's age because they are actively looking around for cues as to how to be in the world. They look to the adults in their life and observe the choices that we make and ask, 'is it okay for me to be me?' They want to know if they have permission to be unique, to be who their soul is telling them to be."

Michael had a sudden wave of nausea pass over him. He knew *exactly* what Leo was talking about as he remembered his father's threats about grades, his wanting so badly to make his parents happy but not knowing what to do, how to be. And his own pressure on Thomas to 'live up to his potential'...but in the way *Michael* saw 'potential'. He had never even really asked what Thomas wanted. In fact, he didn't even really know what Thomas thought at all. He felt sick again.

"God, Leo," Michael sighed. "I get it. So what's the answer? How can I help my kids make this choice?"

"Love them!" Leo exclaimed. "Children want what we all want, what every human being on this planet yearns for. Unconditional love. Love that accepts, completely, whatever they are in that moment. Love that knows that sometimes they are going to fail, or falter, or screw up...and that that's okay!

"What I've figured out as an educator, parent, and son seems so completely obvious but is very rarely practiced: unconditional love and acceptance grants children, and adults for that matter, the safety to explore who they are, to find that special inner self that is capable of astounding creativity.

Leo looked down and shook his head. "But sadly we parents and educators too often offer *conditional* love and acceptance. If you get good grades, don't screw up, don't buck the system, don't cry, act like an adult...which means, don't play too much...then we will show you the affection and give you the accolades that you have earned. We tell them, in so many words, that they somehow are supposed to work, achieve, and perform to receive our love. This conditionality creates adults that are constantly grasping at externalities because they can't imagine that they are lovable for who they are, that they are perfect exactly the way they are today, in this moment."

Michael felt tears welling up in his eyes. It was so clear. All of the pain in his life stemmed from this very fact. Love's conditionality was an assumption he made a long time ago. He saw it in his son, his friends and his co-workers. It was everywhere, and so, so sad. He wanted so badly to reach out to his son right then.

Leo put his hand on Michael's shoulder. "As sad as this is, Michael, we don't need to feel guilty because we simply didn't know any better. We've all been trained in this way...it's the way many cultures are formed and sustained. We can't make ourselves feel bad for being who we are because it was, in large part, formed by a system that has been in operation for a very long time. A systemic misbelief that love is dependent on what we do and not who we are. But the fact is that we are all born of love, exist in love and are comprised of love. There is no other truth. It simply is.

"Which makes the solution just as simple!" Leo said leaning back and smiling. He paused and looked at Michael expectantly. Michael felt like he should know the answer. Leo answered for him. "To show love to everyone! To give hugs! To tell them they matter! To help, be kind, show compassion, accept unconditionally, forgive quickly! This is the secret truth that religions have been trying to teach for thousands of years, and one that for some reason we consistently resist.

"When I realized this," Leo continued, "I became a freak for hugging. I hug everyone, and they think I'm nuts. I have guys trying to squirm away from me because they think I'm some kind of pervert. I thought my boss, the principal, was going to crawl out of her skin as I came around her desk to give her a hug. But, you know, I think she liked it! She had this little smile that gave her away! We all want love, Michael, we all do. No matter how much we resist it. And a good hug heals so many things. So I don't care, I do it anyway.

"And you know what?" Leo was on a roll. His eyes were gleaming. "Kids respond to it really quickly! They don't have any problem whatsoever with love. They brighten up as if you had given them the best gift ever. I listen to them, smile at them, tell them I love them, and they visibly shine! They *shine*, Michael. I don't have to discipline, warn, or shout, nothing that other teachers have to do. When I tell my kids how much I believe in them, and how I see them as wonderful, amazing, beautiful little beings…well, then they just go head over heels. They want so badly to reciprocate that love, because that is their nature. They want to give back, to learn, to listen. They hang on my every word because they *feel the love*."

Leo smiled contentedly. "And it is the most amazing, fulfilling thing I have ever felt. To be loved in return like that. I sometimes weep with joy," he said, his eyes filling with tears. "And yes, Michael, I'm a big fan of crying too. Emotions are wonderful, aren't they?" Michael didn't answer, as this was not something he had ever considered a possibility, that emotions could be good.

"But I think we've gotten a bit off track. That happens with me sometimes, Michael. I live with everything on my sleeve! Let's talk about Thomas and how we can get him to make 'the choice', okay?" Leo said waving the folder.

Over the next thirty minutes they talked about Thomas's interests and exactly how he showed excitement about certain things over others. They talked about what Thomas did at home, from how he moved and carried himself to how he spoke and what he focused on. Leo seemed to want to know everything. How did Thomas act out? How did he cope with anger or fear, and what did he do when he was happy? Was he physical or did he like mental pursuits? Michael thought it was amazing that a man with so many students could be so interested and curious about his son. Thomas was a very lucky boy to have this man as a teacher.

At the end of the hour, Leo summarized the meeting and gave Michael some things that he and Maria could focus on. Michael then took the risk, as they were walking to the door, to tell Leo about his father and the recent family difficulties. It just seemed so easy to be open with this man.

Leo took Michael by the shoulders and looked directly into his eyes. "Michael, it will all be fine if you remember one thing: show unconditional love and acceptance to Thomas at all times. Kids perceive and understand a lot more than we give them credit for. If they feel that there is a loving and understanding environment, they can hear almost anything. If they feel they are free to express their feelings and to be exactly who they are in each moment, they can endure almost inconceivable hardship and heal with a speed and completeness that we adults have forgotten. Just be present and be loving."

And at that, Leo grabbed Michael and gave him a bear hug that almost took his breath away. To his own shock Michael found himself hugging back…a manly, slap on the back type of hug, but a hug nonetheless. When Leo let go they both were smiling. *Damn*, Michael thought, *this guy is something else!*

Chapter Ten

Over the next few weeks Michael spent his time working, talking with his father, meeting with Louise, and reflecting on the events in his life. Mercifully, his relationship with his wife had calmed somewhat, allowing him time to focus on the challenges at hand. He was fairly certain that Maria was giving him some space, and he loved her for that. It seemed like something was unfolding for him, Michael felt, though he couldn't tell toward what end. It was as if events in his life were being orchestrated and information was coming to him unbidden.

Michael's conversation with Leo was still ringing in his ears. He suddenly became very aware of his children's dreams and fears, seeing them as he was now seeing his own. He was even starting to see the child-like strivings and frustrations in everyone in his life. He could see the frustrated musicians, the playful artists, the serious mathematicians… all represented in adult form yet somehow still yearning for expression. It now made so much sense to him why some of his co-workers were angry and resentful. How could one be happy living with unexpressed childhood dreams? Looking at it that way, life's kind of a bummer!

Although he wasn't sure, Michael was wondering if Louise was purposefully provoking these feelings in him. His past few sessions with the psychologist had not been much more than a bitch session. Louise would ask open-ended questions, then sit attentively while Michael vented, grieved and talked about everything that crossed his mind. And as he noticed in his first session, whenever he seemed to be going in circles Louise had an uncanny way of asking a very pointed question that triggered a series of deep feelings and memories in Michael. He hadn't wept or done anything embarrassing, he thought to himself thankfully, but he definitely had begun to feel things, painful things, rising up inside of him.

He just wasn't sure where to go from here. Certainly this process was helpful, as he could see connections between feelings he had as a child and sensations that were present today. But he wanted more. He wanted to feel better, and most of all he wanted his life to be smooth and happy. Venting felt good, but he wanted . He wondered if Louise would be open to moving a little quicker, perhaps cut to the chase and tell him what was wrong with him and how he could fix it. Michael remembered that she said he was perfect as he was, but that was bullshit in his mind. Everything could be made better, including him.

This belief was a cornerstone of his life, and he felt it deeply. His grandfather had said to him once that nobody was perfect, and each one of us had a responsibility to make ourselves a little bit better every day. To learn something new, practice something we already knew, or to expand ourselves in some tangible way. As a child Michael had latched onto it completely, and now it was a major source of his strength and success.

There was a nagging feeling inside him, though, that maybe he had confused things. What if things happening perfectly? What if it was not so much that he had to achieve an image of perfection, but to be perfect in the process of just being who he is? This thought made his head spin. What if everything was right as it was, and that all of these events were somehow orchestrated in a perfect, structured way. What if all of this learning, and all of these seemingly random, yet somehow synchronous events were perfect in their own right?

Maybe Louise could help with this. He was seeing her this after-noon, and wanted it to be more than just another bitch session. Michael wanted answers and solutions, things that would clarify rather than confuse. As he got up to grab lunch he felt a wave of the satisfaction that comes with a good plan. This is what Michael was good at: planning and directed action. Controlling outcomes, not so much. But at least he had something to work with, something to act on. And that was better than just sitting there wondering what the hell was going on.

Michael walked into Louise's office and sat down in the small lobby. As usual Louise was right on time, greeting him with her usual warm, motherly smile. Michael felt some of his determination begin to ebb away, his demand for answers seemed overly harsh and logical in the presence of this woman. Whenever he was with her, he got the feeling that his analytical thought process was almost quaint, like those old Bill Cosby shows where children are trying to explain something complex in their own limited vocabulary. It was cute, but also such an understatement of the reality of the situation.

They sat down in the usual 'knee-to-knee' position and paused. Louise looked at him, tilted her head and then smiled in a knowing way. "I can sense something has shifted inside you Michael. Would you care to tell me about it?"

Michael was dumbfounded for a moment. Did she just read his mind? Certainly she couldn't know what he was thinking in those few seconds. "How did you know that?" Michael asked incredulously.

Louise laughed softly. "There are many ways to communicate, Michael. Many people have become accustomed to thinking that we only communicate through words, but that's only a small fraction of the information that is conveyed between people. We can talk more about this later, but suffice it to say that, with practice, you can learn to tap into an astoundingly vast source of information about your universe. Some would call it 'intuition' or 'gut feel', but either way it's a fine tuning of perception that allows us to see deeply into each other, the physical world and, tantalizingly, the non-physical world. We are babes yet when it comes to this capacity, Michael, but I assure you it's real."

"So when scientists say that we're only using about 10% of our brains, is that what they mean?" Michael asked, pleased to know something on this subject.

"Yes," Louise responded, "in a general sense. But because our brains and our bodies are really one system, we're really only using 10% of our entire beings' capacity to . And this doesn't mean that we can read more books and cram more knowledge inside ourselves. This means we can step beyond our own self-imposed restrictions and be much more than we ever thought. The other 90% is a frontier of amazing possibility, Michael."

Michael was impressed. This sounded to him. If we were constantly evolving and growing in every way, then wouldn't it be true that our capacity as thinking beings would also be growing?

"But," Michael countered, "why does it seem like we're stuck thinking the same old thoughts and doing the same old things? Sometimes I feel like I'm not growing into my new capacity at all! And look around... how many times does history have to repeat itself before we learn anything? How many wars, how much anger, conflict, hatred do we have to endure before we get it? And I mean not only for the human race, but for me as an individual. Louise, I gotta tell ya', I'm getting sick of my own thoughts! I came in here today with the intention to get some answers, because the only thing I seem to be doing here is becoming aware of my own limitations and the stupid, crazy patterns that I seem to perpetuate!"

Again Louise laughed softly. She seemed to never get perturbed! "Wow, you have said a lot there Michael! I can really hear your frustration, and want you to know that it's OK. You are experiencing awareness, which for many of us can be an incredibly frustrating, even frightening, experience. It's all natural and part of the process."

"I wish that made me feel better!" Michael joked. "Can you at least help me with what's holding me back?"

"Yes, yes," Louise said putting up her hands. "I forgot that you consider yourself an analytical learner." She paused and put her hands in her lap. "Would you be willing to follow along with me while I explain some concepts to you? I encourage you to ask questions along the way, but this may take a good bit of our session. Will you agree to that?"

"Absolutely!" Michael exclaimed. This was the type of thing he felt like he was paying for!

"Alright," Louise started, "let's talk about the concept of 'projection'. Have you ever heard of that?"

"Vaguely," Michael answered, "but please start from the beginning, I want to understand completely."

Louise took a breath and paused, seeming to draw something out of the air around her. "Alright. As we know, the human brain is an amazing and complex organ. It processes more data simultaneously than a building full of supercomputers. In fact, it is so good at processing data that we become convinced that what we are seeing, thinking and feeling is a true representation of reality, when it's essentially a of reality."

Michael looked at her quizzically, so she continued. "When we 'see' something, for instance, what we are doing is taking in a certain spectrum of light waves that are bouncing off of objects within our field of vision. The light enters our eyes and, in the back of the eye, is converted to a stream of data in the form of electrical signals. This data is sent to the brain where it's combined with other sensory data – smell, sound, touch, etc. – to create a holographic image inside of the mind."

"Ha," Michael mused, "a holograph like the 'Princess Lea' image in the first Star Wars?" Michael was a closet 'Star Wars', 'Star Trek'…well, 'Star' anything…geek when he was growing up.

"Exactly," Louise nodded. "Except that this image is, for the most part," she seemed to be struggling with something more complex, "only for our viewing. There is increasing evidence, both experiential and scientific, that this information does not exist solely within the confines of our physical brains, but that's for a later discussion."

"Anyway," she continued, "We use this data to create an image of reality that we can use to navigate the world around us. And luckily the images are fairly accurate, which would certainly be a biological necessity. Any animal in the forest would not survive long if the mind created an image of a tree when it was really a tiger! So we trust the things we see, feel, hear, smell, and touch because the holographs in our mind are fairly accurate re-creations."

"Important, however, is the fact that the raw data we are getting is . Our eyes can only see a certain wavelength of light, our ears only hear at a range of pitches and tones, and our fingers can only feel down to a specific level of granularity. Everything else - higher and lower wavelengths of light and sound, the world of the extremely small or large, and a whole world of smells - is outside our basic senses and therefore not part of the picture that forms in our heads. We get enough to navigate the world though, so it works."

"However, don't forget," Michael interjected, "that man has created instruments to extend his perception, like microscopes and night vision goggles."

"Yes," Louise agreed, "man is very adept at creating tools to perceive. That is part of our brilliance, and why we are destined to become more and more aware as we evolve. But even aside from our tools, we also have room for expansion in the senses we already have within us, that 'other 90%'.

"So we have a reconstituted image of the world that is, at first, just raw perception. This is what most animals have, the ability to perceive an object in the physical world. And so the way we navigate the world is to take that perception and compare it to the ongoing sensory data we continue to receive. In other words, we 'project' the image back onto our surroundings and constantly test its validity.

"For example," Louise continued, "as we walk through the forest we take in the light bouncing off a tree and re-create an image of the tree in our minds. Using that projected image we then navigate to that tree and touch it, creating another image in our mind, the image of texture that confirms and enhances the original visual image. We are creating a richer and richer hologram inside our heads that gives us the ability to see more and more of reality. And again, even though this is limited, it is enough for us to perform basic physical tasks.

"Now with most basic organisms this is enough. They navigate and survive, using genetically encoded triggers and responses. But the higher you go in brain function, the more complex the sensory organs become, the richer the holograms appear and the higher the perception of 'reality'. Because even though it is still only a slice of reality, it is a more robust picture than, say, that of a worm."

Michael laughed at this. "I don't know, Louise, my wife might disagree with you. I am pretty sure she sees my awareness as existing at right around a worm's level!"

"Well, that may be true sometimes, Michael...but not because you aren't getting the sensory input. It's because you have chosen to block out parts of the input that don't fit with your established view of reality."

"Are you saying that I've chosen to be as aware as a worm!?" Michael said with mock horror.

Louise laughed. "Weeeelll..." they both laughed and then she continued, "let's see if I can explain this simply. You see, what differentiates us humans from most animals is our of the sensory data we receive. For example, a monkey may see a tiger (data input), and then interpret it (danger), have an emotional response (fear) and then react (run up a tree). The sequence is fairly simple and based on both genetics and contextual training."

"But a human being evolved with a much richer mechanism. Because we have a larger brain capable of abstract thought, we can look at a similar situation and ask, 'Why?' And this is a very simple but powerful question. Another example: A man is walking through a forest and sees another man running toward him. Now, because man is such a complex being with a variety of motivations, this man may be running for a number of reasons. So the first man reads the contextual environment, looking at hundreds of factors like facial expression, whether or not the running man is carrying a weapon, whether or not he knows the man, etc, then interprets what he sees, has an emotional response (or lack thereof) and reacts. But where it really differs is in the interpretation of the data input, the man running."

"Ahhh," Michael said, "and so we take our own understanding of this situation and onto the 'running man' or whatever situation we're in!"

"Exactly!" Louise clapped. "We search our databanks for similar prior situations, our knowledge of facial expressions, stories that we've been told about people running in the forest, our beliefs about people generally, everything we know on the subject, and then we come up with a hypothesis that we act on as if it were reality. The challenge for most human beings is that we sometimes don't realize that not only is it an picture of reality, but it is picture of reality…and it may be incorrect.

"Illustrations can be helpful here as well," Louise continued. "Have you ever called someone and they didn't call you back?"

"Of course," Michael answered.

"What did you think when that happened?"

"Well, depending on the situation sometimes I got mad, other times I forgot about it."

"With any of the times you got angry, did you find out that there was a good reason for the person not calling you back? Say they had an emergency?" Louise probed.

"Yeah," Michael answered sheepishly. "Once my girlfriend had gotten into an accident and I thought she had been avoiding me. I felt like a total shit."

"So what happened was you projected your beliefs about how people should react, based entirely on your own knowledge, internal stories and experiences, and applied them to a situation, only to find out your projected 'reality' was completely false."

"Yep, that's about right!" Michael nodded.

"It's not that you did anything , Michael," Louise assured. "It's just that this particular interpretation mechanism can obscure the true reality of a situation. We have a lens through which we see the world, a totally unique and complex lens that is crafted through our genetics, our family situation, our experiences with peers and some would say our particular karma. The important thing is not to judge ourselves for our lens, but to become if it. And this can be a frustrating process, because for most of us we have simply assumed our way of seeing things is the only way, the 'right' way."

"Ahhh," Michael sighed. "I think I'm starting to see why I'm feeling so frustrated. I feel like I'm noticing things that I haven't noticed before, like my anger in certain situations. It also seems like there are patterns that have played out over and over again in my life that I can't quite explain. Sometimes the way I feel is like the movie 'Groundhog Day', same shit, different day, as they say."

"And here, Michael, is where we get to the most difficult part to grasp," Louise said, suddenly serious. "It is the most powerful concept of all, and one that very, very few people truly grasp." Louise looked at her watch and said, "OK, we have about 15 more minutes, so I'm going to go through this and ask you to think about it for our next meeting. Just listen and try to take this in. You may feel resistance toward these concepts, which is natural, but I want you to just sit with it and ask yourself over the next week if it is true for you."

"Ooookay," Michael narrowed his eyes. "I'll try to be open minded. Go ahead."

Louise looked at Michael and said, "Good, because the very things you project onto the world are what you end up creating in the world. If you see the world, say, as an angry place, because you grew up in an angry household, you will move through the world projecting 'presumed anger' on people around you…which will then tend to create the anger you are expecting to see. The same is also true in the opposite way. If you see the world as a loving, peaceful place, you will project that onto the world and tend to experience a loving, peaceful life."

Michael couldn't help himself. "But even with this rather Pollyanna outlook, sorry, surely we will still experience angry things and negative people?"

"Yes, and you can experience this negativity while still feel loving inside. That is another thing unique to us humans. We can, once we become aware of our reactions, a different reaction. In fact, it's the only thing we can truly control. Our reactions. In that sense we are 'responsible'…or 'able to respond'."

Louise could see Michael was skeptical so she continued.

"Maybe this will help, Michael. Have you ever seen how someone really upbeat can enter a room and change the whole feeling of the room?"

"Sure," Michael answered, "And I've seen the opposite, too."

"Yes," Louise smiled, "We say a person gives off 'good vibes' or bad vibes'. This is because we actually giving off vibrations. As the good Dr. Holtzman probably told you, our bodies are great vibrating mechanisms that are constantly tuning to our thoughts and, hold onto your hat, thoughts. Our bodies tune into whatever our thoughts are saying and can sense, through the five senses and, especially, the sixth sense of 'intuition', what other people are feeling and thinking. So we literally vibrate with people in harmony or against people in dissonance.

"Now here's where it gets interesting. In every group situation – let's say a meeting in your office – all the thoughts, attitudes, beliefs and feelings will combine into one giant vibration. It may be harmonious or dissonant, but either way we create a sort of 'stew' that reflects the combination of each person's projected way of being. Our projections all combine to create a 'combined reality' that we all feel. Sometimes we call this 'culture' if the rules are apparent to all, or just 'the feel of the room' if it's an ad-hoc group of people. Either way, we tend to 'co-create' our environment." Louise smiled.

"Okay, I think I get this, but then how does that create our reality?

I mean, how does my way of projecting my thoughts and beliefs create my life? I don't get it." Michael was beginning to get another headache.

Louise answered with a nod and a tilt of her head that told Michael he wasn't going to believe this. "Because the universe always seeks balance and harmony. If you are projecting thoughts about a particular thing, then everything around you will seek to equalize with those thoughts. If you grow up believing that you are unworthy of money or that money is evil, for example, then you will have thoughts, take actions and attract people into your life . You will throw away money with both hands. In the same way if you believe you are worthy of a loving relationship, you will create situations that confirm that internal reality. In this way, you are, in part, the creator of your own destiny."

"Yes, uh-huh, I get this now." Michael was nodding his head. "But sometimes I really want something, like a peaceful relationship with my boss, yet I don't seem to be able to create it. In fact, I never have."

"That's because somewhere deep inside you there's a belief that undermines what you want. I call this a 'competing intention'. You want one thing, yet deep down you don't believe you can have it. So you feel frustration, anger and fear that maybe you aren't what you think you are. That maybe you deserve what you want. When the reality is that you are what you don't want by holding onto that belief!" Louise could see that Michael was beginning to get it.

"And here is a helpful key Michael: if you want to experience something different than what you are experiencing today, you have to first align your beliefs to what you want. If you want the respect of others, then you have to believe that you're worthy of respect. For most of us, this is a tall order because we can't even see the underlying belief."

"So how do I notice these underlying beliefs?" Michael pleaded. "I really want to get at this because I'm extremely unhappy right now. I just don't know what to do."

Louise put her hands together and smiled. "I understand Michael, and I can feel your frustration. This is a lot to take in. So why don't you try this: just become aware of your emotions. Emotions are the key to all deep-seated beliefs. They are pointers. Negative emotions are merely indications that you are not aligned with something inside of you, that you have beliefs that are in conflict with your external world.

"Judgments are the same thing…they are simply projections of your own internal negative emotion onto someone else. We judge someone because we recognize in them something we don't like in our own lives. So whenever you have a judgment or anger about something, don't fight it…just notice it. Notice what thoughts preceded that negativity. Try to understand where they came from in your past, and what beliefs you came to hold.

"Do the same for positive emotions like love, joy and gratitude, because those feelings are also based on beliefs that you hold. They key here is awareness, Michael. Awareness of your own internal world. Awareness of your beliefs, emotions and reactions. As you become aware, you can then begin to choose differently, to choose beliefs and reactions that project, and therefore co-create, a world more consistent with your own inner peace and happiness."

Louise then stood, indicating that the session was over. She was nothing if not punctual, Michael thought.

"So let's keep our schedule for next week," Louise said as she walked toward the door, "and please don't be hard on yourself through this process. It's not easy to make this mental shift. Just notice what's going on in your head and let's come back and talk about it. If it helps, you can keep a journal of your feelings and judgments from day to day. Sometimes just reading over them at the end of a week can bring awareness to patterns. Regardless, I think you will experience greater awareness no matter what you do!"

Louise smiled one last time and opened the door. There was another client in the anteroom, so Michael bid her farewell.

As the door shut behind him, Michael didn't know what to think. His head was completely spinning. He had asked for her to be direct, but now regretted his decision. He got the concept of projection, but 'creating our world' with it? How was he responsible for his boss being a jerk? And how can he trace his emotions back to his beliefs? This was a lot to take in.

The sun was setting as Michael walked to his car. He wanted badly just to go home and have a beer, but had promised his Dad he would stop by and say hello. Michael noted to himself that next time he would not schedule anything after his session with Louise. He was having trouble thinking straight. As he drove out of the parking lot he mumbled to himself, "Take it easy, all you have to do is pay attention. No big deal."

Little did he know that this was the first step in a complete transformation of his life.

Chapter Eleven

Michael got on the highway and merged into traffic. He knew he had a bit of a drive to get to his father's house, so he began to accelerate and look for a way over to the far left-hand lane. Just as he began to ebb left, a car in the middle lane moved forward and blocked his path. Michael jerked the car back into the right lane and glared over his left shoulder. "Asshole" he said to himself, as he began to look for another way over.

A wave of awareness came over him. Is this what Louise was talking about? He had always had an issue with a low-level form of road rage…could this be some sort of projection? As he sped forward and around the cars in the middle lane – why the hell is the right lane always clear while the middle and left lanes are full, anyway? – he flashed back to a memory of his Dad screaming at people on the road. Did Michael somehow pick up this habit? What was the underlying assumption here?

Michael tried to remember what Louise had explained. Something about our beliefs creating our 'lens' of the world, which we then combine with our experiences and knowledge to create a projection of our view of reality. But Michael was sure that this guy had just cut him off to be a jerk…or was he projecting that? Did he know that this guy moved forward on purpose? No. Then why did he get angry? Then it came to Michael in a flash: because people are mean and spiteful and, well, jerks.

Yes. That was it. And not only that, people are stupid and ignorant and careless. They cut you off, drive in the left hand lane, and are generally bad drivers. He had grown up hearing these exact words from his father. More memories started to pop into Michael's head. When he was younger a group of older bullies had taken his brand-new bike and broken it into pieces. He ran home to tell his father and they both went back to retrieve his bike, but the bullies were gone. His father picked up the broken bike and cursed about the 'punks and jerks that live in this town'.

The realizations were cascading into Michael's mind like a waterfall. The underlying belief is that people are cruel and careless and disrespectful. This was definitely a current in Michael's life, an assumption that he had never really questioned. But Louise also said that we can't project something outward unless we somehow relate to that feeling. That a projection originates from some picture inside of ourselves that we associate with how *we* are. *Am I cruel and careless and disrespectful?* Michael wondered.

And then it hit him. The memory of Michael interrupting his father while he was working. His father had turned around and snapped, and Michael had heard in his father's tone that he was exactly that: careless and disrespectful. He had judged himself as careless and disrespectful, and now he was projecting it out onto the world. Michael felt sick to his stomach. Then all those people in his life, his boss, co-workers, *his wife, his kids*...all of those times he looked at them in judgment, that was *him*?

Was he creating these situations? Or was he just seeing only what he was trained to see? Before he left, Louise had said something about 'our outer world reflecting our inner reality', was this what she meant?

Michael was so engrossed in his own thoughts that he almost missed the turn to his father's house. He swerved to the right and cut across three lanes to barely make the exit. As he slid down the ramp, he looked to his left and saw a driver flipping him off and mouthing "asshole". Michael felt a wave of rage come over him and raised his hand to return the salute...and he froze. Was he just seeing himself in a mirror? Clearly that guy didn't realize the state Michael was in, that Michael was confused and upset. He didn't know that Michael's father was dying, that his wife wanted to leave him, and that his job was in jeopardy. This man was simply projecting *his* beliefs and stories onto Michael.

"Is this whole world one big projection?" Michael asked to nobody in particular as he dropped his hand.

As he pulled up to the light at the end of the exit he suddenly became acutely aware of the anger that he projected onto the world. The mistrust. The feeling that the world was a harsh, cruel place that needed to be controlled. Just then a car passed closely in front of his bumper. "Jerk", the voice flashed in his head. There it is again! The light turned green and Michael pulled onto the main road. Over and over he caught himself judging people around him. "Stupid guy walking in the road." "Ignorant redneck driving the ridiculously huge pickup truck." "Bimbo doing her makeup while she's driving." "Weirdo singing to himself driving his car."

The little judgments and projections each seemed to have a root belief attached to them. People are stupid, weird, mean, careless, on and on. And Michael had somehow created this world for himself. But what confused him was that he was not controlling their actions, so how could he be creating this world. Sure, he was *interpreting* his world this way, but how could he have actually attracted these people into his life?

Maybe it was what Louise meant by 'co-creation'. That all of us are creating our worlds as we go, so the combination of all of our projections result in the world in which we find ourselves. In this case, Michael realized, he is simply predisposed to experience the people he believes make up the world. And if all the projections combined make up what the world is, and others like Michael saw the world as negative and antagonistic, then that would explain crime and war and unfriendly work environments, and all of the painful things humans experience. It's all self-created. Starting with *me*, Michael thought.

Michael had been so lost in thought that he didn't even realize he had arrived in front of his Dad's house. His sense of time had completely disappeared, and somehow he had gotten to his destination on auto-pilot. This process was becoming a bit frightening, and it was just the beginning. Michael took a deep breath and looked into the mirror. "Ok, let's get grounded," Michael said to himself, as he got out of the car and walked up the driveway.

"Dad?" Michael called pushing open the front door and looking around. He desperately hoped he would not find his father lying on the floor.

"Yeah, down here," his father called from the basement. His dad liked to tinker in his shop when he was bored. Michael had a host of his little gadgets at home: Wooden toast grabbers, hooked banana holders, twirly spinning propellers for the kids. Michael had always humored his dad because it gave him something to do. But why, when he is on his last weeks of life, would his Dad want to spend his time down in the basement working on useless trinkets?

Michael heard his dad's feet slowly and heavily taking each step. His wheezing had become a pronounced, wet-sounding rattle. Michael moved quickly to the top of the stairs to help, but his father waved him off. "I can still walk some," his cadaverous father said breathlessly.

"Hey Dad, you don't look so bad," Michael lied again.

"I told you, stop bullshitting me," his father snapped. "You know I look like hell."

Michael didn't know what to say. He had never spoken to his dad in reassuring tones, and it didn't feel right. It was so strange to see such a force in his life deteriorating before his eyes.

"Okay Dad, you look like shit. Is that better?" Michael forced a smile. Why couldn't this be easier?

"Yeah, and I feel crappy too. I guess this is how it works before you croak," Roy sat down heavily at the kitchen table. "Grab a Coke or something. You want a beer? They're in the fridge."

Michael grabbed a beer from the fridge and thought about how strange it was to be drinking while his Dad slowly withered away. Some-

112

times life seemed both tragic and mundane at the same time.

"Dad…" Michael wanted to ask how his dad was handling all this, but he didn't know exactly how. He sat down at the table, opened his beer and started again. "Dad, how are you feeling about all this? I mean, I know you don't feel well and that you aren't going to fight it, but geez, are you…are you *scared*?"

His father paused and looked intensely at him for a few seconds. Michael saw a number of emotions rapidly pass across his father's face. A mix of derision, fear, anger, surprise.

"What am I supposed to say to that?!" his father barked. "What am I going to do about it? I am dying, and that's that. Nothing I can do, so might as well accept it. Scared? Hell no. I've had a good life. I've got nothing to regret. I had a great career, two great kids, a wonderful wife for most of my life, and a good retirement. It's time to move on. So no, I'm not scared. Why the hell did you ask that, anyway?"

Michael was a bit taken aback at this short outburst. He had never heard his father even *talk* about regret or having a good life or anything else. His father had clearly been thinking about this.

"Well, I don't know Dad, I guess I just wanted to get to know what you're thinking. You know, how you think about things. It's not like this happens every day, you know. I mean, didn't you wonder what Grandpa was thinking sometimes? Weren't you a bit curious about who he was as a man?"

Michael's grandfather on his father's side had passed when Michael was 5, and so he had very few memories of the man. He had vague recollections of sitting on Grandpa Frank's lap and getting those old-time candies from the old-time green dish next to the old-time brown recliner. Michael thought how strange it was that some memories 'keep' while most don't. What was it about that event that made it become a persistent memory, Michael wondered.

His Dad's harsh voice snapped Michael out of his reverie. "My Dad was not a talking man. He worked hard, took care of his family, and died 3 years after he retired. Heart attack. He was lucky," his dad grunted. "I didn't ask him a lot of questions, and he didn't offer a lot of information. His whole family was like that. Dirt farmers who barely said anything to each other."

Michael persisted. He knew he was going to push too far, but he didn't care. He knew nothing about his dad's side of the family and he didn't want his dad to die without understanding his own lineage. "But was he a nice man? What were his hobbies? Did you spend time with him, play ball, anything like that?"

His dad issued a stifled half grunt, half laugh. "My dad and I didn't do shit together. The old man worked hard, came home, did house chores, and if he had time, he drank beer and listened to a ball game on the radio. If I was lucky I got to do chores *with* him, but that was the extent of our interaction."

"Wow, didn't that bother you? It must have been fairly lonely. I know your brothers and sisters had all left home by then." Roy had been the youngest of 4, and a 'mistake' according to family scuttlebutt. This was never spoken aloud, but seemed accurate given what Michael knew.

"God damnit, Michael! What's the point of all this? Jeezuz, I feel like I'm with a shrink!" Clearly Michael had hit a sore spot.

Michael sat for a moment. Anger was flaring up inside of him. He knew that he was asking these questions because he himself had felt the cold loneliness of a distant and disengaged father. Michael wanted, just for a moment, for his father to acknowledge the pain. Just to say he understood.

"Well, hell, Dad," Michael glared at him. "I guess I just want to know how you grew up, you know? Is it asking too much to want to know where I came from? Shit, Dad. I grew up not having any meaningful conversations with you. All I heard was grunts and 'get your homework done'! Why can't you just talk to me, Dad? Why can't we talk about things that *mean* something, about life, about the way you feel about things?! God-damn, Dad…you're *dying* for God's sake! We aren't going to get another shot at this!"

There. It was out. Michael had not intended to speak to his father this way, but the work with Louise had prompted thoughts and feelings that he simply couldn't suppress. It was the truth, and he was glad he said it.

Roy Benson sat looking down at the table. Michael wasn't sure what would happen next. When his father went silent like this, it usually meant an explosion was imminent.

"Wow, Dad, I didn't mean…" Michael started.

His father cut him off. His voice was quiet. "What do you want me to say, son? That I regret the way I was with you kids, with your Mom? Well I don't. I grew up in a world where we didn't talk about things, and I don't know if I can start now. Yeah, I was focused on work most of the time. Yeah, maybe I drank too much when I came home. But this was what we did, Son. I didn't go to a shrink and cry 'boo hoo my life is so bad', like people do nowadays." Michael cringed internally.

"I just took the shit life handed me and worked through it. And now that life is coming to an end. So what the hell am I supposed to do? You want an apology? No way. No way. I worked my ass off for you kids and don't regret any of it." Roy looked at Michael with defiance in his eyes.

Michael shook his head. "Dad, I don't want an apology. I know you did the best you could. I just want to learn from you, and to connect with you. Can't we do things differently now? Can't we talk openly about things that are meaningful? Dad, there are things I want to tell you and ask you. I'm struggling right now in my life, and don't feel like I have anyone to talk to. And you may scoff at me, but I am seeing a counselor, Dad, and a lot if it is because I feel so damn alone. I go to work, do my best but still get my ass chewed, go home to get my ass chewed, and sit here and criticize myself for not doing enough. Hell, I don't even know how to talk to you! I can't seem to do anything perfectly enough to get by in this world. It's like I'm on the receiving end of a shit fire-hose. And I just want to talk to you. That's all!"

For the first time in 35 years, Michael felt emotion rising in him. It was a deep hurt that started as a tightness in his throat and became a tingly-hot sensation in his face. He knew, from when he was a child, that the next thing would be a quivering lip and moist eyes. One of the last times this had happened, he was about 8, his father had slapped him and grabbed him by the shoulders and said, 'don't you cry...damnit. I will *give* you something to cry about, so knock it off.' So Michael had swallowed his tears and vowed never to cry again. But now the feeling was back, and with it came a bitterness and anger he could barely contain.

"Dad, it's your last couple of weeks on earth. I just want to talk. Please."

His father faltered for a moment. Michael sensed that his father was torn between exploding and...and something Michael couldn't identify.

"Son," his father sighed, "I don't know. I don't know how to do this. I am sorry for the way you're feeling right now, I really am. And I do understand. I've been there, trust me. But I don't know if I can do what you want me to do. I don't have the skills, Son. I never had to do this, even with your mother. She was so good, too, she never pushed me. She understood, and she just let me be. God I miss her." Michael could have sworn his father was expressing emotion. He leaned forward and put his hand on his father's shoulder.

"Dad, I know you do. I'm sorry, I don't mean to put all this on you. I really want to connect with you is all. You know I worshipped you when I was young. You were larger than life to me, and in many ways you still are. I just want to share more with you, to know who you are. Man to man, you know?"

His father laughed sarcastically and looked up at Michael, "Well, you got some of your answers. You worshipped an emotionless workaholic who cared more about money and 'success' than his own family. How's that for a real conversation?"

At that moment, Michael saw it. All the pain, all the loneliness that his father had been avoiding became apparent in that one look. Michael felt a wave of compassion as he saw in his father the earnest little boy who so badly wanted his own father to see him, to love him. He knew at that moment that his dad had always been doing the best that he could, and showing love in the only way he knew how.

How similar he and his father were. Both of them seeking love from a parent that was disengaged and unavailable. How long had this been going on? Was this some kind of pattern that had been repeating itself…for generations? Michael was suddenly seeing his family in a whole new light. If Louise was correct, then he and his father had been repeating a pattern of projection that probably started hundreds, if not thousands, of years ago!

The components of the story became painfully clear in that moment: The world is an unforgiving and harsh place; we are all 'on our own'; human connection is dangerous; success, if derived through titles and money, proves value; compassion is weakness; anger is the only allowable emotion; knowledge is king; being right is more important than building relationship; telling is preferable to hearing, unless you are a child, then 'be seen and not heard'. No, this wasn't a story, this was a *way of being*. To the men in his family these messages were assumed…. there was no other alternative. This is what they became and the world they created.

Louise's words rang in his ears: *We create the world we project*. How sadly true. This worldview had manifested in every job, relationship and situation in Michael's life. And his father's life. And his grandfather's. Until now, Michael had never been aware of the subtle decisions he had been making, the choices that confirmed his model of the world. He felt both frightened and empowered at the same time.

"Dad," Michael started, seeing his father with a tenderness that was new to him, "I think I get it. We don't need to do this. I…well…I think I see what you mean. I guess I just want you to know how much I care about you, and how much I respect you. You really are an exceptional man, Dad. You did so much for us, and gave us things that you never had. There's nothing more you need to do. I'm okay just spending time with you."

Roy Benson looked at his son with what Michael thought was a mixture of relief and pride. Michael knew in that moment that his father had never felt truly accepted or unconditionally loved for who he was. Not by his father, mother, grandparents...not even by *himself.* So he had hidden this secret pain through activity, achievement, and alcohol. And Michael knew he was doing the same thing. How could he judge those sins that he himself regularly committed?

Michael stood up and lifted his father by his elbows. He looked into his father's eyes and saw the complexity and depth of this man. He could see the child who struggled all his life to gain the love of those around him, and the pain, the hope and the joy of a man trying to both give and receive love the best way he knew how.

Tears formed in Michael's eyes. "Dad, I...I..." but he couldn't finish the sentence. He hugged his father deeply and hoarsely whispered "I'll be back tomorrow, Dad."

As he pulled away, his father nodded and blinked away his own tears. Old habits were hard to break. This was as emotional as either of them had been for many years, and they both fought the temptation to judge the situation.

Slightly confused and embarrassed, they gave each other a slap on the shoulder and then laughed at the ironic, mirror-like quality of the act. Maria had been telling Michael how much he was starting to look like his father, and now he could understand why. It was not so much the similar physical appearance that was uncanny, but more the almost synchronous way in which they *moved* and *expressed.* In some ways he felt more like his father's brother than a son.

Michael left his father's house feeling like a child who had just experienced his first amusement park ride: exhilarated, scared, nervous, proud. He had inadvertently connected with his father...not through direct appeal but through simple understanding. For a brief moment, he had been able to stand in his father's place and to see the world through his father's eyes. And in that moment, he had felt an overwhelming compassion that seemed to change the dynamic of the whole conversation. In one second of pure awareness, he had connected to his father in a way that transcended all words. He *knew* his father.

Driving home was, once again, a blur. As he parked in front of his house, he stared at the garage door for what seemed like hours. How was he going to explain all this to Maria? There seemed to be too much for Michael to even comprehend, let alone explain.

Suddenly another thought popped into his mind. What about women? Michael had been preoccupied with the way he, as a male, existed in this world and his family, and how his father and grandfather had related to each other...but what about the women in his life and family? It seemed like Michael had almost purposefully left them out, as if they were tangential to his world.

Michael began to identify more family stories here. Women were overly emotional and not analytical enough to be trusted with tough decisions. Generally, women nagged men and created more problems than solutions. Women, from the male perspective, were difficult and maddeningly chaotic. Michael saw that he had internalized many of these views, but now began to question their accuracy.

Was he missing something? It did seem that the women in his life were difficult sometimes, both at work and at home, but was this real or yet another one of his projections? Was he creating this situation or the victim of it? He had memories of this mother and father's relationship, which seemed to confirm all of the family stories that men told, but realized that he really didn't know his mother all that well. She was definitely a force in his life, but one that he regarded with a detached amusement. His father felt more important to him. His mother was, well, just *there*.

Michael immediately recognized that his father had seen his mother in the same way. He realized that he had taken on a deeply ingrained view that women were a source of love, certainly, but were largely to be regarded as a burden to be borne by men who are trying to do the best for their companies and families.

Michael put his head in his hands. This felt like too much. This self-analysis (or was it self awareness?) was spinning him in circles. It was as if all the underlying assumptions of his life had been removed and placed on a table in front of him. Worse, all of the *implications* of his choices were becoming clear. He saw how completely he had crafted his life to mirror what he believed.

He got out of the car thinking how Maria was going to be irritated that he was sitting out front for so long, but then realized this was yet another projection. He didn't *know* that, so why was he assuming it? Because his beliefs about women dictated that response!

"Shit. Shit. Shit." He mumbled to himself as he went to open the door. But then again, maybe if he was able to see it, he'd be able to fix it. What had Louise said? "Awareness is the key"?

As he stepped through the door and took his coat off, he had a fleeting hope that maybe this would be a quick process, that maybe he could just fix all this and move on. But as his wife came around the corner, he could see that this wasn't to be.

Chapter Twelve

Michael walked into work exhausted. Last night had not gone well. When he had walked into the house, Maria had rounded on him with a list of grievances about his lack of communication, the burden of taking care of his father, her own frustrations about their marriage, everything. He had exploded and felt justified about it. She had thrown the kitchen sink at him when he was already worn out from the day, and he just couldn't take it.

But at the same time there was a different quality to the fight. Even though it took on the familiar pattern of accusation then defense, then counter accusation and counter-defense, Michael could feel himself observing what was going on. It was as if he were monitoring his words from outside himself. He could see his stories playing out: his tendency to see women as being difficult, his belief that life was unduly harsh and that people were unreasonable.

Even stranger, however, was the reaction his words were generating. Whenever he heard himself taking the tone of 'you are unreasonable' and 'not again', Maria had gotten even *more* 'unreasonable' and angry. It was as if they were reading lines in a play, except that the script itself was creating the stage, the set and the audience. It started dawning on Michael that he and his wife were jointly creating their reality through their stories. They played the roles over and over…but to what end?

In the past, Michael had tended to blame Maria for all this, but now he wasn't so sure. Although it was just a glimpse, Michael was observing how his own actions and words generated the situation that had occurred. And hadn't he in some strange way intended this? When he walked in the door he had reflected for a moment on all of his beliefs about women…and then all of those beliefs had somehow been validated. Or had they been created? Did he actually create the very situation that he had been envisioning?

But he hadn't said anything! He just walked into the door and was ambushed. Or was he? Now that he thought back on it, there was a pause before she started. She had looked at him for a moment, and then brought up his not calling after the teacher's meeting. And he had reacted…as if he had been anticipating this. Michael had suspected Maria would be bothered by his lack of follow up, and he felt sheepish about it. But if she knew this somehow, then why would she bring it up? Was it because he had been *expecting* her to? Was she just following some unstated instruction that Michael was issuing?

It was all so exhausting. Michael felt like his whole life was being tipped upside-down. The arguing and work and his Dad's illness were one thing, but what was really difficult was the fact that Michael was seeing it all in some sort of new context. It was as if he was being shown exactly how he had created his own world, yet he felt powerless to change it. That was it, the helplessness. But wasn't that also a story? The feeling that somehow the world was affecting him, and he needed to control the world in order to feel safe? Don't be a victim. Wasn't that an oldie-but-goodie in the Benson family?

Michael sighed as he plopped down at his desk. He just wished he could understand what everyone wanted from him. He did not know what more he could do. How was he supposed to please his wife, his boss, his co-workers, his team, his Dad? And now he was being presented with the fact that he was somehow *generating* all this unhappiness! Michael wanted so badly for someone to just hand him a list of things to do to make everything OK. Then he could do what he needed to do and everyone would leave him alone. And at peace.

Fat chance.

Michael's computer mercifully booted without issue. As he opened his calendar, he groaned with dread when he saw his morning schedule. Armand had brought in a consultant to talk with the executive team about the company's compensation and performance issues. For months people at the company had been complaining about their pay, and Armand had wanted to see if this was in any way tied to his team's missing their numbers this quarter. Michael had his doubts but was willing to try anything to get Armand off his back.

Generally, Michael hated consultants. They usually had no idea what it was like to run a company. Most of them had come out of business school and gone right into advisory work. But how could they advise when they had never actually run a business? Sure, some of them were really bright, but they acted as if everything occurred in a bottle. All you have to do is X, and you will get Y. But the world was so much more complicated than that! X impacts not only Y but A, G and F! A company is a system of people and people rarely conform to the logic of mathematics.

Nevertheless, Michael decided to be open to what the consultant had to offer. His own life was so much in limbo that he felt like all he could do was surrender and take in whatever information was proffered. At least it would be better than having to think through all of this himself. Let someone else do the thinking for a change!

Michael got up and went to grab a cup of coffee. In the break room he saw an older gentleman, older even than his father, speaking with another member of the executive team. Surely this couldn't be the consultant he was to meet? Michael had never seen a consultant over the age of 45, and this guy had to be at least 70. Did people still work at that age?

The consultant and his colleague finished their conversation, and as they parted, Michael stepped up to introduce himself.

"Hello," Michael interjected, "I'm Michael Benson. Are you the consultant I'm meeting with at 10?"

The man smiled a kindly smile and slowly said "Oh! Yes, I think I must be! My name is Joseph Weiss, but please call me Joe." He reached out his hand to Michael.

"Well," Michael said looking at his watch, "do you want to start a little bit early? Maybe grab a cup of coffee and chat for a bit?"

"Sure! Why not!" Joe replied. "Give us an extra 15 minutes to get to know each other. And you can get a bit more for your money!" he lightly slapped Michael on the back as they headed down the hall. Michael had the feeling he was talking to his grandfather, and it was both strange yet comforting. He already felt very relaxed in this man's presence.

As they walked into Michael's office, Joe noticed the pictures of Michael's family and began to ask questions. He seemed genuinely interested in Michael's life. Michael talked about how and where he grew up, where he went to college, the companies he had worked for, his family, even his father's situation. Joe was so easy to talk to, and had such an accepting presence, that Michael felt like he could reveal anything and not be judged.

After speaking for about 20 minutes, Michael realized that Joe hadn't said a word about himself. Aside from Louise, Michael had never talked this openly to a complete stranger…and it seemed so natural and easy.

Somewhat sheepishly Michael said, "Geez Joe, I've been rambling on for a while here. Tell me about you a little bit. I know you're a consultant, but not much else."

Joe smiled, leaned forward and gave Michael a bit of background on himself. As it turned out, Joe had been a COO and then CEO of a Fortune 500 company for 10 years. He had worked his way up through the ranks, becoming known for his highly motivational management style. The company he worked for, a major retailer, had experienced massive and rapid growth over his tenure and had become one of the top companies in its category.

Joe explained that he had left the company voluntarily in order to give other young leaders a chance. He felt that he had done what he came to do and wanted to pursue his real passion, 'motivational science' as he called it. He said he believed it was important to be constantly grooming others for his position so that he could be freed up to grow to the next level.

"And so," he finished, "here I am as a motivational consultant. I love what I do because now I get to have an impact on *many* other companies. And as a side benefit, I'm constantly exposed to new situations which keeps the old noggin," he tapped the side of his head, "in top form." Joe smiled self-deprecatingly. Michael couldn't help but think how much this guy had experienced in his life, how much he must know.

"Wow," Michael responded, "you don't often hear of CEOs giving up their positions voluntarily!"

"Yes, I know." Joe shook his head. "Most people think I'm crazy, but I believe life is a series of experiences that need to be savored and then released. Getting attached to a job, being *defined* by a job, is very limiting. I didn't want to become someone so wrapped up in the trappings of my position that I couldn't learn anymore. So I took my bonus and went off to see how I could be of service elsewhere. And, if my health holds up, I want to keep going in the non-profit sector. I feel like I can do some good, and it feels good to help out."

Michael had never heard an executive be so candid about his life. Usually he found people at this level to be very guarded and protective about their stature...but Joe was so *humble, so utterly open.*

"Gosh," Michael laughed. "I'm usually cynical about consultants, but now I have so many questions I don't know where to start. I guess we can start with our company. I know you've spent some time with our executive team, so I'd be interested to know your thoughts and perceptions about our culture and how it might become more 'performance oriented'. You know, how we might get more out of our people. And maybe what we're doing wrong, because as you know we missed our numbers this quarter...by a *lot*."

Joe threw his head back and laughed. "Okay, I get the picture. You're afraid you're screwing up and want to know how to do better so you can avoid failure and its consequences."

"Well," Michael objected, "I wouldn't say we're…or I'm…*afraid*, but yes, we don't seem to be doing as well as we could."

Joe nodded his head and said, "I want to be very clear with you and very open, because I sense that you want to learn. Is it OK if I'm blunt?"

Michael felt taken aback. A consultant had never spoken to him like this. He felt like his Dad was about to lay down the law.

"Sure," Michael said hesitatingly, "I suppose that's what we're paying for." Michael wanted to re-assert his authority, but it came across as hollow.

"OK," Joe began. "Motivation comes from one of two places: Fear or Love. Most of the clients that get in touch with me do so because of fear. 95% I would say. They don't like where they are and they're afraid of the consequences of continuing down this path. It doesn't matter if it's an individual, a team or the entire company. The fear is immediately apparent in the nature of the request.

"Clients that are coming from a place of love – and I don't mean that squishy, movie-type love that most men think is somehow 'girlie', but a love that is pure joy and excitement – these clients call me because they want to be better people, create more meaning, and want to try to do something good in the world. The tenor of that request is *completely different* than the fear-based request. And so are the results."

"So," Michael interjected, "you think we're a fear-based organization? I personally don't sense a lot of fear around here."

"Of course you don't!" Joe smiled. "That's because of the lens through which you see your environment. You have a corporate culture that contains unstated but tacit agreements to see things a certain way. I could easily do a survey that would prove this to you, but I'm going to ask you to trust me for now. The fear is very obvious to me because

I've worked with companies that don't have it...and they operate in a completely different way. You will only see this when you step back and look objectively at what you've created."

"Gosh," Michael wondered aloud, "this lens sounds an awful lot like the concept of 'projection' that a…" Michael caught himself, "that a friend told me about."

"Now it's my turn to be surprised!" Joe laughed. "You know about projection! I don't run across many executives who understand this concept!"

Joe continued, "A culture is merely an aggregation of the projections, or lenses as I like to call them, of all the individuals. A 'group projection', so to speak. Each member of the group subscribes to a particular way of looking at the world, and so creates a reality that the entire group experiences."

Michael felt a surge of understanding. "So not only do individuals create their reality, but so do *groups*!"

"Yes." Joe answered. "And this is either done explicitly or implicitly. Groups will work on 'value statements' and 'mission statements' to explicitly state what they believe, but most of the time these are short-lived attempts to change the culture."

"I can relate to *that*!" Michael chuckled. He had been part of so many ineffective 'cultural initiatives' that he had lost count.

"And most of us can," Joe continued, "because the implicit values and beliefs are deeply engrained and much more persistent than the explicit. Explicit statements of belief are helpful, but they're ultimately meaningless if they're in opposition to our unstated, implicit beliefs. Those unstated, implicit beliefs are so deeply held that we're usually unaware that they even exist. And in most people, they are *fear-based*."

Michael immediately saw what Joe was saying. Many of his own beliefs were about needing to be more, needing to be perfect in a tough world, needing to fight. And if he was honest with himself, there was fear at the bottom of all of it. *Fear of not being good enough.*

Michael looked down and nodded. "Okay, I think I see how this plays out in an individual's life, but I'm confused about how the group acts on these. I still don't see the fear in our company."

"Let me give you an example." Joe offered. "It may seem trite, but I find this in almost every company I visit. An explicitly stated value might be 'we value quality results, not long-hours'. But the implicit value, obvious to those on the inside, is 'political maneuvering and face-time is what gets you ahead'. The former is wishful thinking, the latter is reality. And when these two beliefs exist in opposition to each other, it causes stress because humans are constantly seeking to match their internal reality with the external world. When they cannot, they feel dislocation and fear. This is one of the indicators of a fear-based culture. Do what we say, not what we do."

"Oh my." Michael shook his head. "Yes, we have that very same problem here."

"I know," Joe nodded. "I picked up on that right away. And there are many more conflicting stories. You want to hear some?"

Michael's stomach sank, but he was too curious to say no. "Go ahead," he said.

Joe began to tick off on his fingers: "We want you to take risks and 'be entrepreneurial', but we reserve the right to punish failure. Speak openly, but there will be unstated consequences for what you say. Be autonomous and 'act like a leader', but we will question every action you take. The customer is the most important thing, but profit and 'hitting the numbers' is really what matters. Shall I continue?"

"No mas, no mas!" Michael exclaimed in mock horror. "I get it. And you're right, it is stressful. I see it in myself. I feel sometimes like I don't know what to do to make things right. Almost like it's impossible to be perfect enough to succeed."

"And it is impossible," Joe interjected. "Because the system is set up that way. Not consciously, mind you, because nobody would ever knowingly set up such an insanely contradictory situation. It is set up because there is a subconscious, root belief that *fear motivates*. In fact, it is more than a root belief, it is a *way of being*. From an early age we are shown that in order to gain love we must somehow be perfect, so we live in fear of not being able to obtain that love. Which is ironic, because love is not something that can be obtained! So we end up fearfully chasing a carrot that we cannot reach."

Michael sat, stunned. His whole professional life was laid bare.

"And the result is people in organizations seeking constant affirmation, constant title boosts, pay increases, needing to know 'where they stand' and why they were not invited to this or that meeting. Have you ever noticed how you can set off a 'fear storm' in an individual just by forgetting to invite them to a meeting? Or, have you experienced the organizational mayhem that ensues when one person gets promoted to a new level with a nice title? Everyone immediately asks 'whoa, what about me?' This is the fear revealed. If people were not holding an underlying fear, these events would not trigger any reaction. They would just 'be', and accept." Joe finished holding his arms wide.

"God, this is crazy," Michael said shaking his head.

"Actually it's not," Joe stopped him. "It is perfectly predictable. Humans have a biological need to be part of a group, because in the past being kicked out of the group meant almost certain death, especially for a child. So as children we are genetically programmed to be constantly checking for love, because love indicates that we are safe. If we sense conditional love, love based on what we *do* but not what we *are*, then we do everything we can to 'be perfect' and get that love. We live in fear of losing love, because biologically we cannot survive without our parents. And so we carry that fear with us into adulthood. And our organizations merely reflect this. It is perfectly rational under the circumstances."

"But," Michael countered, "I am not completely sure that all striving for money or titles is based on fear...I mean, we all need to live, right? Maslow and all that?"

"Yes," Joe answered, "we do need to live but our 'human needs' are fairly easy to meet. And mind you that comes from fear as well, fear of starving and dying. But everything beyond that is an irrational fear that persists for no good reason. It has been proven, for example, that once people reach a certain standard of living additional money has nothing to do with happiness. We all know this deep down. We sing songs about it, tell our children this truth, and form religions that call it 'evil'. But yet we still act as if money, and many other external trappings, are somehow the motivator of everything. It is the same type of contradiction we spoke about earlier: Money and title are not important, but we will value you for how much money you make and how important you are."

"OK, I am a bit confused," Michael stopped him, "You say that money is not important yet we need money to live, which is the truth? And what in the world motivates people if not these, what did you call them, 'external trappings'?"

"Ahhh…and this is where we get to the crux of my job." Joe put his finger in the air. "To explain what motivates."

Joe shifted in his chair, took a sip of coffee, then started. "Let's talk a little bit about the concept of 'motivation'. I think we can agree that motivation, put simply, is 'the internal desire to take action in a particular direction'. The more difficult question is how can we, as outsiders to another person's experience, *induce them to be motivated*. This has been the challenge of leadership and management since humans formed groups, and has been the subject of more books than I care to count."

"My personal opinion on the subject is," Joe continued, "that a person's motivation can be triggered for any number of reasons, but only a few of those reasons can drive a person to perform at their highest level over long periods of time. And they are all driven by choice, not reaction."

"Take fear, for example. Fear is a 'reactive' motivator. As a leader I can trigger fear in people quite easily, and can get them to do almost anything using that fear as a driver. Leaders throughout history have done this quite well. Simply tell people they are under threat from some

130

external group, person, or situation, then give them a course of action or plan, and they will execute. This is how most countries go to war. The leader says 'those people are bad and are trying to kill you. You must defend yourself by attacking and killing them. Now get behind me or you are putting the country at risk'. And so people fall in line."

"Now," Joe got up and started to pace. "The only problem with fear is that it eventually consumes the very people who hold it. Fear is unsustainable because it is a *degrading energy*. Fear can cause an immediate response, but will eventually result in a lower state of happiness and a lower state of motivation. The leader then has to 'up the ante', by issuing stronger and stronger threats until people are so beaten down they literally have no desire to do anything. They give up."

"I can understand," Michael interjected, "how you might say this for countries and some organizations, but surely you don't mean companies like ours. I mean we have never threatened anybody! In fact, we are quite nice to people!"

Joe smiled as if anticipating this question. "But fear is not necessarily direct threat. Fear is extremely insidious and is usually quite vague. Peer pressure is an example. The logic goes like this: If people don't like me for what I do, then I will be rejected from the group. If I am rejected, I am unworthy of surviving, being loved. And if this happens I will die. It is the same dysfunctional logic we talked about earlier.

"Of course," Joe continued, "leaders and managers use it anyways, because they literally don't know another way out. And, perversely, it is usually sold as a positive. If you get a raise you are *worthy*…if you don't, well, it goes unsaid that you are clearly *not*. The same with titles, power, everything external. To be recognized is to be valued, to be valued is to be made worthy. To *not* be worthy is tantamount to death…the death of my belief in myself.

"The end result is a group of people motivated by fear of not being worthy. The few who do get promoted feel satisfied for a time, but then they go back to the fear. Eventually, everyone begins to 'stress out' and

131

feel like they are fighting for their very survival...which in some ways they are. The whole organization becomes tired, cranky, and fixated on the 'next fix' of a title bump or salary increase or external recognition. It is a need that can never really be sated, because fear can never be eliminated by feeding it accolades. It only gets stronger," Joe stopped.

Michael got what he was saying and could see it at work in his team, but he did not feel like he was getting any closer to an alternative. "So what is the solution, Joe? I am getting the 'doom and gloom' picture here."

"Sorry Michael," Joe chuckled. "I get a bit carried away with this because many people I work with are in serious denial that fear is controlling their lives. Their lens on the world is so tuned to operating from fear that they have come to accept it as the way things really are. So I really try to drive it home."

"Coming back to the question," Joe sat back down, "of what motivates. So we know fear motivates, but does not sustain. So then we are looking for something that motivates in an *increasing curve*. That is, people get more motivated as time goes on. This is the key challenge, and one that needs to be addressed before *any* organization can realize significant jumps in performance. And I can tell you it is *not* money."

Michael could not accept the thought that money doesn't motivate. He had seen it drive people to do all sorts of things.

Anticipating this, Joe went on, "Money, Michael, can cause immediate action because people equate it with recognition and love, but as far as sustained action it actually *de-motivates*."

"What?", Michael blurted. "How can money de-motivate!? I have only seen it do the opposite! Just open the business pages and take a look!"

Joe nodded. "That is because you have never seen the alternative. You live in a culture that assumes money drives everything. This is your lens. Yet this is not wholly true from a base instinct perspective. Let me give you an example. Numerous studies have been done that look at the effects of rewards on behavior. Now, the old Pavlovian theory was that if you rewarded someone they would repeat the behavior, just like the dog from Pavlov's experiments. And this is true for things on an immediate, physical level. The problem is that as soon as you begin to reward *human beings*, they lose intrinsic interest in it. *It becomes work.*

"In one interesting study researchers gave both children and adults a simple, creative task like drawing a picture. Then they split the groups into two: One group got paid for drawing each picture and one did not. The result was that the group getting paid produced more pictures at first, but over time produced fewer pictures than the group doing it for fun. Every time the study was conducted!" Joe feigned surprise. "The upshot is that paying people to do something might cause a burst of activity, but in the end the 'fun' is lost in the activity."

Michael could tell that Joe was coming to a point, because he was getting more emphatic by the minute.

"So, Michael," Joe tapped on the desk, "now I am going to let you in on the 'big secret' of motivation. Actually it is not a big secret at all, it is simply a truth that has been obscured by our own search for a 'rational' source of motivation. And this is not rational, but it is true: People are motivated by that which has meaning for them. And for every single person on this planet, that base motivator is *love*."

Michael stared at him incredulously. What in God's name does love have to do with productivity? Is this a joke? "Joe, forgive me, but that is the wackiest thing I have ever heard. You think people are going to work for *love*? What do I do, issue a paycheck each month that says 'I love you'? This is nuts!"

Joe laughed a deep and hearty laugh. "That is a good one! A 'love check'…ha! I wonder…" he mused jokingly.

"No, Michael," Joe continued, still chuckling. "You still have to pay people. I have found that there absolutely has to be a basic level of pay that is competitive with similar jobs in the industry. And you have that here. But that only gets people to take the job in the first place. After they get paid, the money become irrelevant to performance. That is when you need to access the love!"

Michael shook his head and started to speak, but Joe cut him off. "What I mean by this is that they have to access the love within *themselves*, because the only way to experience love is to *give it*. Give it to others, give it to what they do, give it to the world at large. When a person accesses this energy, which, incidentally is the direct opposite of fear, then they tap into ever increasing source of intrinsic motivation. And endless source of high performance."

Michael was still baffled. "But how in the world do I get them to 'access the love'?"

"By aligning what you are trying to accomplish with what each person finds meaningful, purposeful, and joyful. Once someone starts to do something that has meaning, purpose and joy to *them*, they reach a state of what Mihaly Csikszentmihalyi calls 'flow'. Time becomes irrelevant, money becomes superfluous, and love flows out of them in a torrent. Performance becomes not only easy, it becomes positively self-reinforcing. Love is an endless fountain of energy!"

"Joe, Joe, Joe!" Michael exclaimed, "I get it...'do what you love'. That is an old one. But there is no way I can guarantee everyone is going to 'love what they do'!"

"No Michael," Joe said emphatically. "It has nothing to do with guaranteeing anything. You can't force it, you can only encourage it. It is alignment, Michael. And most leaders and managers simply don't want to take the time to do what is necessary to achieve it."

"But, Joe," Michael countered defensively, "I am a manager with goals and plans, I am *not* a psychologist!"

"*Really?*" Joe said sarcastically and tilted his head. "Have you ever tried to figure out why your wife was angry with you? Or searched for the deeper meaning behind your boss's comments? Or done your best to understand why one of your direct reports was acting 'strangely'?"

"Well, of course," Michael answered, "But that is simply human interaction, human nature. A psychologist is a specially trained *expert*."

Joe laughed his booming laugh. "Michael, psychologists are merely human beings who happen to have taken a deeper interest in human behavior! We are *all* psychologists, Michael, because we *have to be*. In order to get along in this world we are wired, from birth, to try to understand what other human beings are thinking and feeling. And we learn at an early age that to get what we need or want we must understand how those on whom we depend operate. We are hard-wired to try to figure people out!"

Michael had never thought of it that way, but he knew Joe was right. Most of his time at work was spent trying to get his team, boss, customers and partners to do what he needed them to do, or understand what they were asking of him. Come to think of it, a majority of his waking hours were comprised of a running internal commentary about what others had said or done and what it meant. Or, conversely, thoughts about what he was going to say and how it would have an impact on them.

Joe could see Michael was getting the point. "You see, Michael, we are all in constant communication, either verbally or non-verbally. And because we can only see from our *own* perspective, we must therefore constantly try to understand where others are coming from. Some of us have innate skills or interests that allow us to do this easily, while others struggle."

"Well," Michael laughed, "I seem to struggle with it, because I can't understand why anybody I work with, or live with for that matter, does what they do!"

Joe laughed again. "No an uncommon problem…especially among the male of our species!"

"Why do you say that?" Michael asked. He had noticed that women had an easier time with this 'soft stuff', but thought it was some genetic predisposition to be sensitive.

"Because men tend to be taught at an early age that the intuitive side of themselves is somehow effeminate. That connecting, and understanding people makes them weak. So many of us shut off that 'feeling side' and then go through life frustrated because we can't seem to understand other's behaviors...especially the women in our lives!" Joe's eyes were gleaming. "But here is a secret that you might find strange, Michael: Studies have shown that when they are young boys are actually *more* sensitive and emotional than girls. But in our culture it is common for us fathers, having been ourselves taught that sensitivity is a sign of weakness, to brow-beat this aspect out of our sons. And so men in our society simply deny their innate abilities, resulting in distance, confusion and an atrophied emotional being."

Michael sat for a moment deep in thought. Joe had once again hit on a profound truth in Michael's life, and something he had recognized in his male peers. *Undeveloped*, was the word that popped into his mind.

"So," Joe continued, "Men, in their inability to understand how to 'be' with others, separate themselves...sometimes physically, sometimes mentally, usually emotionally. Men are much more likely to become loners or hermits, and in rare cases lash out at society at large. At the very least we are taught to treat others as objects - 'things' to be manipulated to get what we want. We create distance with one another, tell each other 'it's a dog-eat-dog world', and then wonder why everyone is so selfish. Corporate culture, long dominated by men, is many times a shining example of the selfishness and lack of connection – driven by fear – that each one of us has learned to embody. It is a denial of self that creates a culture of denial."

"And you are saying that women are not capable of this?" Michael asked incredulously.

"No," Joe stated flatly, "but they have less of a tendency to head in this direction. Women are not burdened with a perceived social stigma around connection. As children, women are less often told that their emotions are bad, or that being close with someone is weakness. So they allow their nature to take over and have less of a problem with emo-

136

tional expression and verbal sharing. Women have different challenges, but because they have not, sadly, been founding pillars of our corporations and institutions, their issues have not manifested as strongly in most company's cultures. But the truth is, Michael, that we need both the male and female outlook in our organizations because without this yin-yang energy our organizations become terribly imbalanced."

"Just look at some of the disasters in recent corporate history." Joe continued. "A great many of them are caused by the belief that we are not connected, that somehow one person can, and *should*, gain at another's loss. This is a uniquely male perspective that is sad not only because of the damage it causes, but because of the totally mistaken belief it represents! This belief, that connecting, sharing, caring and being of service cannot be 'profitable' to individuals, is endemic and totally unnecessary. The truth is that all of these things result in more profit for each individual! I have seen it Michael!"

"So what do we do, Joe? What do *I* do? I am still not seeing how all this relates to motivation and performance."

"Well," Joe sat back, "I don't know how you are going to react to this, but what you do is to listen, care, connect and try to understand every individual within your range of influence. You *love them*, Michael. You sit down and ask them how they are feeling, how they perceive things, what their lives are like. You try your best to see from their perspective. Once you understand them, you can help them develop meaning and purpose in their lives. Once they have purpose, it is simply a matter of applying their energy in a direction that is consistent with the company's direction."

"And how do I do that?" Michael asked, "Everyone is so different!"

"Yes," Joe smiled, "and that is when true leaders show their colors. You communicate the grander vision, *the possibility*, of the group. You show how each individual is a very special part of a very powerful group on a very important, meaningful mission. It has nothing to do with intellect, Michael, it is all *feeling*. It is not a 'mission statement'. It is much more personal and emotional than that. The greatest leaders of all time, both good and bad, were able to show how each individual's life had meaning in the context of something greater. And each time this has happened, groups, communities, and nations have been able to achieve things that make simple 'process excellence' seem like child's play."

"The power of the group is unleashed through connection, understanding and constant communication, Michael. Until you can do that, you are playing a game of little league ball where each player is scared to death to do anything wrong. Your performance is inherently capped, because the fear of failure will drain the system before it can rise to new heights. But meaning and purpose has no such limits. There is an endless source of energy that emanates from loving what you do and who you are with. This energy can manifest anything, if you are willing to drop your defenses and let yourself be fully human."

They sat looking at each other for what seemed like an eternity. Michael felt like Joe was peering into his soul. Michael knew, at a deep level, that he had a decision to make, and it scared the daylights out of him.

Chapter Thirteen

Over the next week Michael reflected on his conversation with Joe. Toward the end of the talk, Joe had given him some specific things to do to increase motivation within his team, but they were not the kind of tasks that Michael was prepared to execute. Joe had told him to 'get to know each individual intimately', and to 'become intensely curious about perspectives and thoughts'. Although he saw these as 'nice to have' Michael was hoping for something more concrete, something that he could *do*.

When Michael had objected that this sounded like a lot of 'touchy feely' stuff that had nothing to do with productivity, Joe became very stern. He reflected to Michael that his very unwillingness to reach out and connect with others was exactly what was holding his company back. This had galled Michael slightly...was Joe suggesting that the culture of the company was based on his *lack* of connection? What about Armand? And his team?

Truth be told, Michael did get the point. If he wanted to motivate people to perform to their highest potential, then he needed to understand what made them tick. And to be fair, Joe had been clear that this did not mean that Michael had to give everyone what they wanted. What was it that Joe had said? That "firing someone is sometimes the kindest thing you can do"? That sometimes an individual's purpose did not align with the company's mission. Or, as Joe had emphasized, that sometimes a person's personal issues were simply too deeply entrenched to allow them to perform. In these cases separation was the only solution, and that made sense to Michael.

But this whole 'listening' thing was somehow troubling to Michael. Joe said that most in order to help people figure out their passion he needed to first listen to the fears that are holding them back. To Michael this sounded a lot like listening to people bitch. He was damned if he was going to sit there and let waste his time like that. In his defense, however, Joe had said that there was a difference between 'clearing' and 'complaining'. Clearing, evidently, was the act of saying what you needed to say. Once. Complaining was when a person got 'stuck in their story' and could not seem to develop a new way of looking at the world. Clearing was good, and usually resulted in a person being able to step to a new level of achievement. Complaining was self-defeating, and usually resulted in low performance and eventual dismissal.

Michael stared out his office window and tried to recap what he was supposed to do. Listen deeply, ask probing questions, reflect back what he heard, and then confirm that he understood what they were saying. Then, and only then, would he have earned the right to offer suggestions or to look for solutions to problems. What was that old quote: "Seek first to understand, then to be understood"?

Still, there was something nagging at Michael. Something that made him feel uncomfortable. It was almost...*revulsion*? As if the idea of sitting and listening to all these people was a waste of time. That he should be *doing* something. Telling them what to do. What was supposed to happen after he listened? Some miracle? And what the hell did Joe mean when he said "be of service to your colleagues"? This made him want to laugh. Most of them could care less about him, and he was supposed to 'be of service'?! The only people Michael felt he needed to 'serve' was his boss and his customers. The rest were there to do their jobs and shut the hell up.

Michael felt a sudden shock. That was the voice of his father! This was the uneasy feeling Michael had inside. Joe was suggesting something that went against deeply rooted beliefs about how people should be in this world. *People are either above you or below you, and they should act accordingly.* It was something that Michael had felt as a child…his parents had constantly reminded both he and his sister that they were subordinate to his parents, and that they needed to remember their place in the hierarchy. Hadn't his father said at one point "you are living in *my house* and you will obey *my rules*"?

What Joe was suggesting was that Michael treat every person at his company as an equal, even his subordinates, and that rankled Michael. Even further, Joe had told him to 'be of service' and, yes, 'be humble'. In Michael's story that meant subordinating himself to those who should be subordinate to *him*. A wave of feeling came over Michael that he could not place. He sat with it and then it came to him: Fear. Fear of losing control. Fear of being seen as weak. Fear of being abused.

As Michael sat staring at his desk he realized that he had been operating from a place of fear most of his life. It was not the 'scared to death' kind of fear, but more a subtle wariness of the world…a low grade anxiety that caused him to be constantly on the attack, and always ready to defend himself. He felt he needed this hierarchy to maintain control, yet his obsession with how he 'stacked up' was eating him alive.

Michael acknowledged to himself that this was not a comfortable way to exist in the world, because it was a battle he could never win. He could try to be perfect in every way, to become *everyone's* better, but that was laughably impossible. Someone was always going to know more, to be stronger, to have more money. It was a Sisyphusian battle, Michael thought, recalling his college mythology class and the story of Sisyphus who was tasked with rolling a rock to the top of a hill only to have it roll down the other side…and then to repeat this endlessly. It was a fight Michael could never win, because by his hierarchical world view he was always going to be 'below' someone.

It dawned on him that this was what Joe was suggesting. That in order to motivate people, we had to give up our sense of better or worse, higher or lower, and simply sit with *everyone* as equals. To show respect by listening to people and doing our best to understand them deeply. Only then will they feel free to release their fear and explore their passions. This was the key, Michael thought: Helping people release the blocks that keep them from high performance! He finally understood what Joe was getting at. Each person was holding themselves back, keeping their fullest energy and true ability in reserve. *And our job as managers and leaders is to help them 'take off the brakes' and move into the fullest version of themselves! To BE OF SERVICE!*

Michael sat back with a smile on his face. He saw it clearly…at least intellectually. When he thought about actually doing this, however, he felt a wave of dread come over him. In truth, he was much more comfortable executing on tasks and hitting milestones. This had nothing to do with quantifiable activity. This was what every hard-core quant-jock detail-oriented git'-er-done manager hated: touchy feely, qualitative interactions. C'mon, Michael rolled his head, *listening*!?

In some ways, this was good timing because he had a session with Louise after work. There were so many things he wanted to discuss with her, because he had been overwhelmed with awareness for the past week…right up until this very moment. Michael was beginning to see stories, patterns, feelings that were ruling his life, and frankly making parts of his life a living hell. He was seeing so much fear, anger and negativity and, although he became internally defensive at the thought, could see how it had created situations that confirmed these thoughts. He could see his own projections clearly, but could not see a way around them. They were so deeply engrained in his life that he was afraid, almost panicked, that he would have to live like this.

At that thought Michael shook his head, stood up and grabbed his coat. He thought maybe a bite to eat and a call to his Dad would clear his mind before his time with Louise. With that in mind, he walked to his car.

Chapter Fourteen

Michael plopped down in front of Louise, "I think I'm going crazy."

Louise smiled and nodded. "Well, that is to be expected, I think," she said reassuringly.

Michael shook his head as if trying to clear the confusion that had been plaguing him over the past week. "I just don't know what to think anymore. Everywhere I look I see projections, old stories and assumptions that have clouded my thinking."

"Until now," Louise offered.

"Well, that's the problem," Michael countered. "I seem to still be having these thoughts, only I'm now conscious of them. And I can't seem to stop! It's like they have a life of their own, coming in unprompted. The worst part is that I can see how unhappy they make me. So many of my thoughts are angry or sad or fearful. But I don't know what to do about them! What am I supposed to do, Louise, really?" Michael had never felt such exasperation as he did now. He felt totally unmoored.

"Oh Michael, I think I understand. Am I correct in saying that you feel out of control? Perhaps like you don't understand who you are anymore? Is that right?" Louise probed.

"Yes! And I don't know what to do, Louise!" Michael pleaded.

"And what is it that you're supposed to do, Michael?" Louise asked softly.

"I don't know, be better? Fix myself? Get through this? I have to do something!" Michael almost shouted.

As Michael became more agitated, Louise seemed to become calmer and more centered. She sat for a moment looking deeply at Michael. "What if I told you that you are perfect right now, right here? What if I told you that you are exactly where you are supposed to be? Would you believe that?"

Michael sighed. "I don't know Louise. Everything I have come to believe, everything I know about life says I should constantly be improving, that I should be dissatisfied with myself. To believe that I am perfect right now is to stop growing, isn't it? I mean, how can I get better if I am satisfied with the way I am today?"

Louise nodded and smiled. "And this is the challenge we all face, Michael. It's the conundrum of our society. However, I would like to offer you the possibility that you can pursue growth and at the same time accept who you are today. You can open yourself to new possibilities and yet still love where you are. They *can* coexist. You don't have to deny yourself, or others, in order to improve. Fear dictates that we must change because we are not good enough. Love suggests that we are *always* good enough, *and that there are additional ways to be even more.* Love is growth, fear is retraction."

Michael nodded. He had heard this enough over the past few weeks that it was starting to sink in. "Ok Louise, I do believe this. Then how do I become 'more'?"

"You already are!" Louise said laughing. "This is the beauty of growth. It is much simpler than we want to believe. For some reason we are given the message that growth is hard work and we come to a mistaken belief that we must be in pain, we must struggle to grow. But growth is more natural than that. Children don't have to struggle to grow, they just *do*. As adults we many times resist growth, thinking that we need to make it happen faster, that we need to force it. But we don't. We are growing everyday, and your awareness is an example of that growth. It's part of an inexorable process that we are all going through."

"So this confusion and pain is normal?" Michael asked incredulously.

144

"Not only is it normal, Michael, but it's also *wonderful*. The first step in moving forward on anything in our lives is to first see the challenge. That is 75% of the process. In many circles this is called 'awakening'. When we first become conscious of how much our stories and beliefs have dominated our lives, and have made our experiences unpleasant, then we begin to 'wake up' and see that we can choose a different way of being. And this choice, Michael, opens up a universe of possibility."

Michael sat and pondered this for a moment. "So all this is good? All this awareness shows that I'm growing?" he asked.

"Yes, Michael, I can assure you of this. Everyone goes through a different process and has a different reaction when 'waking up', but universally this increased consciousness is both necessary and consistent with our natural process. Sometimes it's uncomfortable, as you can attest, but it's certainly not 'bad'. In fact, the discomfort mainly comes from *resisting* what is happening...but we will talk more about that later. For now, please be patient with yourself because everything is perfect just the way it is. Perfection, you see, is in the process. Everything in the universe is proceeding perfectly, and you are part of that process. So, by inference, you are proceeding perfectly as well!"

"Wow. I feel a bit better about it then. I thought maybe I had screwed up somehow, or that I was massively failing at life." Michael said, relieved.

"I can assure you that you can't fail at life, Michael. You can only learn. This is true for all of us, and I really want you to believe this before we continue." Louise took on a rare, stern visage.

"But what if I had somehow become a killer, or a rapist, or something like that? Or more realistically, what if I failed to put my kids through school, or my wife left me, or I became a raving drunk? That's not what I would call 'success'!" Michael protested.

"Well," Louise began, "then your life would be a series of learning experiences, but it would not be a failure. Success and failure are judgments placed on situations by our culture, our family and the stories that we have decided to adopt. For one culture success may be going into the priesthood and failure marrying anyone outside of the 'clan'. For another culture, success may be having lots of money and a big house, and failure being uneducated and poor. We impose these judgments based on the stories we hear growing up. But the truth of the matter is, Michael, that there are just situations. There is no success or failure."

"Man, this is hard to get my head around," Michael said in disbelief. "Most of my life has been built on some notion of how success was defined."

"Yes, this is true for most of us. And I will shock you even more by suggesting an even more extreme version of this. You are likely going to jump out of your chair at this one! Are you ready?" Louise kidded.

"Oooookay…" Michael squinted.

Louise leaned forward and whispered, "There is no such thing as good or bad."

Michael sat with that one for a moment because it touched a nerve. 'Moral relativism' was a philosophy that he had come to equate with anarchy, permissiveness, and the degradation of moral values. In Michael's mind it meant a complete lack of social order and control, because if nothing was good or bad then 'anything goes'…and he saw that as a cop out by 'New Age' thinking.

He started slowly, calling on all of his collegiate philosophy training. "Yes, Louise, I've heard this before. This is called 'moral relativism', and it gives everyone an excuse to justify their behavior. All I have to say is 'my culture is different' and I can justify killing someone. And you would say 'go ahead, there is no right and wrong'. I don't buy this because it leads to a total breakdown of moral structure."

Louise smiled lovingly. Michael found it amazing that she never seemed to get agitated.

"I hear what you are saying Michael, however, I invite you to consider that this has nothing to do with permitting or disallowing any type of behavior. The central point is the difference between *restricting* a

146

behavior and *judging* it. Do you understand what I mean?" Louise asked.

"I'm not sure. I thought they were the same thing." Michael answered.

"No, certainly not. We can agree as a society to restrict or allow a behavior, and make laws to that effect, but judging the behavior is an emotional process that's universally destructive. Almost every society on earth struggles with this difference. We can restrict, detain and sanction someone for making a choice that we have agreed as a society as 'outside the bounds', but when we step into judgment and condemn them as 'bad' and having done a 'bad act', then we simply put more anger and pain on top of an already painful situation."

Louise continued. "As an example, I'm a black belt in Aikido."

Michael was stunned that this demure woman was a martial artist.

"I know, I know," she laughed. "Nobody can believe it. Anyway, in martial arts fighting is seen as the absolute last resort, while anger is seen as a detriment to clarity and speed of action. The whole point of martial arts is to develop the ability to be centered in the face of violence. To be peaceful in all situations. If I were to condemn my opponent and see him or her as 'bad', I would be creating internal discord and diminishing my ability to perform. If someone were to attack me, I can only note *the fact that I am being attacked*, and respond with enough force to keep myself safe. I cannot label the attack 'good' or 'bad' because I don't know what's going on in the larger picture. All I can do is end the attack… ideally with as much peace and compassion as I can show."

Michael was beginning to see a larger picture here. "So I can stop someone's behavior but not judge it. I think I can see that. But it's still hard for me to see that there is no 'bad' or 'good'. What about raping a child? Or torturing someone? Isn't that universally 'bad'?"

"No," Louise said provocatively. "All we can say is that it is hurtful and unloving. That is a fact. But to judge it as 'bad' means that we put ourselves in the position of the universal arbiter of some notion of 'right' and 'wrong'. It is the human desire to play God, to claim to know

God's mind. Most wars are fought because both sides claim to know the 'universal truth', when in fact no one individual or culture knows the intent or unfolding of the universe."

Michael was confused…this went against everything he was brought up to believe.

"Okay," Louise smiled. "I can see you're getting frustrated." She thought for a moment before continuing, "There's an old Zen parable about the farmer who lost his horses because the gate to his barn was left open. The farmer came to the Zen monk and said 'It's horrible, I have lost my horses.' The Zen monk replied cryptically, 'We shall see'. The farmer was angry because he felt the monk was less than sympathetic. The next day, the farmer came to the monk and said, 'Good news! I found my horses, and a good thing they had escaped because my barn burned down the next day due to lightening. If they had not gotten out, they would have surely perished!' To which the monk replied, 'We shall see.' The farmer, once again confused, went back home to discover that an army troop had come by and, seeing his fine horses, conscripted both the horses and the farmer's son. Distraught, the farmer once again went to the monk with is tale of woe, to which the monk again replied, 'We shall see'. A few weeks later the son had returned home a great hero, with a large sum of money granted by the emperor for his deeds. The farmer was elated…and you can see where this goes.

"You see, Michael, we can't know if something is 'good' or 'bad' because we can't see how things are unfolding, what the ultimate outcomes will be. We can only do our best to do the most loving, compassionate thing in each moment and have faith that the universe is opening in a way that makes sense."

Michael immediately saw his personal objection to this. "But what if the universe or life or whatever is *not* opening in a way that makes sense. What if I just don't buy that?"

Louise nodded knowingly. "Now you have hit the central point. Faith. Do you have faith that everything is moving toward a loving outcome, or do you fear that it is not? This is the choice, and it can dictate our whole life. We choose in every moment to love and have faith, or to doubt and have fear. And the truth is, the only thing that exists are facts, raw data, of which we can only perceive a small portion, so we must choose...to have faith or to doubt. It's a very personal choice, Michael."

"But what does this choice have to do with my own mental state? All these projections I've been having? All of my anger and frustration?" Michael asked, exasperated. He noticed he was having this feeling a lot lately.

"As soon as we doubt the world and seek to control it with our judgments and condemnations, we create our own hell. We create a world where we see good and evil everywhere, and because everything is a projection, we first see it in ourselves. And because we cannot tolerate evil, we learn to hate the evil that we perceive within ourselves...which results in a never ending cycle of self abuse and self judgment. We can only know for certain what we are *experiencing*, Michael. Everything else is a guess. So all judgments we pass on the world are reflections of what's inside us, and self-judgment is painful." Louise finished.

Michael was stunned by the simplicity of it all. All of the anger, judgment and fear inside of him had only been destroying...*him*. And by sowing discord in the world in which he was operating, he was perpetuating the things from which he wanted freedom.

"Louise, I think I see, but *help*! I don't *want* to judge myself! How can I let go of this?" Michael actually felt tears of rage filling up in his eyes. Every time he asked someone for an answer they seemed to point back to him!

"Michael," Louise lightly touched his knee, "the answer is very simple, but also very challenging. I want you to open your mind a bit, because the key to joy, happiness and to creating the life that you want is counterintuitive. Can you do that?"

"Yes," Michael responded. "I really am sick of the way I've been living. I'm willing to try anything."

"OK," Louise started, "then first I want to make sure that we have a clear intention around what you want to create. Everything in this physical world, *everything* Michael, has been created because a consciousness *intended* it to be created. In fact, the only 'real' thing in this universe *is* consciousness. Everything else stems from that. A famous scientist and philosopher called consciousness 'the ground of all being', because before anything can exist there must first be a thought, an intention. I know this may sound crazy, because in our world we think that our thoughts are *reactions* to the physical world, but in reality they are *generating* the physical world."

Michael reflected back on what Yoda had said some weeks earlier, that science was beginning to notice that consciousness and physical matter were intertwined. So it was not outlandish to Michael that somehow consciousness could generate physical outcomes.

"Yes," Michael interjected, "like when we build a building. First comes the thought, then the plan, then the physical outcome. I'm familiar with this. And this is how projection works, correct? We think certain thoughts and then recreate them in the world?"

"Yes, very much so," Louise was nodding. "Except that it's much, much more complex than we might suspect. In fact - and brace yourself for this - consciousness is not confined to each person's body. Consciousness is a *force* in the universe...very likely the fundamental force. The common denominator. And it is shared. As individuals we are simply different viewpoints that act as a conduit for this vast, shared consciousness. Collectively we anthropomorphize this as a separate 'God', when in reality we are *all* this energy we call God. We are all part of a huge, vibrating energy field that experiences the physical world according to the lens that we call our 'senses'."

Louise paused to gauge Michael's reaction. "How are you feeling about all this, Michael?"

"Well, I'm not sure I get it 100%, but I think I know what you're talking about. The point is that we are all connected and our separation is somewhat of an illusion, right?" Yoda's talk was actually helpful, Michael thought!

"Yes. And as we become aware of this illusion, the facade of separateness, we begin to see that everything we're experiencing is the working of a world we have all jointly created. If we live in a country at war, it is because we, as a group of people who form this country, have created for ourselves a culture that is fearful and warlike. We get to experience that which we have jointly created. The same is true of individuals, companies, the planet, everything, Michael. Through the thoughts we have we *create our world*, which is both our problem and our solution. Angry, fearful people create angry, fearful situations. Happy, joyful people create happy, joyful situations. It is a *choice*, and that choice *begins with intention!*" Louise said emphatically boring into Michael's eyes.

"So, Michael," Louise opened her palms to him, "what do you intend with your life?"

Michael sat somewhat stunned. Louise was asking him to choose his life. He had never thought this a possibility. For some reason, he had always seen the world as a giant machine of which he was a simple part. He knew he could influence it, but *choose* it?

"Wow," Michael said, "I'm not really sure. I've never thought about this before."

Louise's face was becoming more and more intense. "And that is why you have experienced your life as being a random set of events that happen *to* you. Without a clear intention, our lives form according to the ebb and flow of the forces around us. Without a clear intention, you get a life without clarity. You actually get what you are unknowingly asking for: randomness."

"So," Louise continued, "choose, Michael. Say right here, right now that you intend for your life to be…what? It can be anything, Michael, but you must choose it."

Louise became completely still. Michael sat staring at his hands. He didn't know how to begin.

"Well," he hesitated, "I guess I would like to be happy and, and joyful and peaceful and at ease with everything...is that what you mean?"

"Yes, however, I encourage you to express this with forceful intention. Remember this is what creates everything. Pure, unwavering intention. You don't 'guess' you want these things. You *intend to create them.* You say 'I intend to create a life of happiness and joy'. If you want to be even more powerful, you say 'I AM happy and joyful'. The strongest intentions are those that presuppose the outcome. The 'how' is just a matter of flow...the most important thing is to *know* that this will happen," Louise paused. "Do you believe this Michael?"

"I'm not sure. If I'm not happy now, how can I say that I *am* happy? I would be lying...right? It wouldn't be real!"

Louise smiled. "As we talked about earlier, reality is perceptual. And so is time. In fact, time is nothing like what we think it is. So think of it this way...you are *telling the truth in advance.* By declaring that you already *are* what you want to become, you create it in this moment. You don't have to wait. This is where you have faith, Michael, because your mind and body will react to whatever suggestion you give it. If you say 'I intend happiness in my life' or 'I am happy', you will subconsciously begin to change your internal story from unhappiness to happiness. You will, through projection, create a world of happiness around you. It really works Michael."

"Wow," Michael shook his head. "This is counter-intuitive to my logical mind, but I think I get it."

Louise laughed. "Your logical mind is very limited, Michael, try to keep that in mind!"

"Ok. So here goes." Michael took a deep breath. "I am happy, I am joyful, I am in a loving relationship with my wife and children, I am happy in my job, I am in a good relationship with my boss, I am working well with my team, I am experiencing financial success, I am at peace with everything in my life, I am not ever angry."

"Great!" Louise almost shouted. "I'd like to offer one thing though.

The last one, 'I am not ever angry' is phrased in a negative. You want to phrase this in a positive way, because your mind does not interpret the 'not'. All it hears is 'I am angry'. You want simple, positive declarative statements that craft your ideal world. You can do this with anything... work situations, home life, personal outlook, anything. And it is very powerful, especially if you can conjure a positive, loving feeling while you say these things. Keep a deep belief that these things are already happening, and at some point you will realize that they are!"

Louise stopped and peered at Michael again. "So how does that feel?"

"Strange," Michael answered. "But also good. For a moment there I felt hope and my internal negative stories...well...*paused*. I feel a little relieved that it's indeed possible to create happy things in my life."

"They are more than possible, Michael, they are already happening. Remember, the future is merely a concept. The only thing that is 'true' is now. So if you say these things are true now, then they begin to be true...*now*."

"Ok, I got it. But what happens when my stories come back? I came in here feeling besieged by all this negative crap floating around in my head that kept popping up as I went through my day. How am I supposed to keep these positive things in mind when my mind does not seem to be under my control?!"

"Ah, and now we hit on the second component of creating the life you want: *acceptance*. And it's active component, *forgiveness*." Louise turned her palms up and looked up in the air. She looked like a religious figure in that moment.

"Michael," Louise continued, "when you were a little boy and you began to learn your stories about the way the world works, and how love is given, or withheld, you didn't really have control over that, did you?"

"No," Michael answered. "It was just the world I knew. I really just followed along."

"Yes," Louise nodded, "you assumed that the way your parents acted was the way things were. And so you learned how to behave from the way they behaved. You did the best that you could. And, because your parents are human, so did they. Your whole family took their unique ways of looking at things, their understanding of the world, the way that they experienced life, and then created a series of rules of 'how life is' and 'how we think and act'. You did not consciously choose these things, they were presented to you, right?"

"Sure," Michael agreed. "That makes sense."

"But then as you grew older, there were things you began to notice that you didn't like about your parents. You started to see some of the flaws in their thinking...so you became resentful because you wanted to be your own person and didn't like their way of doing things. In your teenage years you may have rebelled. Or maybe you simply internalized their messages completely and never really questioned anything. In either case, you could not help but to carry some of your parents' 'way of being' forward. We all do."

"Now," Louise continued, "some of these beliefs and 'ways of being' suit us. They make our lives happy and joyful. Warm things like loving interactions with others, laughter, the joy of learning, creative expression...if they existed in our family, then we carry them forward happily. Other things, however, don't feel so good. Fearful outlooks on the world, angry interactions, grudges against others, a negative view of work...these all create painful circumstances that, *once we become aware of them*, we don't want in our lives. Both of these positive and negative thoughts are our 'stories' that we project onto the world. Until now you had not chosen your stories, you had simply lived them, and in doing so, you were doing the best you could."

Michael was nodding vigorously. This made total sense to him. Choose the positive stories over the negative stories.

"But what do I do with the negative stories? Or the negative people in my life?" Michael asked.

Louise lowered her head and very softly said, "First you accept that everyone is doing the best that they know how…including yourself. You accept everyone completely, and you surrender any judgment of them or yourself. For all of us are doing the best we can with the life we have been given. *If we knew any better, we would do better.* This is the root of compassion. To understand that every life on this planet is experiencing reality in the only way they know how. Even the cruelest murderer thinks at some level he or she is doing what he or she is supposed to do."

"But aren't there some things that are out of bounds, some actions that are pure *evil?*" Michael could not get his head around the idea that cruelty could be justified by anyone.

Louise was shaking her head gently. "This is a longer discussion, Michael, but let's just say for now that evil exists only as a concept, not as an actual separate entity that is waiting to ambush us. When we call something or someone 'evil', we are finding a way to distance them from us, to assure ourselves that we are different from them. In reality, we all have the capacity to do harm to one another, and that is where we create 'evil' and 'hell'. 'Hell' exists not as some terrible place, but as the real-world consequences of unloving, hurtful choices. We create our own evil and hell, and this is what humans find so objectionable. We want to believe that we are not responsible for terrible acts, so we make up a concept called 'evil' to place the blame somewhere else. In this way, someone who is evil is not worth thinking about, not worth considering. We can justify torturing, killing, anything when we have decided something is 'evil'."

"So even a serial killer deserves compassion? Even a child rapist?" Michael blurted incredulously.

"Yes," Louise said flatly. "And that's what every major spiritual teacher has tried to tell us for thousands of years. But this is very, very difficult for human beings to accept. And herein lies the challenge. Because we know that projection is how we perceive reality, if we refuse to forgive and be compassionate toward others, then we are holding judg-

155

ment and anger within our own minds. And if we hold judgment and anger internally, *then we also create it externally through our actions.* So we end up in a living hell of judgmental and angry life situations. We live what we have created in our minds!"

Michael pondered this for a moment. "So in reality, forgiveness and compassion gives us internal peace and freedom?"

"Exactly!" Louise clapped her hands. "The Buddha said, 'Anger is like holding a hot rock you are waiting to throw at someone. You only burn yourself.' Forgiveness is dropping the rock."

"Wow," Michael shook his head. "I think I'm really getting this. So if we forgive others, we release the judgment and anger within us. If we do that, then what? Certainly the problems of the world don't go away."

"Well," Louise answered, "Forgiving others is the first step. The harder part is forgiving ourselves."

"Huh?" Michael tilted his head. "Forgiving myself? I don't get it… if someone else murders another person, why do I need to forgive myself?!"

"And this is the most challenging concept to grasp, Michael, so I'm going to explain it and then ask you to pay attention to your own thoughts over the next few days to see if it resonates with you."

"It all starts with projection and meaning making," Louise continued. "As we discussed earlier, we take in data from the world around us, create an internal image, give that image meaning, then project that meaning back out into the world. So in this logic, we can only project things we have already experienced some way internally. *The internal feeling comes first.*

"OK," Michael nodded.

"Good, then let's take the case of a thief. If we see someone stealing something, our internal response may likely be judgment and condemnation. We identify them as 'bad', which usually is accompanied by a visceral anger inside. We may even hate them. But what we miss is that this feeling had to come from somewhere. It had to exist in some form

156

inside of us *before* we saw this person stealing something. We just applied an already-existing negative emotion to an input of data from the outside world. Somewhere during our lives we internalized what it meant to be a thief. We may have been accused of being a thief, or seen others judged for being thieves, and we took that negative emotion and buried it inside of us. The external event is merely the trigger of a feeling that already exists." Louise looked at Michael with anticipation.

"Ok," Michael nodded, "I get that. We learn how to react. So why must we forgive ourselves for this?"

"Because at some point we must let go of this negativity and judgment within us. We have been carrying it around for our whole lives, and it has caused us endless pain and suffering. Our whole lives have been built on a series of mistaken notions about the world, and we must forgive ourselves in order to let go of these notions." Louise could see Michael was still not getting it.

"What about this," Louise started again. "What if you find out the person is not actually a thief, but is instead someone breaking into their own car because they have been locked out. Now you find yourself carrying anger and condemnation around for no reason at all. It's made obvious in that one moment that all of that feeling inside is your own... and that for some reason you chose to think and feel this way. At this moment, most of us will justify our reaction and avoid the awareness that calls our attention to the fact that we are carrying a load of negative assumptions around with us. But there is another choice, Michael. We can forgive ourselves for carrying this stuff around. We can release it, and *choose to think and feel a different way.*"

"Ahhh," Michael smiled. "So we essentially forgive ourselves for the thoughts and ideas that create the projections in the first place! We let go of the sponsoring thought, and then the way we perceive the world changes!"

"Yes," Louise laughed, "and when you let go of those thoughts, you can choose other thoughts that are better geared to what you are trying to achieve: internal peace and happiness"

Michael was enjoying this game. "And because my internal state changes, my projections change, which in turn changes the way I experience my world."

Louise had a huge smile on her face. "There is a saying that I love: your outer world is a reflection of your inner reality. Once we change our inner reality, our outer world by definition begins to change."

"OK!" Michael exclaimed. "I really think I see this. But let's get down to practicality here. How exactly do I forgive myself? I mean, I'm not sure if I have ever consciously forgiven *anyone* before…how am I supposed to forgive myself?"

"Great question, and this is where things get challenging," Louise joked. "Forgiveness is easy in concept but hard in practice, mainly because we are not used to doing it. Jesus encouraged us to forgive over and over and over, as many times as it took until we got it right. And that's great advice. The idea is to identify the sponsoring thought that is causing anger or judgment, and then to forgive ourselves for feeling the need to create that thought. To forgive ourselves for buying into the mistaken notion that we are supposed to live in fear and judgment."

"Great, OK." Michael leaned forward. "Let's take an example. A couple of days ago, a guy cut me off on the highway and I felt anger and judgment toward him. How do I forgive *myself* for this?"

"Good," Louise nodded, "This is a good example. First, Michael, what assumptions did you make?"

"That he was cutting me off on purpose, and that he was being a mean person." Michael answered.

"Good," Louise continued. "And what values did he violate, according to you?"

"Well," Michael hesitated, "the value to be nice to each other in public. The value that we should be kind to one another." Michael was walking on thin ice because he knew that he was definitely not always nice to other people in public, especially on the highway.

Louise sensed this and pushed. "So you made an assumption that this man was purposefully breaking a value that you hold dear, correct?"

Michael was feeling boxed in. "Yes, I guess so."

"And you judged this as bad, condemned this man as 'evil'?" Louise was leaning forward.

"Yes." Michael said softly.

"Can you remember a time when you acted this way yourself, Michael?"

"Yes. Many times."

"And so what are some of the beliefs about the world and yourself that come to mind when you think about this? What are some of the fundamental notions?" Louise was speaking more softly now.

Michael sighed. "That the world is an awful, crappy place. That people are jerks. That…that I am an uncaring jerk. And that I'm supposed to be this way." Michael put his head in his hands. He realized at that moment that he had spent most of his life acting under the assumption that he had to be tough in a tough world, and that being tough meant fighting for what was his…and as a consequence becoming the very jerk that he judged others to be.

Louise was very tender at this moment. "Michael, we forgive ourselves for judging ourselves as bad. For buying into mistaken notions about the world being bad. For judging others as bad. We forgive all of it…and then we become free."

Michael stared at her. He understood the words but couldn't feel the feeling.

"What does forgiveness feel like, Louise?"

"It feels like joy, Michael. It feels like a release. It makes everything seem easier and lighter. When we forgive we find compassion easily. We begin to see that every human action is either an attempt to give love or a call for love. We can look at each human act, no matter how painful, and see that the person responsible is coping with judgments, fears and anger, just like us. Everyone is given situations in which they

159

are forced to choose. Some make self-affirming choices, others don't. But we all have made self-destroying choices. Forgiveness is the deep understanding that we are all struggling with our own issues in the best way we know how."

"To err is human, to forgive divine," Michael whispered.

"To forgive is to recognize our own divinity, and to move into a higher place of being. To forgive is to make the choice of love over hate, faith over fear. And that choice determines the way our lives unfold. In every moment, Michael, you choose how your life is unfolding. I can only recommend you choose with awareness."

Chapter Fifteen

Strangely, Michael was getting used to the dislocation he felt after his meetings with Louise. As he sat in his back yard the following weekend, having a beer and staring up at the sky, Michael was finding it easier to notice and trace the judgments and stories he had been holding all of these years. Each one had its origins in some event that occurred long ago. Some were so old that he couldn't find the source memory that generated the core belief.

Like an archaeologist in search of ancient fossils, Michael had looked through old picture albums, spoken to his sister, and even tried to pull information from his father. Each time he was reminded of a particular event, thoughts and feelings would arise that placed him right back in that moment. The terror at being dropped off at school for the first time. Blissful joy when his father agreed to play catch with him in the back yard, then swelling pride as he expressed admiration for Michael's throwing arm. His anger at being dumped by his girlfriend, then his subsequent head-over-heels love when he met his wife. As he looked back, everything connected in a way that made perfect sense. He saw how logically his life had unfolded given the beliefs he had internalized and the consequent choices he had made.

Michael even began to notice the judgments he held against himself. He had initially had a difficult time accepting the whole idea of self-judgment. He felt that he certainly had judged others, and even judged God to some extent, but the idea that he somehow held negative beliefs about himself was confusing. It wasn't until he looked back into his life and re-experienced old thoughts and feelings that it became clear. When the bully had stolen Michael's new bike, a gift on his 6th birthday, and smashed it in front of him, his rage and hatred of the bully came present. So did the feeling of being victimized. When he experienced this feeling again, he saw how he had internalized a belief that the world was not safe. He also saw how he had judged himself as weak for not being able to stop the bully, and how that feeling of weakness had resulted in an over compensation of 'toughness' that continued to this day. And how, in trying to be 'tough', he had himself become the bully in school, at home and at work. He judged himself viciously whenever he perceived he was being weak, then secretly hated himself when he overcompensated and acted like a controlling, judgmental bully.

This victim-judge dynamic was unnervingly persistent throughout his life. Michael had early memories of wanting his father's attention, feeling that his father didn't really care about him except when he did something good. So he tried to be a good kid. He tried to excel in sports, but didn't have the size and aptitude to move to the higher levels. School came easy for Michael, but he never felt like his grades were good enough. His father never seemed satisfied, and his mother paid him lip service for his accomplishments. The underlying message was 'you're doing OK, but it's still not good enough'. He had always felt so angry and hurt that he had to do so much just to get a nod of affirmation…a little bit of love.

And so he saw himself as the victim of uncaring parents. Especially his father. So in a desperate attempt to gain his father's love, he had become very harsh with himself. He held a deep belief that he was not good enough, and that meant that he was required to keep moving, keep achieving in order to create a momentary sense of value and well being. Michael had also judged himself as unworthy of success, because if he existed in a constant state of imperfection then how could he possibly accept that what he had earned was truly deserving? Deep down

162

he knew he had spent his entire life judging himself as inadequate, and had used that judgment to motivate himself to perhaps gain a little bit of the love for which he yearned.

It was true, as Joe had said, that this fear-based motivation had achieved results. Michael was certainly well off by any standard. But at what cost? At this age he had hoped to be comfortably relaxing in his executive position, issuing orders to others and reaping the benefits of his long achievements. Instead, he felt like he was caught in an endless cycle of momentary achievement followed by thoughts of 'still not good enough'. With each new goal came the hope that maybe this time it would get easier. Maybe with money will come peace and happiness. Maybe with this new title. Maybe with marriage, kids, a new home. But peace never came. A sick joke, like a marathon where, at mile 25, someone moves the finish line to a point over the horizon.

Michael thought, with another self-judgment, how he couldn't seem to appreciate what he had. As soon as he got something he thought would make him happy, his mind jumped in and said 'yeah…but…' and quashed any notion of satisfaction. He shook his head as he realized he was now judging himself for judging himself! Endless loops of being the victim of an unfair world and judging himself for being weak and unable to overcome his own limitations. It was circular. He was both the jockey and the horse…beating himself to go faster but hating the pain and self abuse.

Michael took a swig of his beer and looked around his yard. Really, objectively, his life was very, very good. He had a wonderful house, a beautiful yard, an amazing wife and two beautiful children. So why did it feel so empty? He was trying to find reasons to be grateful and happy in this moment, but something inside of him kept negating those positive feelings. He felt like his mind had established some 'upper limit' of happiness. When his level of contentedness reached a certain point, an internal governor would kick in and remind him that things could always be better. But he had yet to find this elusive 'better'.

Maybe Louise was right. Maybe self-forgiveness was the way out. An image popped into Michael's mind of the old 'Chinese finger trap', where a person puts an index finger of each hand into a flexible tube only to find that they cannot be removed by pulling them back out. The trick was to push the fingers closer together and then delicately remove the trap with the other fingers. The idea was to surrender control, not try to force your way out. Could Michael simply let go of all these judgments? Just release them? Forgive everything and everyone?

Somehow Michael wasn't sure that it was going to be that easy. These judgments were very old stories that held a great deal of power in Michael's mind. But he knew he had to try, because his life had gotten to the point that he was simply unwilling to continue holding this much dissatisfaction.

As he sat there, he had a thought. What if he simply tried to stop thinking? He had heard that meditation was essentially the act of turning off the mental thought processes in order to experience inner peace, but he had never actually tried it. Could it be that simple? Certainly his old stories and frustrations could not be jettisoned that easily, he worried. But then again, why not give it a chance?

Michael put down his beer and closed his eyes. He took a few deep breaths and tried to relax. Stop thinking, he commanded…and for a moment he did. His thoughts went blank and he felt an almost giddy sensation as he realized that he was actually doing it. But then he remembered that he was thinking again, and commanded himself to stop it. Again, his mind stopped for a moment, but then more thoughts began to appear. He heard noises that he tried to identify, wondered what time it was, thought about his wife getting home, remembered that he had a customer meeting the next morning, felt an itch on his leg, had a memory of his Dad, saw his Mom's face…an endless stream of mental noise that he felt powerless to stop.

He sighed and opened his eyes. This was not going to be as easy as he thought. Michael suddenly realized that his mind was not in his control. It was as if a hyperactive child had gotten into his head, and he could not turn off the chatter. The subjects changed as fast as his mind could process. If this is where the stories were coming from, then Michael could understand how he had been inadvertently allowing himself to be controlled by them. They were not rational, intentional thoughts, just random noise from the ether.

Michael shook his head and tried again. Louise had told him that awareness was the first key step, so he thought he would simply try to notice his thoughts. He took a few long, deep breaths and…observed. But as soon as he noticed the first thought, about picking up his kids from school, it vanished. Each time a thought began to enter his mind he merely became aware of it, acknowledged it…and each time, the thought would then disappear.

As Michael practiced this for what seemed like minutes, the most remarkable thing happened: he felt joy! Something inside of him bubbled up and burst into his awareness. For the first time in many, many years, he felt a giddy, peaceful joy! There was no thought, just a feeling. His whole body relaxed and he felt a jolt of energy run through him. He started to chuckle to himself as he realized that all his mental chatter had been denying this feeling that was already inside of him. Michael instantly remembered that, as a young child, he had often felt like this. Free. Happy. Giddy.

And then the phone rang. Michael snapped out of his reverie and looked around. He didn't know how long it had been, but it seemed like time had all but stopped. As he looked for his cell phone, his mind came back on line and all the thoughts flooded in. But this time it was different. He now saw that his thoughts were like a tic, a habit that until now he had taken as his natural state of being. He had been living according to thoughts that he had chosen a long time ago, and had been totally unaware that he was…addicted to them! As Michael picked up his phone, he felt a surge of hope as he realized that he could choose to think other thoughts. He was not trapped by his own mind!

Looking down, Michael saw it was his wife calling. He unlocked the phone and before he could say hello, his wife was talking, clearly under stress. The story was short and caused Michael to grab his keys and head for the door. Maria had been visiting his father when he collapsed again. She was following the ambulance to the emergency room, but needed to pick up the kids in a half hour, and so asked Michael to take over at the hospital. He agreed and hung up the phone. *So much for serenity*, he thought.

"Déjà vu all over again" Michael thought as he raced up the hospital stairs. This time he ran into his father's doctor, who happened to be seeing a patient at the moment. He stopped him in the hall.

"Hi Dr. Peterson," Michael panted. "What happened?"

"Well, Mr. Benson, we really don't know. It looks like your father has lapsed into a coma and we're not quite sure why. His organs are shutting down as the cancer spreads, but we usually don't see this type of collapse. We have him on pain medication to make sure that he's comfortable but there's not much else we can do. As you know, your father doesn't want any heroic measures to be performed,"

"Is he..." Michael hesitated to say the words.

Dr. Peterson put his hand on Michael's shoulder. "We don't know how long it could be, Mr. Benson. Your father could stay like this for a day, a week, or a month. But we do know that he...well...he will not survive much longer even if he does wake up. I just want to make sure that you have your chance to say goodbye." The doctor looked awkward but was doing his best to be clear.

"I understand," Michael mumbled. He felt numb. He realized that he hadn't truly accepted his father's condition until right now. How easy it had been to act as if nothing was happening, that his father would live forever.

Michael turned and walked into his father's room. He looked at the figure lying in the bed and had to strain to see the vibrant, powerful business executive of 10 years ago. This person didn't even look like his father, but of course he was. 50 pounds lighter, sunken cheeks, rattling breath. Michael slumped into the chair next to the bed and took his father's hand.

"God, Dad, I thought we had more time." Michael felt warm, unfamiliar tears running down his face.

As he looked at the emaciated figure of his father lying in the bed, he felt a wave of compassion for what this man had been through. All of his judgment and anger at his father evaporated in the face of the stark reality that his life was about to end.

Michael reflected how strange it was, this event called life. We are born, learn, experience, and then live the best life we can with what we have been given. His father was a flawed man, an angry man, but Michael knew now that he was doing the best he could with what he had. Roy Benson was a child born of innocence just like the rest of us, and had done his best to live a life of meaning and purpose. Michael knew this was the source of his compassion: that his father was no different than himself, or from any person. Everyone is doing the best they can.

"Dad," Michael stood and looked into his father's face, "I just want you to know that I love you and I forgive you. I know…," tears coursed down Michael's face, "I know that you were doing what you thought was best. I know that this was your way of showing us love. And I am sorry if I judged you. I think I was angry because I wanted love in a way that you couldn't offer, and for that I treated you poorly. I treated you how I thought you were treating me…with disrespect."

Michael sat back down in the chair and put his head in his hands. How often had he tried to 'get even' with is father by treating him with contempt and derision? And how much of that anger had he carried into his workplace, his home life, his friendships?

"Dad, were you like this when you were my age? Did you treat your father this way?" Michael asked, knowing there would never be an answer.

It began to occur to Michael that his father likely had similar feelings

167

and ways of interacting with the world. There was an intergenerational pattern emerging, one of loveless relationships and harsh judgments of the outside world. Michael knew that his grandfather was a judgmental and withdrawn man, as was his father, and as was he himself to a great extent. Michael wondered if this was how projections and stories got learned, through generations of unconscious training. If this was the case, then Michael could understand how organizations and societies came to be so selfish and angry and fear-based. We are all simply trained to be that way. We don't know any different.

As he sat looking at his Dad he felt a love and understanding that he had never felt before. All of this comes to an end, and we can only do our best to be as loving as possible while we are here. Death is the final arbiter, and it does not negotiate.

Michael stood and took a deep breath. He could hear his sister coming down the hall, and wanted to be as strong as possible when she was here. He felt like he had to be the 'man of the family' now that his father was passing on. *What a strange feeling*, he thought. He had always pictured his father in control, in the picture. Now Michael was going to pick up the mantel. But which mantel? His father would have been strong but harsh...he would have pushed his sister to 'buck up' like he did with his wife. No crying, just accept and move on.

Is that what Michael wanted to be? He saw that he had a choice *in this moment*. The choice to be who he wanted to be, to express the love and care and concern that he felt had never been expressed in his family, or to continue the pattern. As he turned to greet his sister he knew the answer, but also suspected that following through was going to be more challenging than he expected.

Chapter Sixteen

A week had passed since Michael's father had lapsed into a coma, and yet there was no perceptible change in his condition. There was something unsettled about waiting like this. It was one thing to deal with known tragedy, something concrete with an answer of some kind. But to sit and wait, not knowing what was going to happen, this was in some ways worse than had his father died. The tension in the family was tremendous. Michael could see how families tear themselves apart when a loved one is trapped in limbo like this. He couldn't imagine how people coped with a years-long bedside vigil. It must absolutely wreck a family.

Michael's sister had been having a really hard time of it, which was why he secretly, and abashedly, hoped that his father would pass on sooner rather than later. At least the grieving process was known, and he could do something to help his sister get through it. Instead she was sitting at home or at the hospital consuming herself with worry. This was the difference between Michael and his sister. While Michael could deflect his emotions and rationalize what was happening, his sister dove into her feelings and lost herself in grief and emotional flooding.

The hard part for Michael was his judgment around his sister's emotions. Because he was strongly discouraged, if not punished, for expressing his feelings, he felt that his sister should exercise restraint now and then. It seemed unfair that he should repress everything while she blabbered on with no control whatsoever. But this was the way they were brought up. His sister was the 'emotional one' while Michael was the 'analytical one'. The only problem was this wasn't true. Michael many times had felt deep pain and fear, but had simply dismissed them as unacceptable for a boy or a man.

So Michael pretended that his feelings did not exist, and masked them in a stoic façade of 'doingness'. But the energy it took was tremendous, and it was wearing him out. Compounding this was the confounded awareness of it all. He saw himself repressing and judging his emotions, but could not seem to act in any other way. He wanted to cry out in anguish, to beg his Dad not to die, but a terrible fear arose in him whenever he felt the energy begin to bubble up inside of him. Michael felt that if he let this pain come out he was going to destroy everything…and that he might lose control…and what?

It wasn't as if he was going to die or hurt anyone. So why was he so afraid of expressing his feelings? This loss of control seemed to be a key. Was it that he thought that somehow he was going to lose control of his life, of himself? And what would happen then? If he did cry out and sob and carry on, what would follow?

He would be embarrassed. And what would that mean?

That people would laugh at him. And then what?

Then he wouldn't be able to look at himself in the mirror. And after that?

Then he would have to disappear from the world. And that would mean…

That he would die.

Michael sat for a moment staring at the wall in the bathroom. He had been getting ready for work and had totally lost where he was.

Somehow Michael had equated his expression of emotion with death. Actual, physical death. He wondered how in the world he had gotten this notion in his head. But he had to admit that the thought of weeping openly in front of others generated a fear…no, a terror…that in some ways was worse than death. He felt like if he lost control of his emotions he would be drawn into a whirlpool of energy that would rip him apart. And so he kept a tight lid on everything inside of him. Michael had become a master of control because he thought he needed to in order to stay alive.

"God", Michael said to the wall. But it made total sense looking back. There was something about the men in the family that *assumed* this was the way to be. After all, emotion was weakness, and weakness meant failure, and failure meant death. Hadn't that been the subtext of the family for years? Yet another mistaken notion picked up inadvertently.

Staring into the mirror, Michael took a shot. "I forgive myself for believing that my emotions are bad and that I will be harmed for expressing how I feel."

Then he had an idea. What if he – right here, right now – changed this story? He looked at himself with determination. "In reality," he said to himself, "my emotions are a natural part of me and they are necessary to my survival. It is good to express emotion." As he finished, he could not help but laugh a bit at himself. Michael wondered what his co-workers would think of this…their hard-ass boss talking to himself in the mirror!

Finishing up his morning routine, Michael grabbed his coat and headed out the door. As he pulled the car out of the driveway he saw his neighbor, Jim, taking out the trash. He waved, then groaned to himself as he remembered that he had promised to go to a 'community meeting' tonight to discuss issues the town was facing. Jim was a consultant who had worked with many different cities and towns across the nation, and had volunteered his time to organize this session. Michael groaned again as he pictured the typical town hall meeting with lots of yelling and arguing.

Michael thought briefly about cancelling, using his father's illness as an excuse, but something told him that this might be a valuable evening. Connecting with the community sounded vaguely appealing as he thought about it…maybe it was his newfound awareness. Anyway, Jim was a nice, smart guy and Michael had promised he would be there, so he might a well see what it was all about.

Heading out of work that day, Michael had second thoughts. He had had yet another rough day and did not feel much like listening to people complain about the trash and noise and everything that he imagined would be a part of a community discussion. Nevertheless, he headed toward his small downtown as he reflected on his day. He was beginning to notice that there were some patterns in the way he worked. For the most part he was a productive person, but he saw that his interactions with people at work created frictions, little tensions that made the work not only less efficient, but terribly draining. Small misunderstandings led to ongoing email arguments that became insulting and highly disruptive. A small slight in the hallway or, heaven forbid, an exclusion from a meeting, and there would be repercussions for days. Michael's workplace felt like a larger, more complex and more resourced highschool sometimes.

Michael mused about his role in this ongoing drama. Given the concept of projection, he knew that he was somehow both helping to create and sustain the situation, but he couldn't get his mind around how he was doing this. Michael pictured himself a reasonable guy. He was clear about the goals, communicated effectively, and expected people to perform to their highest abilities. But this simply didn't work all the time. If things were going smoothly he knew it was a fluke...just a matter of time before something blew up. Michael wondered if his pessimism was the issue, or if indeed the people he worked with were inherently unreliable over time.

And then there was Armand. His boss had been completely unmanageable from the start. An intelligent guy with a huge ego, he was both maddeningly present and distant at the same time. Detail-oriented to a fault, Michael knew that Armand was aware of everything yet seemed not to engage with people beyond the superficial. His boss seemed to be a ghost that haunted his office from time to time, terrifying him but never really taking a form that could cause actual harm. An annoyance.

Michael thought again about his role in this relationship. Was he creating this dynamic? Another wave of awareness struck Michael. His relationship with his boss was very similar to his relationship with his father: distant, fact oriented, unemotional, disconnected…yet also with a yearning for approval and love that, when denied, resulted in anger. Yes, Michael thought to himself. This was his relationship to Armand. If he was honest, he wanted approval badly and blamed Armand for not giving it to him. In order not to be let down, Michael maintained distance yet stoked a simmering resentment that Armand never reached out.

It suddenly became clear! Michael realized he was recreating his childhood family dynamic at work. He had established a relationship with each person in which he had embedded silent expectations, judgments and hopes. And those unstated assumptions had created the dynamic he was experiencing!

The depth of this realization hit Michael as he searched for parking near the town hall. It was just as Louise had said. He was creating his world as he went, unknowingly encouraging others to act toward him in a way that he understood. And other people were doing the same. When those expectations meshed, things went well in the relationship. Co-dependency was created. If a colleague was looking for an argument because that is what she was used to in her life, and Michael gave her what she wanted because he was expecting conflict from women, then they both created a reality for each other that was affirming of their world view. Reality agreed with what they both thought was 'the way the world works'.

Michael sat in his parking spot and lightly pounded his fist into his forehead. But what to do? Louise said to release all judgments, to choose to act otherwise. How? Was it like the experience Michael had with meditation? Did he simply need to 'let go' of all expectations and judgments? It seemed to be the answer, but Michael was struggling with the sheer force of habit. In this moment he felt like his whole life consisted of a huge number of stories that he was now realizing were *not true*. His world, the world of defined people and situations and structures, was not real…a creation of his mind.

Taking a deep breath, Michael got out of the car and tried to let go of his confusion. He hoped Louise was right, that everything was unfolding the way that it should. He worried that if he let go of all these stories he might end up in some sort of mental limbo, anchorless in a cruel, relative world. Michael laughed…his fear was not death but insanity. Letting go was tantamount to going into the nut-house, because thinking 'nothing' was simply not an option that made sense.

As he walked into the town hall, Michael chuckled to himself that maybe this was the nut-house he was destined to enter. He pictured the health care town hall meetings a few years back and shivered. People lining up to scream into a microphone was guaranteed to send Michael to an early exit.

Strangely, however, the room behind the sign was very quiet and peaceful. People were chatting in small groups, there was soft music playing in the background, and, best of all to Michael's growling stomach, there was food from various restaurants in town. Grabbing a plate, Michael headed for the buffet.

Munching happily on a Thai basil salad, Michael surveyed the room. It was not at all what he had expected. In Michael's experience, mainly gained from television, town hall meetings were set up with the leaders sitting on a dais above and in front of the audience. Each leader had a microphone, and the audience shared one. Or, the format of the presidential 'town hall meetings', where a selected audience sat in a circle around the candidate, who walked like a gladiator in the ring waiting to be given the thumbs-up-or-down from a slavering public.

But this room was completely different. There was no dais or, to Michael's amazement, even a regular order to the chairs. There were some chairs in circles of 8, others in small trios of 3, and a mix in-between. There didn't seem to be any particular purpose in the arrangement, yet

174

it seemed ordered anyhow.

Michael looked around to see where he was supposed to sit, but couldn't find any clear indication. As if anticipating Michael's thoughts, his neighbor approached him with a big smile.

"Michael!" Jim Thornton said as he reached to shake Michael's hand. "I'm so glad you could make it!"

"Me too, Jim," Michael said, half truthfully. "I'm really curious about what you do in these meetings. It doesn't look like any town meeting I've seen…on TV, I mean. I've never been to one myself."

Jim laughed as he looked around the room. "Yep, this is a bit different for everyone. I think you're going to like it. We try to emphasize 'maximum involvement' as you'll see. Most town or community meetings use what we call the 'leader-led' model of governance. But we don't believe in that."

"Leader-led?" Michael asked quizzically. "Isn't that what government is?"

Jim paused for a moment as if assembling his thoughts. "Well…sort of. I guess I'm referring to the psychological model behind government. Certainly there are people we elect who we want to represent us, our 'leaders', if you will, but that's where I believe things go south. In most democratic models the citizens have somehow come to a notion that by electing a leader we are therefore no longer responsible for what happens in our community, state, country…our world. We look to the leaders and say 'fix it', and when the leaders don't, or can't, fix it, we scream bloody murder as if we're the victims of some grand conspiracy."

"Like the health care debate a few years ago," Michael interjected. He had been dismayed and disgusted at the image of people standing at a microphone screaming, sometimes obscenely, at anyone proposing anything that they didn't like.

"Exactly," Jim nodded. "We lose sight of the fact that we are responsible for the form of government we have, the leaders we elect, even the issues on the table. Democracy is supposed to be *participative*, yet we've taken that to mean we cast a ballot, refuse to compromise, deny our own involvement, and then blame everyone else when things don't go the way we want. The sad reality is that we have willingly ceded our own power and choose not to take it back by refusing to get involved. We are the architects of our own frustration!"

"Wow," Michael said, "that really syncs with some of the realizations I've been having lately. We really do choose and create this, don't we?"

"Absolutely," Jim said with finality. "But these meetings are another way. So sit and enjoy, because I think you'll find it enlightening." Jim looked at his watch and glanced back at Michael. "Find a seat anywhere, I have to get the show on the road." He clapped Michael on the shoulder and smiled as he turned and walked away. Michael was starting to like this guy.

Michael wandered around the room, picked a chair at random and sat down in a trio of chairs. The smaller setting seemed more comfortable to him somehow. A minute or so later the other two chairs were filled, one by an elderly black woman and the other by a 30-something Asian man. Michael politely said hello and turned in his seat to listen to Jim start the proceedings.

"Hello everyone," Jim started, standing in the center of the group of approximately 90 members of the local community. "I'd like to welcome you and thank you for coming to our first of, hopefully, many of these meetings. My name is Jim Thornton, and I am so very happy to be here with all of you."

As Jim continued, Michael noticed how careful he was to include everyone and mention, by name, their contribution to the meeting. Michael felt very much like this was a meeting organized by and for the community…as if he were part of a very large family where everyone's contributions, no matter how small, were recognized.

Jim then laid out the ground rules for the meeting. First, he asked everyone to be mentally present. He emphasized that nobody had to promise to agree to, or to do, anything specific, just to engage with oth-

176

ers and participate in the way that felt natural.

Second, he asked that everyone stay for the duration of the meeting. If someone had to leave for an emergency or other very important engagement, he asked that they stand and announce their departure and tell everyone why they had to leave. This also applied to late arrivals. Jim explained that he insisted on this ground rule because it showed respect for the group and led people to commit their time more seriously.

Last, Jim asked that everyone simply listen and have fun. He explained that the idea wasn't to solve every problem or to even come to a conclusion, but to generate a discussion where new ideas and new leadership were welcomed. He finished with what Michael thought was an interesting quote: "No matter what happens we cannot fail, because by merely coming together today we have already succeeded."

It struck Michael that this concept was at the root of the word 'community': to 'commune' with each other, regardless of the outcome. And, Michael realized, this is what Jim was referring to earlier…that we have lost our sense of community, of connection, and that we see each other as individuals at the mercy of some distant and arbitrary system run by distant and uncaring leaders. *Jim was right*, Michael reflected, *we have succeeded simply by coming together like this.*

Jim then explained the structure and announced the topic of this meeting. The topic was whether or not the town should use tax dollars to subsidize the opening of a health center that would cater to lower income families and urgent care walk-ins. The discussion would be comprised of two 45-minute discussion sessions, with the groups changing members between sessions. During the discussion, each person would be granted 5 minutes to offer their opinion on the topic while the other group members listened. During this process Jim asked that people simply listen and not interject. Once everyone had spoken, or chosen not to, then the group could engage in open discussion. Each group would be responsible for holding a respectful dialogue, as defined by that group.

After each 45-minute session, and before people rotated to new groups, there would be 30 minutes of 'open mike' comments during which anybody could say anything he or she wanted. At the very end, Jim would ask for commitments to take actions that had been suggested by the group. Nobody was required to do anything except be present and to focus on the subject at hand.

When Jim was finished, he looked at his watch and said, "Your 45 minutes begin now. I will announce when you have 10 minutes to go, and when the session is over. Have fun!"

Michael turned back and looked at his two group-mates. This process felt somewhat strange to him because there was no leader, nobody structuring or guiding the conversation. So he defaulted to his 'take charge' disposition. "Well," he said, "who would like to go first?"

And so over the next 3 hours Michael sat and talked with people he had not only never met, but people that he very likely would never have even encountered in his very narrowly defined social experience. He heard about the challenges of being elderly, and learned that a diminutive octogenarian can have more spirit than a high-school athlete. Michael saw how difficult it was to be gay and ostracized by a highly religious and traditional immigrant community. He looked into the world of a teacher struggling to teach an over-sized class while raising a downs-syndrome daughter.

Each person that spoke saw the issue from a different perspective and had a unique take on the solutions. Michael himself had come into the meeting with a fairly simple worldview, one learned from his family and, most importantly, his father. He did not believe in government subsidies because they were economically inefficient. He believed that each person should work to support him or herself, and that each person was responsible for his/her own health and well-being.

But he also saw that his perspective came from life experiences that were not necessarily the norm. His education had been paid for, and he always had a job with health insurance. Michael had never had to search for a job while his extremely expensive COBRA payments ate into his savings. He had never had a debilitating disease that virtually ensured an inability to get health coverage. As he sat and heard the myriad of situations and stories, he realized that everyone wasn't so lucky.

Much to his chagrin, he also realized that he had used a fairly broad brush to describe people who used community health services. These were not all illegal immigrants seeking to live off Uncle Sam's dime. Many of these people were simply average citizens trying to stay healthy in a system that many times didn't work for them. Independent consultants, nurses, teachers, retirees...Michael realized that he could easily of have been one of these people in a different life.

The most striking thing for Michael was how much each of these people wanted to do the right thing. When it was his turn and he suggested that perhaps this was not the best use of the town's funds, everyone listened. Certainly some of the people disagreed with what he said, but Michael was amazed at the genuineness of their arguments. Regardless of perspective, Michael felt that they all wanted to do the best thing for the community and each other. He could not paint anyone with a broad brush anymore because each person was so entirely unique in his/her opinion, approach and outlook.

This open, tolerant discussion had an interesting affect on Michael. He began to soften. It wasn't that he changed his mind, but he began to see that the issue was more complex than he thought. He saw that in a way each person was right. Each person had a perspective and a set of life experiences that were valid and that he couldn't deny. And so Michael listened and learned and began to seek common ground. In reality, he began to see himself as a part of a much larger picture, and that felt both comforting and unnerving at the same time. In some ways it was easier to keep himself walled off in his own beliefs, living under the illusion of separateness.

After 3 hours and a great deal of conversation and sharing, Michael had a very detailed picture of the topic, the perspectives, and the challenges his community was facing. He felt truly educated. Regardless of the final decision on the health center, Michael knew he would accept the outcome because he had been a part of the conversation.

Jim stood and looked out over the crowd. There was a different feeling in the room now, an intangible but palpable *connectedness*. Jim started slowly. "Regardless of your position on this topic, I think you will all agree that this was a meaningful night. We heard from each other, we listened to each other, and I truly believe we care about each other. We have covered virtually every angle on this decision, and I think now is the time for next steps."

Jim began to list potential action items and asked if anyone felt called to participate further. Much to Michael's surprise, Jim found many potential volunteers willing to canvass the community, set up the next meeting, take a straw poll and draft a proposal. Even more shocking to Michael was everyone's willingness to look at alternate sources of funding, and not to rely on tax dollars. This was not a 'step up to the feed-wagon' social program...people in his community were willing to work to bring this service to the town. Michael's father wouldn't have believed it, because it flew in the face of the notion that all people wanted was a free ride.

Michael, however, heard a nagging voice in his head. 'What about you, Michael? What are *you* going to do?' At first he rationalized that he was far too busy with his work and family and father to participate further, but then he saw people volunteering he *knew* were similarly busy. So why was he feeling so resistant?

As the meeting wound down Michael was relieved when Jim asked if anyone would be willing to commit to participating in further discussion on this matter. This was a question Michael could answer in the affirmative. As he raised his hand, he noticed that virtually every person in the room had raised their hand as well. They were a team now, a team that had elected themselves as members. Michael felt touched and inspired.

As Michael walked toward the exit, Jim walked up and asked excitedly, "So, what did you think?"

Michael smiled at Jim and shook his head. "It wasn't what I expected. At all. But yes, I enjoyed it very much. I'm still not sure if the health center is the right idea, but I really respect all the people I heard from tonight. I had no idea we had such a diverse population!"

"Yes," Jim smiled, "we pre-select for that. We want as many diverse opinions as possible, which makes the discussion so much more interesting. And don't worry, you don't have to agree or even compromise. Just trust the process and be open to learning…you'll be shocked at the secondary benefits."

"Secondary benefits?" Michael looked at Jim quizzically.

Jim nodded, "The benefit of connection.

"We are wired to connect with everything in our environment, especially each other," Jim continued. "Our brains are designed to sense thoughts, facial expressions, pheromones, intentions and anything that tells us how we fit, how we are part of the bigger picture. And when we are successful, we feel a sense of completion, a sense of wholeness. We recognize that we are part of something greater, and that our separateness is an illusion. This realization is a powerful and wonderful feeling that brings communities together."

Michael remembered again what Yoda had so many weeks earlier: *Everything is connected right down to the subatomic level. Separateness is an illusion.*

"I get it," Michael said, "but it seems that with technology and our value on individual achievement we're moving away from this, not toward it. Our whole society is built on the concept of individual potential, isn't it?"

"You've hit the nail on the head, Michael," Jim nodded soberly. "As a society our social intelligence is under siege. We don't know how to *be* with each other anymore, and you can see it reflected in the loneliness and dislocation that our citizens, especially our children, feel. People are taking record amounts of anti-depressant, anti-anxiety and pain killing medications just to feel *good* again. I think it's a direct result of the loss of connection to each other. A loss of connection to a major part of the life force that runs through us all."

"Yeah, I get what you mean," Michael offered hesitantly, "but haven't we come pretty far as a society by emphasizing individual excellence? I mean, I really believe that the human drive to be excellent is at the root of all social progress. Don't you?"

"Of course!" Jim said, waving his hands. "We wouldn't be where we are if individual people did not invent, create and accomplish amazing things. This is an enormous force, but it's only half of the equation."

"Okay," Michael smiled, "I'll bite. What's the other half?"

"Love," Jim answered, looking directly at Michael.

"But…" Michael started.

Jim interrupted. "Before you tell me that love doesn't 'work', let me explain some concepts that might make it easier to digest. First, there are two basic forces in every living thing, but especially in human beings. One is 'power' and the other is 'love', and they are not defined in the way you might be used to. 'Power' in this case is the drive to self-actualize. It is the growth of every living thing into the best version of itself. Some would call this an evolutionary force, but I think it's bigger than that. It's the force that causes a tree to not only become the biggest tree it can be in any given forest, but to also adapt itself to the contextual conditions to allow itself to be even better than it might be 'programmed' by its DNA. It grows and adapts.

"In humans," Jim continued, "this 'power force' is what Maslow called 'self actualization'. It's every human being's desire to become the best possible version of him or herself. This force is what drives us not only to grow physically, but to grow mentally, emotionally and spiritually. We are driven to learn, through curiosity, and to grow, through an insatiable desire to be 'more'. Every human being has this drive, as does everything in nature, but for humans it can become stunted through mistaken notions about our lack of ability, lack of opportunity, etc. Each person has this very powerful force inside them, but some people lose touch with it and flounder."

"OK," Michael nodded, "I get that. It's the choice people make whether or not to believe in the possibility of themselves, to access this force inside of them."

"Absolutely!" Jim exclaimed. "When people believe in themselves and do the thing that is most natural to them…the thing they *love*…then a huge wave of potential is unleashed and they achieve great things. It is actually natural for us to accomplish great things if we can find the flow within ourselves. This is the definition of 'power' that I'm referencing."

"Got it." Michael nodded. This made complete sense to him and was consistent with his self-reliant world-view.

Jim motioned for Michael to grab a seat in the nearly empty room. "So that leaves us with the second force, the other half of the equation," Jim paused for a moment, "which is 'love'. Now this love is *not* the squishy, mushy love that makes 10-year-old boys say 'eeew'. This is a force just as strong as 'power', but is completely misunderstood as weak and ineffectual."

"So how do you define 'love' in this case?" Michael asked. "Because I must confess that I don't have much experience in anything beyond romantic love…"

"You don't?" Jim smiled knowingly. "Have you ever yearned to be accepted? Have you ever felt pride at the accomplishments of a group to which you belong? Are you touched when someone in a group reaches out to you and welcomes you? Isn't there just a bit of emotion when someone really hears you, and when you in turn hear them? And when they accept you regardless of what you say or do?"

Michael immediately thought of the elderly African American lady in his first group. She had been so kind and so accepting of him. And she cared so deeply about her family and her community. Michael felt the warmth radiating from her. He was surprised and mildly embarrassed when he felt tears welling up in his eyes as she described the challenges she had getting to and from her doctor.

"Yes," Michael said quietly, "I've felt these things."

Jim reached out and touched Michael's shoulder. "*That* is love. Love is the desire to connect to each other, to return to the 'oneness' from which all life emerges. It's at the core of every major religion…before things got confused in translation. It's the simplest concept of all: that we came from One, exist as One, and will return to One. Some would say this is the essence of God: the consciousness of pure love. And as much as we are driven to actualize ourselves, we are also driven to connect to one another in loving community."

Michael sat for a moment and thought about the implications of what Jim was saying. If this was true, then society had certainly gone to one extreme over the other. Every message Michael could remember was to 'take care of number one', to win by all means necessary.

"Well," Michael sighed, "I see this in theory, but in practice…well with war and greed and all the seemingly disconnecting activities that we humans undertake…reality tells me otherwise."

"I know," Jim said. "And this is why I do what I do. I believe, at a deep level, that we all *want* to connect, but that we've simply forgotten how. In the past at least we connected to family or tribe or region, but now it seems that we have isolated ourselves into groups of 1. Everyone is an enemy and everyone is out to get us. Just look at our media and politics. Everything is about what divides us, who is special, who gets more than others. But this is temporary, because we will destroy ourselves if we continue to live like this. When we destroy habitats in the name of wealth, kill each other in the name of 'right', poison the earth in the name of progress, well, then we are literally destroying an aspect of our own beings. We create a hell on earth."

"OK," Michael laughed, "now I'm depressed!" Michael again fell back to his take-charge nature. "So what can we do? We have tried every system possible, haven't we? What's left to try?"

"A lot." Jim stated flatly. "The key is to create systems that include both power *and* love in the operational approach. But what may seem strange is that this has a lot less to do with governance than it does with the way we see ourselves and our worlds.

"OK," Jim leaned back and shook his head, "I'm going to go off on what might seem like a tangent but is actually quite relevant. It has to do with how we govern ourselves and our institutions. To date we, and I mean the larger 'we', as in the human race, have tried many forms of governance throughout history. For the longest time it was based on family or clan. One person, usually an elder, was deemed to have the knowledge, personal power, or experience to manage the affairs of the group.

"As the family and clan groups began to merge and grow," Jim continued, "the question of leadership became more complicated. If there are two elders, who leads? For most of our history it was decided by force of arms, the strongest taking power by killing or subduing the others. But, as we know, the ability to conquer does not necessarily mean the ability – or right – to govern. So kings, emperors, and other leaders needed something else to justify their position…which became 'divine right'. God is on my side, goes the logic, so I can do what is necessary. And for the longest time the 'little guy' was forced to go along because resisting the king meant not only physical death but also spiritual death, because to resist the king or emperor was to resist God."

Michael nodded, thinking, *This is history 101.'*

"So you get all this," Jim agreed, "but here's where it gets interesting, and brings into focus the two human drives of power and love." Jim leaned forward, "Although the Greeks invented democracy, it wasn't until the seventeenth and eighteenth centuries when philosophers began to see potential, power and the innate worth of each human being. Prior to this it was widely accepted as fact that only certain people had value. In some cases it was 'nobility', in others 'the educated', and up until recently 'race', or even more recently 'wealth'. But in each case there was a distinct divide between those who ruled and those who were subjects.

"But then, slowly, a new concept began to take shape that included both democracy and a new form of economics called 'capitalism'. The emphasis of both of these systems was both the acknowledgment and, more importantly, the *harnessing* of the individual potential of each citizen. The notion was, and is, simple: let people freely choose their leaders, engage in unrestricted economic activity, and create laws to enshrine these rights and the power of human actualization will drive humanity forward. The entire U.S. system is predicated on this concept.

"But," Jim winced, "there was this sticky notion called 'equality' that people could not get their heads around. Ideally, we would like everyone to have an equal chance at success. But what we quickly found out was that freedom to self-actualize – 'power' in my definition – sometimes became quite nasty when put into application. It was, and is, easy for individuals to take this notion of self-actualization to the point where they can justify using and abusing others to enrich or 'actualize' themselves. It's simply another version of 'might makes right', except this time it's justified by the notion that in order for me to actualize myself, I can do anything I need to do, including what amounts to legitimized theft. It's the separation notion again...because I feel separate from everyone and grew up with the notion that I must care only about myself, then I must do what's necessary to get as much as I can. Every financial meltdown, scandal, and crisis in capitalist history stems from this sorry fact."

"Jim," Michael interrupted, "I can see where you're going, but the truth is that there are some people that are simply better at some things than others. People are *not* equal. To claim we must somehow ensure that everyone is equal is *communism*, and we all know how that turned out!"

"It's funny you should mention communism, because that's where I was headed," Jim smiled. "You see Michael, communism was at first a fairly noble idea. Now, before you call me a 'commie', let me explain. Going back to what we talked about earlier, we know that there are two forces that drive the human spirit: power, or the desire to become the best version of ourselves, and love, the desire to connect with and care about others. Democracy and capitalism have leaned toward the 'power' side, emphasizing freedom and individual human potential. But as we have seen, without love and care, 'power' can quickly become controlling and abusive.

"Certain philosophers, Marx being one of them, began to notice the abuses and the huge disparities in wealth and began to ask, as the Black Eyed Peas' song goes, 'where's the love?' Essentially 'socialism' was merely an attempt to take care of those who were being left out of the equation, which was about 99% of the population at the time. Capitalists had become the new kings, and the employees were the modern serfs. So political philosophers at the time came up with 'socialism', a system that they thought had the care of the downtrodden at the heart of its proposition.

"The problem was that both socialism and communism, when put into practice, *forced* the top 1% to give up their wealth. It was not voluntary, but a denial that the top echelons of society, in many cases the best and brightest, did not have the right to their own power. The concept of 'love' swung too far away from 'power' and became not only ineffectual, but abusive in and by itself. The 'father state', instead of being a loving presence, became a terrorizing authority, denying all individual human potential for 'the greater good'.

"The essential struggle that humans have been wrestling with, the struggle to *both* use our power and love one another is represented in our choices of government. And none have been perfect to-date, because systems that emphasize individual power can become abusive while systems that emphasize love and care can become ineffective," Jim shrugged and laughed.

"So the question becomes, Michael, can we create a way of operating that both ensures that each individual has the freedom to actualize him or herself to the greatest possible extent *while at the same time* caring for each other and ensuring that each other are supported in times of crisis? Can we include both 'power' and 'love' in our community life? I

187

believe we can. I heard a quote the other day that I just love: 'what we need is tough minds and tender hearts'. The ability to act intelligently while at the same time caring about others."

Michael sat for a moment and thought about what Jim was saying. It just seemed so far-fetched in this divided world. Sure, this would be nice, to have the best of all worlds, but weren't these notions, 'freedom and equality', and 'power and love', mutually exclusive? Wouldn't including one take away from the other? Ayn Rand seemed to think so, and Michael tended to agree. He said so to Jim.

Jim thought for a moment and then answered, "Michael, what you have identified has been the limiting factor in human governance for the past 10,000 years. It's the mistaken notion that in order to be free I must be selfish, and in order to be equal I must give up all personal power. This is how financiers justify amassing unheard of wealth at the expense of the larger community and why socially concerned people can be so ineffective. Power without love is abusive. Love without power is ineffectual. But both presume that they cannot include the other, and that is the point you've identified."

"So?" Michael said, "What's the way forward?"

"Individual awareness, Michael," Jim stated flatly. "And that's what you did here today."

They both sat for a moment, and then Jim broke the silence. "Michael, let me ask you this. Do you feel more compassionate, more identified with the people you met today?"

"Of course," Michael answered.

"Do you feel that you had to compromise anything about yourself to feel this way? Did you have to give anything up?" Jim probed.

"No, not at all. In fact, I think I gained a lot by being here." Michael started to see what Jim was getting at.

"So," Jim smiled, "you still have your freedom to be who you are, you've grown, and yet you can also see other's positions and care about them. Democracy has not changed because we can still vote on the issues. Capitalism has not been challenged because we can still all agree that freedom to do business is important. But we have now come together as a caring community – yikes, a 'commune' – and have heard each other and expressed an intention to do both the best thing for ourselves and for our community. This is the secondary benefit: reestablishing a connection and learning from one another in the process. Although we still don't know what the outcome will be, just by reestablishing connections with each other we have increased our chances for success immeasurably."

"Wow," Michael marveled, "that sounds like a *primary* benefit to me!"

"I think so!" Jim smiled again. "We need to have faith that by both being the best people we can be, and at the same time caring about others, we can live in both peace and prosperity. Unconditional love for ourselves *and* others…which are, after all, the same thing anyways."

Michael and Jim sat in silence for a long time. Michael reflected on what Louise had said, that it all starts with acceptance of all things, most importantly ourselves. It all made so much sense now. All of the screaming and war and division in the world was based on the notion that we are separate, that we need to fight for things. As long as we isolate ourselves and are unwilling to listen to each other, we will suffer. And we isolate ourselves because we harbor anger and fear and hate within us.

These revelations were stunning to Michael, because the implications were so personal. If he wanted the world to be a different place, he was going to have to be a different person. If everything was connected, as it clearly seemed to be, then his own thoughts and attitudes were as much responsible for the world as anyone else's.

Michael stood and, quite uncharacteristically, gave Jim a hug. He felt so much goodwill toward this man, who clearly cared deeply for this community and for the human community at large. Although Michael still felt daunted by the personal challenges he knew were ahead, he was relieved that at last he had something larger and more meaningful to hold as an ideal. It felt good to *know* something for once, and Michael had no intention of letting that go.

Chapter Seventeen

Walking through his office the next day, Michael could not help but to see the workings of power and love. The striving, working for more money, promotions, achievements were obviously reflective of the individual drive to power. The 'achievement story' was so built into the modern business culture that it was almost unnoticeable anymore. People are *expected* to achieve; to not move forward is considered an admission of personal failure. The term 'up or out', coined in the 90's, was the operational belief.

The question Jim had asked was quite another story. 'Where is the love?' kept running through Michael's head. Every company Michael had worked for had a culture skewed to the 'power' side of the spectrum. Feeling a sense of connectedness and care was relegated to the occasional team off-site or the spontaneous get-togethers organized by individual groups. Aside from these moments, the mood was decidedly 'get all you can get, and if possible more than anybody else'.

Michael did not believe this was entirely dysfunctional, because this type of business culture could be extremely productive. But he was beginning to see what Joe, the performance consultant, had meant about operating from fear. If everyone was out for themselves, and if their personal worth was judged solely on their individual achievements, then of course the culture would be fearful! The price of constant comparison was constant insecurity! Michael saw how this fear could lead to abuse. If power wasn't accompanied by care and compassion, then it would be tempting to treat everyone with suspicion and to control everything as much as possible…because otherwise we might 'lose' to others.

And looking back on his life, Michael reflected that he had often felt this way. It wasn't that he hated the people around him, he just constantly compared himself to everyone else, and many times, he found himself lacking. It drove him to gossip, cut other people down, take credit for things, and grab the limelight whenever possible. He never felt good about himself after this, but something deep inside claimed that this was necessary to get to the top. Now he could see that this was his own fear of not measuring up, of not being good enough.

His gnawing, subliminal anger was also understandable in this context. What was it that Louise had said…that 'anger is merely fear in its most aggressive form'? Michael thought of the rage he had felt at not getting an adequate raise or when someone in the company resisted his ideas. And God knows the anger he felt when his wife pressed him. Could all of this come from deeply sown fears?

The answer, Michael knew, was yes. He felt a great deal of internal pain knowing that he had been operating from fear for all of these years, and he deeply regretted the emotional toll it had taken on others. Wincing, he recalled the underhanded and mean things he had done to others in the name of self-preservation. The pointless arguments and offenses in the name of 'being right'. So much damage had been done in the name of power, because in seeking the best version of himself he had acted in the worst possible way. He had confused the means with the ends, and regretted it deeply.

At that moment Michael determined that he was going to bring more love into the equation, to balance out his own internal drive for power. He did care about people, and knew that his actions in the past were merely misunderstandings around how he was supposed to be. Although he didn't know what he could do about the larger culture – the country, his people, even his company all seemed too big for him to affect – he did know that he could do things differently himself. And he resolved to do just that.

Walking back toward his office, his assistant ran up and handed Michael a piece of paper. With tears in her eyes, she lightly touched his arm and said, "I'm so sorry, Michael."

For a moment Michael paused as he read the note. His brain was struggling to register what his eyes were seeing. His father had passed away, and his wife and sister urgently wanted him at the hospital.

"How long ago?" Michael asked.

"No more than 5 minutes," his assistant answered.

Turning, Michael jogged to his office and grabbed his coat and keys. As he headed for his car he noticed something curious: he felt nothing. There was no emotion present at all. If anything, there was a sense of relief, which made Michael wince with self-admonition. He felt like he should feel sadness or frustration or something, but there just wasn't anything there.

The trip to the hospital was a blur. Michael's brain was occupied with next steps: the viewing, the funeral, the will. A brief flash of curiosity about his father's net worth, followed by another round of guilt. Looking at his own thoughts from a distance, Michael wondered at the mental gymnastics he was going through to avoid the feelings looming just over the horizon. Or maybe he really didn't feel anything…maybe he didn't care?

Running up the hospital stairs had become Michael's exercise over the past few weeks, yet another in a series of random thoughts. 'The hospital stair-master,' his brain gabbled, 'the right combination of exercise and stress can help you lose weight like a pro.' Nonsense, nonsense. He commanded his mind to be present as he rounded the corner to his father's hall. A moment of wonder arose that his father kept getting the same room, and then Michael stopped as if he had run into a wall. Lying in the place where he expected a corpse was his father smiling at the group standing around his bed. Everyone, including the doctors, looked at Roy Benson as if he were a foreign object, something bizarre that had dropped out of the sky before their eyes.

Michael cautiously walked up to the bedside and looked at his sister, his wife, and the doctors and nurses. "What...I...didn't he?" Michael stammered.

"Mr. Benson," one of the doctors started, "I mean Mr. Benson junior," he said, smiling at Michael's father. "We thought...well, we were sure that your father had passed, but he...he...*came back to us*." The doctor looked at the family and shook his head. "I am sorry for the shock to all of you, but I've never seen anything quite like this. I was sure...well, I guess not so sure. There is precedence for this in medical journals, but I've never personally experienced such a dramatic...*return*. I'm sorry, but I'm somewhat at a loss for words." Dr. Peterson shook his head and said, "I'll leave you alone with him for a bit."

Leaning over the bed, the doctor looked into their father's eyes and smiled, "Roy, we're glad to have you back. Let us know if there's anything we can do to make you comfortable." He then turned and walked out of the room.

As if on cue, the entire family reached out and grabbed Roy Benson's hands. In turn their father looked at each of them, lingering for a moment on each pair of eyes. Michael noticed a strange look in his father's eyes, one that he had never seen before. It looked like *peace*.

"Dad," Michael began softly, "how are you? What...what are you feeling?"

That look on his father's face. It wasn't just peace, it was also a very loving, knowing look. Roy Benson had lost all of the anger, seriousness and impatience that Michael had assumed were innate to his father's being. The man in the bed before him bore no resemblance to the man he had come to know over the past 40 years.

Roy Benson smiled slowly and looked again into the each of their eyes. There was something so peaceful and loving about that moment. Michael, his sister, and his wife all looked at each other as if to acknowledge that something profound had happened.

Speaking at first in a croak, and then strengthening, Roy Benson beamed at them. "You are all so beautiful. So incredibly...luminous."

Michael looked at his sister and wife and they all smiled. This was definitely a new version of their father.

"What happened, Dad?" Michael asked. "We thought we'd lost you."

Roy turned his head and looked at Michael. "Oh, Michael, you can *never* lose me. I...I understand that now. None of us can lose each other. This, this..." Roy looked around the room, "...is only a show. I don't know how to explain what I want to tell you, but...but this is only the beginning. I see now. I see."

Chills ran up the back of Michael's spine as he looked again to his wife and sister.

His father continued. "We are all connected, you and I," his father lifted his withered hand and motioned to each of them. "We have never been separate. We are all...love. Pure, unending love. I felt it. In one rush I saw it all. Each one of us is a part of God. We are all perfect and divine. Everything living is made up of light...I can see this light everywhere now. Oh, it is so beautiful." Roy Benson sighed in wonder.

Michael was getting waves of goose-bumps listening to his father, but he didn't completely understand what had happened. Clearly his father had experienced something profound.

"Dad," Michael asked again, "can you tell us what happened to you? You were gone for a long time."

Roy Benson smiled an impish smile and looked directly at Michael. "Son, time is not what you think it is. There is no time...there. I moved on, but he wanted me to come back for one final experience."

"He?" Michael asked half from fear and half from wonder. "Dad, are you talking about God?"

Smiling, with tears in his eyes, Roy said "Yes, Michael, God. But I don't mean he...or she...just a wonderful, forgiving, completely loving *presence*. Oh Michael, son, I can't tell you how beautiful it is. It is pure loving light, and it is the same light that makes up everything living in this world. It is the pure light of creation, the light of God. It…he… she…is completely, totally accepting of everything that is, because it created everything. I…I really can't describe this to you in words, it is beauty beyond all understanding. It is more real than this world, Michael, and I don't fear it anymore. Dying is just the beginning, son. It is."

Roy was staring into Michael's eyes, and for the first time Michael felt the thing he had always wanted to feel as a child: Love.

Tears began to fill Michael's eyes and his father, seeming to understand everything at once, said to Michael, "Yes, son, I love you. I have come back for one reason…to experience the love that I feel for all of you. And to tell you: I…love…you." Roy Benson slowly looked at each of his children. "I have been given a chance to see my life as it was, and to come back and say the words I have always wanted to say. I don't know why I have been given this gift, but I do understand that it is a *gift*. All of life is a gift. You are all part of me, part of God, and I love you all so deeply and dearly."

Michael's sister and wife were weeping openly at this, and Michael had tears streaming down his face.

"When I began to cross over," his father continued, gaining strength, "I saw my whole life in a flash. Everything I had ever done, everything I had ever thought or said, it was all there as if I were re-living it again. I saw how cold I had been in my life, I saw the pain of my father, I *felt* the pain and loneliness of each one of you. I also experienced the joy of being a father and husband and the pride that my father had in me." Roy Benson's eyes were wide with wonder. "I could feel everything that happened in my life…not just my own experiences but also all of yours. I had *all* perspectives…and at the same time I felt his accepting presence. There were no words. Just…just one *thought*."

Roy Benson paused as if trying to make sense what he had experienced.

Michael softly prompted his father. He felt compelled by an intense curiosity, "What was it, Dad? What was the thought?"

His father looked up into the air. "Well," he began, "it was sort of a thought with a question. The best translation would be: 'Did you learn to love?' But it wasn't accusatory or judgmental, just a completely accepting and forgiving presence that encouraged me to see my life as a series of choices to…to either *love or to not love*. I saw my whole life in a flash, and saw every moment where I had been loving…and not loving. And I see now so clearly that the whole point of life is to *learn to love*. Michael, I see this so clearly now."

Roy looked around again and continued, "But the same voice, or thought, said to me that I was being given another chance to tell you, to express what I have been feeling all of these years. I see now that my pain blocked me from letting you know how much I love you. How much I love your mother. But she knows now. She was there. She loves me so much, and she loves all of you too."

Michael's father looked at them with tears running softly down his face. "Everyone was there. Your mother, my dad and mom, my sister, all of them are pouring love into each one of us. Oh, I so look forward to seeing them again."

Roy Benson looked almost child-like in his demeanor. Michael saw his *real* father for the first time. The loving, caring man under all of those layers of pain and anger. Michael felt so blessed to have been given this chance to experience his father this way.

"Dad," Michael picked up his father's hand again, "I love you too. And I'm so glad you came back to us. We're so happy to have this time with you."

His father smiled and shook his head, "But I won't be here for long, son. I'm being called back home soon. I am here only to experience and express this love to all of you. To express my love of life. This is a gift beyond all measure. This moment is more precious to me than anything. I just want you to know that you are deeply loved, not only because you are my son but also because you are. You were created in love, exist in love, and will return to love. My children, *you are all love*. We are *all* love."

The family sat in silence for a long time. Roy Benson drifted in and out of sleep while they all held his hands.

The Doctor came in, breaking the reverie. "How is he?" the Doctor asked.

Michael smiled and nodded at the Doctor. "Just fine, Doc. Just fine."

Michael's wife and sister moved to the side to let the Doctor approach the bed, and Michael motioned them outside. Once in the hallway, they spontaneously hugged and began to whisper how much they loved each other. Years of unexpressed emotion suddenly surfaced. Through the sobs, Michael tried to express the sorrow he felt for the uncaring things he had said and done over his lifetime, how much he had wanted to love each of them. They all took turns trying to apologize and forgive and accept, which all came out in a blubbering, incomprehensible stream. Then Maria started to giggle, and they all broke down laughing. Nurses walked by looking and smiling, not knowing what to make of this half-crying, half-laughing trio in the middle of the otherwise sterile white hallway.

Standing back and looking into each other's eyes, nothing more needed to be said. For the first time in his life, Michael felt complete. He actually felt what he had been hearing all these months. *Connectedness*. Michael understood now what his father had experienced: we all come from the same love and are connected by that love, so the only way we can experience true happiness is to connect back to our true nature. *To understand who we really are*. Everything else is window-dressing.

The rest of the day passed quietly with the three of them taking turns holding Roy's hand. At midnight the Doctor came in and told them that their father would likely last a week or so more, and that they should get some sleep.

Gathering their coats, they walked arm in arm out into the cold night. Michael looked at his sister, and then his wife, with admiration and love. "You both mean everything to me," he said, and they turned

198

and went home.

Chapter Eighteen

Michael sat looking at Louise, who as usual had a serene smile on her face. He had been telling her about his most recent realizations and experiences and was surprised at the excitement he felt. Michael had come so see Louise as somewhat of a mentor more than a psychologist, and found himself looking forward to sharing the inner workings of his mind. He had seen the projections and judgments, finding them in many of his thoughts and words. He was still having trouble letting go of these mental stories, especially the self-judgments, but was increasingly aware that through awareness and concentration he could simply let go.

And then there was the almost-death of his father 3 days ago. Michael was still trying to process what his father had said. If everything Roy said was true, then there was an afterlife…a *God*. Michael had been brought up Methodist, but was not practicing in any real sense of the word. An occasional Easter or Christmas service, or a wedding or funeral, was the gist of Michael's religious experience. But this was something completely different. Someone close to him had *experienced* what he had heard in the occasional Sunday sermon. This was not words being read from a book, this was a person just as agnostic as Michael, describing something otherworldly, something *divine*.

Louise had listened to Michael's recounting of his father's experience with complete acceptance. More, it was with a sense of *knowing*. Louise did not seem to be surprised in the least, nor was she doubtful of what Michael was telling her.

Michael narrowed his eyes a bit and said, "Geez, Louise, I thought maybe you would be a bit taken aback by my story. Doesn't this surprise you in the least?"

"No," Louise replied, shaking her head. "To be honest I have worked with quite a few people who have expressed stories such as this. It's quite common, you know, to experience Spirit first hand. And you don't have to die to do it!"

Michael shook his head. "What do you mean that you don't have to die? I am just getting used to the idea that there *may* be an afterlife, and you are telling me that we have access to some other world now?"

Louise chuckled softly and tilted her head. "Well, it's a bit more complicated than a yes or no…but, well, yes, we do."

"Okay," Michael rubbed his hands together, "it's back to sch ool time. More detail, please." The science geek in him was very curious how Louise was going to present this concept.

Louise looked at him warily. "Am I being interrogated here?" she half joked. "Because I don't have all the answers. I have simply spent a great deal of time listening, reading and experiencing things and have come to some conclusions."

"I get it," Michael assured her. "I have my own mind and can decide for myself. But I have found many of your insights to be dead-on, even though I did not at first want to believe them. So I would like to hear your opinion on this. Do you believe there is a God? Do you believe in an afterlife? Is there such thing as a soul? I really want to hear your thoughts."

"Wow," Louise laughed. "That's a tall order! Okay, I'll give you my best shot. But I want to clarify something first. There's an old saying that 'my finger pointing at the moon is not the moon'. Do you understand what this means?"

"No, not really," Michael admitted.

"It means that as I speak, my words are trying to describe something to you that you must see for yourself, and not just believe in my words. I believe that each religion on earth has tried to describe the true nature of God and spiritual reality but has had its words mistaken for the reality itself. Every religion was founded by someone who experienced the true nature of things, the truth of God, energy and oneness. But when they tried to describe it to others they were misunderstood, persecuted and vilified. Most people could not grasp what these individuals were saying, so they denounced them as heretical. They mistook the words for the reality."

"Okay," Michael interjected, "Like Jesus, the Buddha, and other saints?"

"Exactly," Louise answered. "And it became more challenging when these ideas were written down. People began to *worship the book* that contained the words instead of trying to experience the essence of what the words were trying to say. They mistook 'my finger for the moon itself'. So when I try to describe these things I want you to not take anything I say as 'gospel'…pun intended! I am merely one person, inherently limited because of my language, brain and experiential history, trying to describe what I have personally come to know. In order for you to believe any of this, *you must experience* it yourself. Nobody can tell you the truth…you can only know the truth."

Michael sat and thought about what Louise was saying. It made sense. Part of the reason Michael had fallen out with organized religion was because he felt that there was an underlying premise to 'shut up and believe', to not question. But Michael believed that we were given brains for a reason, and that it was his right – no, his duty – to question and to think. He wanted to understand, not simply be told what to believe.

"Yes, Louise, I completely understand. I promise I will take all of this in and think about it. I won't take your word as the truth."

Louise leaned forward. "But do please think about it. Read, think, ask questions. Look around. Experience your world fully. This is the only way to see the truth behind the façade. I came to my beliefs through a very thorough process, Michael. I read about every major religion, listened to many enlightened and wise people, meditated and thought for months, and only then did I begin to see the truth in things. And it is *my* truth. I encourage you to find *your* truth, because in the end I do believe that when we all seek our own truths we come to the same conclusion anyway."

"And what is that conclusion?" Michael asked.

Louise waved her finger and smiled, "I will tease you with that and answer it later...again, only from my perspective."

"Okay," Michael said feigning disappointment. "So how do you want to do this?"

Louise thought for a moment and then said, "I know you as a logical person so I am going to start from the beginning...the very beginning. The creation of everything. Have you ever thought about how everything got started? The universe, life, existence itself?"

"Of course," Michael responded, "but it's such a huge question that I just shrugged it off as 'unknowable'."

"And indeed it may be," Louise nodded, "but most of the world's religions have mystical branches that come surprisingly close to a common working theory. And strangely, quantum physics is fairly close to confirming that this theory may indeed have a some validity."

"Interesting. I'm dying to hear this," Michael interjected excitedly.

"So let's start with modern science. As you probably know, there is a philosophical approach right now that holds that the universe is more like a 'great thought' than a 'great machine'. This approach sees consciousness as the only thing that is *real*, and that this consciousness is what brings the material universe into being. The question, in the case of the 'beginning' of the universe, is how does consciousness play into all of this? And this is where the mystics of every religion may have had an answer."

"Yes," Michael added remembering his conversation with Yoda. "I see the challenge of this line of thinking. It presumes that consciousness is not a *result* of the physical universe, but the *cause* of it. And if that's the case, then consciousness came first."

"Exactly!" Louise exclaimed. "And this is what most religions and mystics have been trying to say for thousands of years. That at first, before anything physical, there was simply a presence. An awareness. A pure light that was nothing but love and joy and peace. The universal source of all things. God. The unexplainable. This pure loving presence of simply 'I am'. It's the same awareness that now exists within you and me, which is why every saint has proclaimed that *we are all God*. We are all this awareness."

Anticipating Michael's question, Louise continued. "But the question remains then, if there was only love and light and joy in the beginning, then why did the awareness, God, create the universe? Well, this is where the 'great thought' comes in. Because there was a part of God that wanted to understand what he/she/it was…and I will alternate between these genders because it helps in discussion…and that meant he needed to know what he was *not*. The closest thing I can use as an analogy here is that if you were floating in space with nothing around you, you would not know if you were up, down, going fast or slow, or just sitting. Because there is nothing *relative* to you, you would not even know where you were. You would just be somewhere undefined. This is as close as I can get to describing the theory of how God perceived things in the beginning. Just pure, floating love."

"Ooookaaaay…" Michael responded with skepticism.

"Now," Louise interjected cautiously, "I want to remind you here that these are just theories, and you need not believe them. But they are interesting and do relate to what science is discovering today. And whether or not you believe what I'm saying, is unimportant. What is important is that you *think* about these things."

"Ok," Michael nodded. "I was judging, and I see that. Go ahead."

"So, in the moment that God expresses the desire to understand what she is not, the relative universe is created. From pure energy, matter comes into being in one instant. All of the rules of the universe, all of the physical laws and opposing forces are consequences of this singular, intentional thought. The universe is the way it is because a hugely powerful consciousness made it so. And this consciousness then *became the universe.* It underlies all things. It is the same consciousness that we express when we say 'I am'. It is the thing that holds the universe together, and it is the thing both from whence we come and to where we will return. It is our soul."

Michael found this interesting, if only because he had never heard anyone try to logically explain the existence of God and the universe.

Louise continued. "In quantum physics they are finding, most disconcertingly to the 'mechanistic' or 'dead' view of the universe, that consciousness does indeed affect everything. The very act of perceiving changes that which is being perceived, because the two are inextricably interrelated. If consciousness is 'the ground of all being' as many theorists are saying, then our consciousness, our soul, can both create and manipulate the material world. Our consciousness is the original, pure energy of God and acts through us every day. When we express our intention to do something, we express that energy in 'creativity', which is the same force that God used to create the physical universe in the first place!"

"Wow," Michael shook his head. "This does make some sense to me, and explains what we were told in Bible school about Jesus healing, creating food for the poor, etc."

"Yes," Louise nodded, "and there are many saints throughout history who have claimed this ability. And every one of these people have said that we all have the capability to perform miracles if we are able to access this creative source within us. But we live deluded by the physical world. We create our own suffering by thinking that this universe is real when in fact it is simply an aspect of a larger underlying reality."

"This brings me to a question I have had for a long time," Michael interjected. "I get why God created the physical universe in this theory, but why all the suffering? Is all this pain and hardship necessary?"

Louise thought for a moment. "I would have to say no, it isn't. But the creator of our universe does not create our suffering. This is the ironic part of our existence. *We* create our suffering by resisting *what is*. We resist our own true nature and therefore suffer because of our choices."

"Okay," Michael stopped her. "You lost me. Is the system set up for us to suffer?"

"Let me try another angle at this. One that is a bit more logical." Louise took a breath and started again, "In this theory, God created this universe to know herself, to experience the pure love that she is. That means that God is at the base of everything that exists: the planets, molecules, rocks, water and, especially, life. This physical existence is, and science has proven this, a vibratory shift…a change in vibration from pure light energy to solid matter. Matter is made up of light that has changed from a higher to a lower vibration. This light, then, is at the core of everything, and this light is God.

"Now what's up for debate here isn't whether light is the base component of all things physical, because science readily accepts and has proven that," Louise continued. "The big question is that of consciousness. Is this light *conscious*? Does it have awareness of who and what it is? As you know, one side says no, it is a dead universe and all things are random. The other side says yes, we live in an aware universe that is alive and aware. I happen to believe the latter, because there is far too much synchronicity and patterning for everything to be dead and random. Added to that, I have had personal experiences with God that tell me that this universe is not only alive, but it is only one aspect of the deeper reality."

Michael was nodding and remembering his father's words: "There is more."

"So to answer your question about suffering, we have to see that everything is happening for a reason. There are laws and structures in the universe that ensure that everything is unfolding and evolving in an ordered way. Cause and effect are basic tenets…and so we reap what we sow. We have made choices that virtually ensure our own suffering. God is merely a bystander, honoring whatever choices we decide to make."

"But can't God intervene and stop the suffering? I mean, if he or she is the creator of and energy behind all things, then how can he want to see his own creation suffer?" Michael asked confusedly.

"Because as part of the laws of creation there is one that I might call 'freedom of choice'." Louise answered. "Again, I'm going to ask you to suspend your disbelief and follow this logic. If God created this universe to experience himself, and each facet of the universe is part of him, then each one of us is also a part of him. Yet he has given us the ability to choose, which is the most powerful way to experience and learn. There is a reason many religious texts refer to us as 'God's children', because we are indeed smaller versions of *him*. In the Kabbalah, an ancient Jewish text, it is said that in the beginning there was only one light, but because this light wanted to experience itself it fractured into a trillion pieces, each piece being an aspect of the one light…and each piece given a chance to choose its own path. Each piece of light is an individual soul. Each individual soul is an aspect of God…or a way for God to perceive the universe."

Michael sat back, stunned at the implications. "So you are saying that we are all…well, God experiencing himself?"

"Yes, we are all aspects of God experiencing *what is not* in order to experience what she *is*. And because God is love, suffering is an experience of what is *not* love. But, again, the universe is not designed to be an unloving place…it is just a set, a stage where we are given the chance to make choices and see what happens. It is truly as if we were children. When you have a child, you let them experience the world as it is. Certainly you try to protect them, but part of growing up is being allowed to make choices that result in pain…so that we can learn and do better next time. This is exactly how God created the universe. So that his children…aspects of himself…could experience the love that he is by making unloving choices."

Michael nodded, "I get this, but what do you mean by 'unloving choices'? How do we *choose* suffering? I certainly don't…suffering seems to come randomly to me."

Louise laughed. "I know it feels that way, but it really isn't. Your life, as we have discussed in earlier sessions, is a culmination of all of the choices you have made. And some would say that your soul, before it came into your body, chose everything that is happening to you, and in you, right now."

"Now you lost me again. My soul made a choice for all this?" Michael waved his hands exasperatedly around the room.

"This is more difficult to describe than I thought," Louise mused out loud. "So let's continue with God's intent in this theory. If God fractured into trillions of individual aspects of himself in order to experience this relative world in a way that would help him realize himself as pure love, and each individual bit of himself has its own free will to choose its path, then yes, each soul makes a choice about what it is going to experience in this life. Each soul chooses what experience is going to be most helpful in allowing it, as an aspect of God, to know itself as pure love. So it chooses challenges that will best help us, the human being, realize who we really are: divine beings having a human experience."

Louise continued. "But nothing is set in stone, only circumstances are chosen. Each soul comes into a child that has a unique chemistry, biology, brain function, predisposition, family life, social experience, the dynamics at play here are mind-bogglingly complex. Each soul also agrees with other souls as to what it wants to learn, and these other souls are your parents, siblings and close friends. This whole world is, in this theory, a massive mix of intentions and contextual situations. No one life is exactly like any other. Each life has its own situation and consciousness, and each life chooses the way forward it thinks will help

209

it learn the most. And these choices, which are merely our responses to outside factors, determine how our life unfolds."

Michael interjected, "So if we choose an angry or fearful way of living, we live an angry or fearful life?"

"Yes!" Louise exclaimed, "And the opposite is true as well. If we choose to be loving, compassionate and kind, then we experience that kind of life. Our emotions are *guides*, they tell us when we are off track or on track. As we talked about earlier, the concept of *sin* has been misinterpreted. Originally it meant to be 'off track', meaning that our choices were leading us to suffer, away from our true loving nature. If we think that money leads to happiness, for example, eventually we will make choices that will result in suffering because we are trying to find love in something material, something that can't deliver what we want. We 'miss the mark'. These choices are not wrong, there are just consequences to the mistaken belief. If we treat people badly, we will only be condemned to hell in the sense that we will be forced to live with our own choices. We create a hell on earth: a life without love."

Michael sat for a moment and thought about this. He could see clearly how his own choices had led him to painful outcomes. Whenever he seemed to strive after things like power or money he felt more and more isolated, more in conflict with those around him. But if he chose to let go of those things...what then?

"So let me see if I have this straight," Michael started. "In your telling of things, we are all aspects of God and we are all in our bodies, which are kind of like robots, and we move around in these bodies making choices that help us experience what love is and what love is not."

Louise laughed loud. "I like the robot analogy. And in a sense you're right. But remember, it is about a thousand times more complex than that. Our souls are made of pure light, which vibrates at a very high frequency. Our bodies are matter, which also vibrate but at a much lower frequency. When the two come together they must merge, and this is a complex process that I don't fully understand. But I do know that when these two entities come together there is resistance, because each is oscillating at its own frequency."

"Whoa, okay, back up again!" Michael waved his hands. "So when the soul comes into the body, there's resistance?"

Louise looked slightly worn out from trying to explain herself. "I don't think it's resistance as much as a difference in frequency. It's what we call someone's 'vibe'. When someone is very kind and easy to be with, we say they have a 'great vibe', which means that their soul is in resonance with their body. They look healthy, act kindly, and overall are wonderful to be with. This is the light of their soul shining through."

"But when someone is out of alignment, say very angry and mean, we can think of their body being in dissonance with their soul. They have a 'bad vibe' because their soul, which is pure love, is in conflict with their body and mind, which is choosing to be very unloving. Many of these people get sick because their bodies cannot take the stress. They are 'in resistance' to the true loving reality that is their soul, and so suffer the consequences."

Louise paused and thought for a moment. "The good thing about all this is that we can only take so much suffering before we step back and ask 'what's my role in all of this?' We 'wake up' to the fact that we have been making choices all of our lives that have resulted in suffering. It isn't that we have chosen the random events that happen 'to' us, but that we have chosen our response to those events. This is why some of the most aware and loving people on the planet are those that have had a tragic experience in their lives. They have experienced frightful pain and seen that they always have a choice: to love or not to love. And they choose love."

"And if we don't choose love?" Michael asked.

"Then we will keep experiencing suffering until we do." Louise answered. "This is the beauty of the system…it is a never-ending source of feedback. We are eventually forced, by our own suffering, to choose a more loving way to be. There is no way to avoid this…we will all eventually learn *who we really are*. We will all find our way back to our source, which is the pure love and pure light and pure peace that is God."

"Wow." Michael sat for a while with this. He had never heard "God" explained in quite this way. For the first time in his life he had a notion that he could understand, and perhaps even believe.

"But Louise," Michael started hesitantly, "how do I experience this 'self'? I know you said not to believe what you're saying, to find out for myself, but I have no idea where to begin even if I wanted to. Is there some magic secret?"

Louise laughed. "No, there is no one right way to find out about yourself. Each one of us is entirely unique. We all experience this world in a different way. Many saints, sages and seekers have tried to explain how to do this, but each one of us must explore this territory on our own."

Michael looked disappointed. He had hoped there was some magic bullet.

"Some people," Louise continued, "have experienced their 'true self' in one massive realization, either through a difficult trauma or very intense experience. In these rare cases the person in the experience is forced to surrender all notions of the 'false self' and to drop everything they previously believed. It may be that they lose everything they own, or have a near-death experience, or witness the death of someone very close. Or it could be simply that they are ready to receive the truth. However it happens, they are given the gift of instant awakening."

"That sounds a bit painful!" Michael joked.

"I guess it's a matter of preference," Louise smiled, "because the rest of us seem to choose the other road, which is a longer learning process punctuated by brief moments of realization. Most people go through their lives fairly blind to their true self…their real potential. They may receive a prodding here or there, or spend a good portion of their lives unhappy, but only get glimpses of their true selves. For some it only happens when they die. But rest assured, we can't avoid the realization.

It happens for all of us."

Michael appreciated this idea. He felt he was on the longer road. "I can see what you're saying, but certainly we can speed things up? Can't we do *something* to be happier and more loving?"

Louise nodded knowingly. "And you are, Michael. The first step in the road to realization is to become aware that our projections, judgments, fears and angers are not our true selves. They are well-learned stories that muddy our vision. We distract ourselves from who we are by looking to the outside world for answers. We blame others for our problems. We seek happiness in money or material possessions. We look for affirmation through power and accolades. We measure our self-worth by who loves us. All of these things are distractions because all the love, safety, peace and happiness is already available to us. These things exist within us. *They are the real 'us'.*"

Louise paused to see if Michael was getting this. "Michael, you don't have to believe anything I'm saying, in fact I hope you see it all with skepticism. But I want you to know that everything you want is already inside of you. To find happiness you first must let go of all the things you are not. Surrender the chatter of your thinking mind and allow yourself to be. The real you will surface. This is the simplicity, and challenge, of meditation. To let go of the mental noise that keeps you from being happy."

"But it's so difficult," Michael said with exasperation. "I notice all the garbage my mind puts out, but I can't seem to stop it. I think I understand why the 'fast approach' to realization might be better. Those people are lucky."

"Indeed they are, but again each one of us goes through our own process in our own way. The key is to be patient with your process. We are all evolving toward this 'realization of self' and are doing our best in the process. You can speed up the process, but you cannot force it. Just by becoming aware of your mental chatter you have taken a giant leap. You don't have to push it now. Just keep your mind open, keep learning, and try to be as loving as you can. In fact, there is a whole school of thought that suggests that simply being kind, compassionate, forgiving, and loving to those around you will do the trick. But surprisingly most of us find that difficult."

Michael nodded vigorously. "Yes, in fact there is a part of me that goes back to my rational, business, Ayn Randian mind-set that says 'this is all a nice fantasy, but there is a cruel and difficult reality that requires defense against evil and action to achieve'. I see people meditating and smiling and think that there's no way those people would have ever built the institutions, civilizations and wealth that we enjoy today. To live in bliss and 'without need' will drive us all to sit in the mud like aesthetic yogis. Sorry, but there's an awfully strong argument to this."

Louise didn't look offended at all. In fact, she seemed to be nodding with encouragement. "This is good Michael. I want you to challenge this, because it shows thought. For thousands of years many religions and spiritual seekers lived purely of the heart, and they abandoned much of the physical world. But that does not need to be the case. With the advent of science we began to value the human mind, which was a glorious leap for the evolution of man. But in the process we have lost much of our heart. We have become convinced that living in the mind is the only way, and that isn't true. The truth is that we have both a mind and a heart, and we can combine those."

"I'm not sure what you're saying," Michael pushed. "Are you talking about a compromise between religion and science? Because I just don't see that happening."

"Oh, Michael," Louise exclaimed, "it's already happening! Science is being exposed to conundrums that are not readily solvable with the mind alone because of the role of consciousness in everything material. And religion, which used to operate solely on faith in a historical figure's teachings, is having to answer legitimate questions posed by thoughtful followers. In essence, the mind is looking for a heart, and the heart is seeking a mind. This is a unique point in human history, because for the

214

first time we are struggling to both think and feel."

Before Michael could object, Louise continued. "In this new world we can continue to be action-oriented thinkers who accomplish things…but also caring, compassionate individuals with a deep faith in the power of love. We are becoming complete. In fact, I believe that as we begin to re-connect to our hearts, and to each other, our power to achieve will increase *exponentially*. Fear-based achievement was based on a notion of control…the mind's belief that it can force people, including our own selves, to be better through the badgering of internal beliefs. It works, but only for a time."

Michael reflected on what Joe had told him about fear-based cultures. "And then people burn out," he finished for Louise.

"Yes, and they end up in my office," she smiled. "As a society we have used the logical mind to achieve many great things, but we've done so at the expense of our hearts…and our sanity. But this is actually a blessing because many people, having first tried anti-depressants, anti-anxiety medications, drugs and alcohol, end up finally looking inside themselves. We are realizing that we gave something up in our rush to achieve, and are collectively seeking a solution. Everything is evolving, Michael, everything."

Michael sat silent for a long moment. Everything made so much sense now. All of the pain he felt at never seeming to have enough, or be good enough. He saw all of the endless, heartless striving around him. The business world was full of people who claimed to be 'motivated by money alone', yet were obviously and painfully unhappy. Divorces, theft, violence, scandal…wasn't it obvious?

Breaking the silence, Michael said, "I'm beginning to see it now Louise. I really am. I'm not sure I buy the whole creation story you told, but I do see that everything is evolving. Sometimes I become so depressed, though, at the seeming futility of things. Everywhere I look, including inside myself, there is a pointless scrambling for things and achievement and ego-boosters. The world seems lost in insanity sometimes. Religions that justify killing for words in a book, politicians who create fear and acrimony to get elected, business-people who greedily take at the expense of everyone else. I feel like this has been the nature of humanity since the beginning. I just get so depressed."

Louise touched him lightly on the knee. "It's all part of the general 'waking up', Michael. All of this strife and fear keeps prodding us to look deeper for our answers. As long as we keep looking to others, to the material world, and even to a 'separate God' for answers we will continue to feel like life is a painful struggle. The God and the love we are looking for is inside, and the only answer is for each one of us to find it in our own way. You can only choose to be the best person you can be, Michael. And only you can make that choice."

Michael sat with this for a moment. Then Louise looked him straight in the eye and said, "Each time you choose to love, forgive, be compassionate, or be kind, you move all of humanity forward. We are all inextricably connected, Michael, so your only responsibility is to realize the love within you. Everything else will take care of itself."

Chapter Nineteen

The sun was warm on Michael's skin as he walked through the park. He had decided to walk to the hospital straight from his appointment with Louise. The conversation with Louise had him thinking, and he wanted to digest what he had heard. There were two distinct parts of him operating. One declared that all of this was a bunch of mumbo jumbo designed to keep people from focusing on the here and now, but the other wanted so much to believe what now seemed to make so much sense.

Childhood memories of Santa Claus came to mind. Michael remembered the pain and embarrassment when his father had abruptly walked into his room a few days before Christmas and declared 'there is no Santa Claus, you're too old for that'. Michael had been 7 at the time, and probably was too old for that fantasy, but nonetheless he felt like something had been torn from him. What was the harm in believing? Why was his father so threatened by the notion that his son would believe in something so wonderfully pure?

From that day on, Michael had adopted the notion that to believe in a higher power, a higher goodness, was an embarrassing fantasy in a world that valued material reality. Money, power, success, intelligence, dominance…these became his idols. But it was also true that something had been lost. He had lost his heart. Michael had given up the warmth of his 'childish notions' for the cold hard reality of the modern world.

Perhaps Louise was right, we *have* thrown out the baby with the bathwater, so to speak. In our striving for logic and reason we have lost our heart and emotions. Love and care had become niceties in a harsh and cruel world. But was this really necessary? What was the harm in believing?

If Michael believed that an unconditional, powerful and *conscious* love was at the root of all existence, then what would happen? Deep down, Michael felt that it would be the 'Santa Claus' situation all over again. People would make fun of him, belittle him, accuse him of believing in childish fantasies. But what was the alternative? To live in a cold, mechanistic world where 'care' is relegated to mere evolutionary advantage? To see everything as self-serving? Michael had believed this most of his life, and found it only created an empty and cynical existence.

Michael shook his head. Recently he had felt an inkling of what it would be like to live a life of faith, to feel the warmth that comes from love, and it was an awful lot better than the alternative. So what if people thought he had gone 'soft'? What had Louise said, that 'it's none of my business what you think of me'? Michael laughed to himself. How true. The only thing that mattered was that Michael felt love and joy and peace inside. Everything else was detail. Then it really didn't matter if he believed the things Louise told him; feeling happy inside was all the confirmation he needed.

Rounding the corner Michael saw the hospital and thought about his Dad. Even though he had doubts about the universe that Louise had described, he could not doubt that his father had experienced something extraordinary. Roy Benson was not the type to believe in just anything…but Michael could tell that his Dad had experienced something well beyond intellectual thought. Something profound had happened, something that Michael had felt intuitively. Certainly a skeptic might be able to claim that his father had experienced an elaborate dream, but Michael knew that this was more. Whatever it was his father had experienced, it was strong enough to completely change a man who had previously prided himself in his stubborn rationality.

Michael found his father sleeping in his room. Whereas previously he had seen the ravages of illness on his father's face, this time he saw a peacefulness that was as inspiring as it was new. Even though his prognosis had not changed, Roy Benson looked 20 years younger, as if he were simply asleep in his own bed. Michael felt a rush of love for this man who had spent so many years in an empty house, his wife gone and kids who felt too distant to offer affection. Tears filled Michael's eyes. He felt such compassion for this man – this soul – searching for the love he thought he would never find.

"Well Dad, it looks like you finally found it," Michael said to his father as he took his hand.

Faintly, his father stirred and opened his eyes. Turning his head, he smiled at Michael. "Hello, Son," he squeezed Michael's hand. "I so love to see your face. You are so beautiful, do you know that?"

Tears streamed down Michael's face. All his life, this was the love he had been seeking.

"Son, I don't have long. I know it's my time. But please don't mourn for me, because there is so much love where I'm going. And Michael, son, we will never be apart. I will always be with you, caring about you and loving you. All those years I thought I had lost your mother, and now I see that she was with me all the time. I just didn't realize that we are all part of the same thing, Son," his father shook his head and smiled. "I just didn't know."

Michael's throat was closed with emotion, so he nodded and looked down.

"I'm sorry if I was cold toward you when you were a child, Michael. I loved you so much, but I didn't know how to show it. My world was so very conditional, you see. I thought I was supposed to mold you, to create a son who would be accepted and respected by the world. I think I got this from my own father…he was so afraid that I would end up loathing myself as he did. Oh, Michael, it's all so clear. We are all trying so hard to love but can't seem to figure out how. Everyone is so confused.

"So I'm sorry, Son. I hope you can forgive me," his father said as his eyes filled with tears. "I love you so much."

Michael leaned over his father and hugged him. For the first time in his life he felt true forgiveness. For the first time he let himself love someone unconditionally. He sobbed quietly as he felt himself let go of a lifetime of pain and anger. He felt then how clearly these things had blocked his heart. Years of withholding and fear flooded out and vanished like mist in the sun, allowing Michael to experience a sense of true freedom for the first time.

For the next 3 days Michael sat and held his father's hand. To Armand's chagrin, Michael had taken an abrupt vacation to spend as much time with his father as possible. In the past Michael would have been consumed with thoughts of work, looking at his iPhone every 5 minutes to see what new crises he could bring into his consciousness. But now all that had faded away like a bad dream. What was real was in front of him in this moment. The only thing that mattered was letting his father know that he wasn't alone, that he was loved as he made his passage.

They talked of many things when his father was awake. Michael shared fond memories of family vacations, laughter, and the quirks of each family member. His father recalled the times with his mother, before she had fallen ill. Roy Benson spoke of his youth, meeting his beloved wife, and the love he felt for her. Michael had never heard most of the stories his father told, stories of youthful hope, excitement, promise. As his father spoke, Michael could see the young man looking forward to his life. The wonder of a new family, the newness of his first job. As he sat and listened, Michael realized that he related to this man. He deeply understood the challenges that he faced and the dreams that he held.

And Michael realized that as human beings we share so much more than we think. We are all born with a 'spiritual wonder', looking at the world as if it were an amazing playground to be explored and understood. Then we experience confusion at the pain we experience from other humans, and we get scared. We wonder if the world is safe, and if our lives at home are less than a haven, we begin to build defenses. Those defenses keep us from loving one another, and so we begin our great journey of separation. We try to reclaim that love through attachment to the material world because we have come to believe that our worthiness for that love is bound up in how much we make, what we do, what we own, or who we know. But at some point we look around, or are forced to look around, and we wonder how we got to where we are. And that scares us.

Michael looked at his father. Hadn't he spent his whole life trying to gain the love that he so badly wanted? And now, as his father lay here dying, he awakens to the reality that the love he wanted is already within him. In one transcendental experience, his father saw that love is not something to be traded and sold, but it's something that just *is*. That giving love to others is the most nourishing, most natural and the safest thing we can do.

In that moment Michael felt an enormous surge of gratitude for everything in his life because he was being given a chance to awaken before he died. He felt grateful to his father for this learning experience, and grateful to his wife for seeing in him something greater than he knew. He even felt gratitude toward his boss, who in his own way was driving him toward one inescapable conclusion: that something had to change. There was so much opportunity to be bigger and more powerful. For the first time, Michael could now clearly see the possibility of purposeful life.

On the third day of Michael's stay at the hospital, his father heaved a long sigh and stirred in an uncharacteristic way. Michael's heartbeat rose as he intuitively recognized that the inevitable had come: his father was about to die. The rational side of him wanted to call out for help, to save this man, but he was frozen in place. In his gut he knew that there was nothing to be done, that Roy Benson's time in this world was coming to an end. He quickly stood and took his father's hand.

Turning ever so slightly, his father opened his eyes and looked in Michael's direction. Michael could feel that his father was not looking *at* him, but *past* him, somewhere above his left shoulder. His father whispered hoarsely, "She wants me to come."

Michael felt the chills running up his arms. He moved closer to his father and whispered, "It's OK, Dad, go. Go to her. We're OK here, Dad. I love you so much, but I want you to go." Tears streamed down Michael's face.

Roy Benson took one last breath and, with a sigh, left his body.

What struck Michael in that moment was not sadness, but the sheer peacefulness of his father's passing. All of the pain and suffering was gone, and he felt a deep knowing that his father's soul had moved to another place. Michael's mind was rapidly trying to process and explain what had happened, but there was nothing to be grasped except the absolute reality of this experience. Roy Benson's life on this earth was complete, yet something else was beginning. Michael felt with absolute confidence that this empty shell in front of him was but a vessel, something that temporarily contains the essence of who we really are.

Standing slowly, Michael walked to the door. He felt as if he was having an out-of-body experience as he approached the nurses' station.

"My father died," Michael said softly to the nurse behind the counter.

The nurse walked around to Michael's side. She had tears in her eyes as she touched his shoulder. "He was such a sweet man, Mr. Benson. You were lucky to be able to share this with him." She spoke with such tenderness that fresh tears came to Michael's eyes.

"Yes," Michael said. "I am a very, very fortunate man."

"Go and call your family, Mr. Benson, we'll take care of everything here." The nurse smiled and guided him to a chair.

Michael sat at the window and noticed for the first time that the sun was setting. It never seemed so beautiful as it did then. This life was a cycle, just like the rising and setting of the sun. As he absently picked up his phone to dial his sister, he said quietly to himself, "Thank you for your light, Dad, and happy journey."

Chapter Twenty

The next day Michael found himself wandering through town, drawn to the anonymous hustle and bustle of humanity. Michael couldn't help but to think that each one of these people, so busy on their errands, was going to die. It wasn't a morbid thought, just a reflection on the seeming pointlessness of most of human activity. We create to-do lists, cross off the completed items, then make a new list. We become consumed by the daily doings of a life that, in the end, will seem quite short. Distractions, obsessions and attachments while away the time until we look back from our last hour and ask 'what happened?'

Michael did not want to wait to answer that question. He already knew that most of his life had been squandered in petty concerns over right and wrong, better and worse, higher and lower. He was tired of allowing his mood and sense of self worth to be determined by the external world…a world that, if he were honest with himself, held nothing but endless wanting. Michael knew there had to be more than this, but he didn't want to wait until his own demise to truly understand what that was.

For the second time in so many days, Michael walked through the park near the hospital. He smiled to himself that in all the years he had lived in this town, he had never even *noticed* this park. And now it seemed to have become a central figure in a tragic play about the purposelessness of life.

Plopping down on a park bench, a solitary figure caught Michael's eye. Moving slowly down the asphalt path leading through the park was an elderly black lady. Although her pace was glacial, she seemed to move with a determination born of years of suffering. Michael felt warmth toward this woman so steadfast in her approach to life. In a way Michael felt envy, for he had doubts about his own strength.

As she got closer Michael realized that this was the very same woman he had met at the community meeting. He racked his brain for her name…Florence, was it?

When she was a few feet away he cleared his throat and asked, "Florence? Is that you?"

She looked up and smiled, "Well, well. What a small world! Imagine seeing you here in the park!"

Michael stood and moved to shake her hand.

"Oh no," she laughed, "a handshake just won't do! Give me a hug young man!" and with surprising strength she wrapped her arms around Michaels bent shoulders. "Besides," she continued, "it looks like you could use some love right now."

Michael winced at the accuracy of her perception. "Is it that obvious, Florence?"

Florence Johnson looked Michael in the eye and with a twinkle said, "Yes, it is son. I didn't get to be this old without coming to know how folks are, you bet. And besides, something told me to come through this park today. I figure now that it must have been to see you!

"And call me Flo," she said with firmness. "Only my long passed mama called me Florence. And that was only when I got under her skin!" she chuckled.

Michael took her by the elbow and helped her sit down on the bench. He felt once again the warmth he had felt toward her in their first meeting. It felt like he had known this person a long time, longer than he could mentally comprehend. Michael felt completely comfortable and at ease in her presence. There was a force about her that instantly pushed away any doubt about the goodness of life. She was…

226

luminous.

"My Dad passed away yesterday," Michael blurted out unintentionally. In Flo's presence he felt like a child seeking the warmth of someone he could trust, someone *safe*.

Flo turned on the bench to face Michael. "Oh son," she said taking Michael's hand, "I am so very sorry to hear that. How are you doing?"

Michael wasn't sure if it was the question itself, or the way she asked, or simply the way she held herself, but he immediately began to sob. A voice far in the back of his head protested that this was embarrassing and unbecoming of a business executive, but the flow of emotion was too strong. Flo's presence seemed to draw feelings out of him that he had not allowed himself to have. Grief, guilt and pain all came out in a rush.

Flo sat quietly with Michael and patted his hand, softly whispering "there, there" as years of emotion came rolling forth.

After a few minutes Michael began to feel the intensity of his sadness weaken. The tears gave way to a deep sense of release and relief. He took a deep breath and sheepishly looked at Flo. "I haven't ever done that in front of a stranger," he said.

"Oh," she laughed, "feels good, doesn't it? Besides, we aren't strangers," she said with a twinkle in her eye. "We go waaay back!"

Michael looked deep into her eyes and got that feeling again. Like he knew her. "Well, Flo," he said, "I do feel comfortable with you otherwise I don't think I could have... *let go* like that."

Flo smiled and patted his hand again. "Well I think it is beautiful, caring so much about things. We don't do enough of that anymore." She shook her head, "We need to let people know how much we care about each other. We've lost a lot of that, you know."

Michael nodded. "I thought maybe I had lost the ability, Flo. Like I didn't care about anything anymore. Only recently have I come to realize that I have feelings, you know? I thought I was dead inside." Tears began to fill his eyes again.

"Now, now," Flo gave Michael a squeeze, "none of *that*. You were just hiding what you had, all that life and love and care. We do that sometimes. We get scared of the world and we think we have to be tough to get along." Flo concocted her face into a grimace that made Michael laugh.

"Yeah," he said still laughing, "well, I don't feel so tough now."

"And that's good, son! Real good!" she said with emphasis. "We need to be vulnerable sometimes, to learn that we can't control everything. Why, I spent I good portion of my life trying to control what was happening in my life. It only leads to pain, son, and frustration." Flo shook her head.

"Life is a force, Michael," Flo said with seriousness. "And it only goes in one direction. We can fight it, rant about it, and try to manipulate it, but we will only tire ourselves out. I know. I tried to save a son from killing himself, keep my husband from drinking, and keep my grandbabies from hanging around with the wrong people. And through all my tears and pain I realized that the only thing I could control was me. All the rest of them are on their own paths, and I can't do much about that."

Michael looked at her. He had no idea what this woman must have seen in her life, the pain she had endured. Being an African American woman of her age must have meant she saw unimaginable discrimination in her time.

"Flo," Michael asked softly, "how did you do it? How did you learn to get through it all?"

Flo shook her head and smiled. "I don't know son. I used to spend so much of my time angry, so much hatin'. I hated white people, you know. When I was marching back in the 60's, this white woman watching us go by, she looked at me so hateful like. Then she spit at me, Michael. *Spit*. To her I was nothin' but an animal. And I had so much hate in my heart for a time. And I hated my husband for his drinkin', and God for puttin' my son in so much pain. I looked around and I saw that the world was just an awful, hateful place."

Flo sighed. "But then I came to see that it was just burnin' me up. Eatin' me up inside. I was living in hell, Michael, a living hell. People talk about goin' to hell, but I tell you hell is what we make here. We make hell inside of ourselves by takin' and hurtin' and hatin'. Every time we blame somebody or yell about how the world is doin' us wrong, we add another log to that fire of hell inside of us."

"And the worst part is," she continued, "we work it so everyone around us feels our hell. We drag 'em down with us. Now it don't happen cause we want to do that, it is just that our hell *infects* them, surely as a cold would infect a person. So we look around and our lives become the hell we are feeling, the loneliness and despair looks back at us as sure as we are lookin' in a mirror."

Now Michael lightly touched her hand, "But Flo, you are the sweetest person I have ever met. I just can't imagine you even being angry."

Flo chuckled. "That is what old age does to you, son. You learn. Your Daddy knows that now. The closer we get to death the better we can see. We come to understand that separatin' ourselves from other people is just being scared. Hatin' other people is easier when you don't know them. But hate and fear and loneliness hurts so bad inside that eventually we can't take it anymore. So we look up one day and decide to try something different. If all that bad stuff hurts so bad, why not try some of the good stuff? Why not try to have faith and love and care? I mean, it can't be any worse, right?" Flo shrugged her shoulders.

"And you know what I did, Michael? I started caring for people, listenin' to them. Takin' time to hear their story and care about what they were sayin'. Seein' them as people with struggles, just like me. I started to have faith that everything was goin' to be OK, and that there maybe was a God up there who cared about me too. And you know what happened, son?" Flo's eyes watered a bit, "I started feelin' love *inside*. Everything started to get beautiful, you know what I mean? Instead of seein' hate and fear lookin' back at me, I saw lovin' and carin'. And that

229

changed me. It wasn't a hard kinda change, like quittin' smoking, but it felt *natural*. Like I was goin' home."

Michael and Flo sat together for a moment and held hands. Something was moving in Michael, something profound. He saw the rightness of what Flo was saying, and for the first time in his life, he felt the peace and love he had been seeking.

"I don't want to wait until I die to feel that, Flo," Michael said softly.

"No, I suspect nobody does." Flo nodded. "But you have to make a choice, son, because this world of separateness will eat you up with its fakery and promises. You find yourself gettin' after things that don't matter and before you know it you will be takin' from others cuz you think the world don't have enough for everyone. You make yourself crazy with wantin' more and never gettin' what you want. So you gotta decide, Michael, what's important to you. You want to reach out to this world and be a part of it, or you want to stand back and keep yourself thinkin' you're safer that way? Cuz you ain't safe. You will be hurtin' worse than you can ever imagine."

"I know," Michael said. "I've been doing that my whole life."

"They got a sayin' I heard once, I think it is a Buddha sayin' or somethin'." Flo looked at Michael. "It says to 'die before you die'. I like that. 'Cause when we die I think we come aware that we are all connected and we are all part of the same love. So if we can figure a way to die before we die then we can feel that sooner, and that's sweet. When I made my change I took to lookin' at every person as if they were gonna die tomorrow, and it was funny but I came to be more sympathetic to them. I saw them as fellow creatures workin' to do the best they can with the limited time they have. I saw them as special, and it gave me reason to love 'em."

Michael smiled at Flo. She was such a beautiful, wise woman. He felt like he was in the presence of his own mother, but with a lifetime of learning behind her.

Flo began to stand up and said, "Well, I suppose I have to get to the store and get my sale eggs before they sell out."

Michael jumped up to help her and found himself at a loss for words. "Flo, I…" he stammered, "I would like to see you again if I could."

"Well," Flo replied, "I come by here every week at sale time, so I think you can find me. Bein' 92 years old don't allow me to move too quick you know!"

Michael reached out and gave her a gentle hug. She cluck-clucked and said, "Now ain't hugs nice? Reminds us that we are all still here!"

Flo shuffled down the walk and out of the park. Michael watched her go with a sense of peace, because for the first time he really knew what he wanted to do. It wasn't a thought, but a feeling. He knew deep down that there were things he wanted to change, and he was not going to wait until he died to face them. He was not going to look back and wish he had done it differently. He was going to do it differently *now*.

As he made his way out of the park his problem-solving mind came on line. He had opened a new chapter in his life and he was determined to do it right. He picked up his pace and thought, "This just might be *fun*."

Chapter Twenty-One

The office did not seem the same anymore. As Michael walked through the hallways he didn't feel the sense of dread and foreboding that he had once felt. The tension had been replaced by a peacefulness that Michael couldn't explain. Looking at his co-workers as he passed their offices, he felt a newfound appreciation for their presence. Each one of the people who worked for him or around him had made a choice to be here, and he felt grateful for that. For the first time he was able to see each person as a unique and beautiful soul who was doing the best they could do with the life they had been given. It felt wonderful.

Michael closed the door to his office and sat down at his desk. He was determined to follow through on his decision. Things were going to be different from now on, and he wanted to quietly set his course. He felt strange doing this only a few days after his Dad had passed, but he also felt that this was the most important thing he could do for both himself and the people around him. And he was pretty sure his Dad would approve because he was going to consciously advance all of the skills that he had been taught…with some special additions.

Taking a deep breath, Michael looked out of the window and went over the past 6 months. So many things had happened, and he had learned so much, but strangely everything seemed to be…*ordered*. Information and awareness had come to him with almost perfect timing, as if someone or something had put together a curriculum for a specific purpose.

"And now it's time for my final exam," Michael said to himself.

Taking out a piece of paper, Michael wrote across the top 'THINGS I HAVE LEARNED' and placed a number 1 on the first line. He sat staring at the paper and then, almost involuntarily, began to write:

1. Everything is connected.

Michael recalled his conversations with Yoda, his doctor, and Louise about the state of science and the interconnectedness of all things. He now understood that all physical matter resided in a field of energy, and that 'separateness' is only an illusion. He also saw how the non-physical, energetic properties of matter influenced each other through vibration, how even thoughts had vibration and could influence both other thoughts and physical objects.

Although Michael had at first resisted this notion that thoughts could influence matter, he had recently come to see that this happened all the time. The collective thoughts of a society can bring either creation or destruction, and individual thoughts can result in hostility, lack and unhappiness as well as love, peace and joy. All things are sponsored by an original energy and return to that energy. To try to separate ourselves from our world or each other is to fight against the very laws of nature.

2. Emotions are indicators

One of his biggest realizations, Michael reflected to himself, was the idea that emotions are not something to be avoided, but instead to be observed and felt. Emotions arise to guide people in their growth. Painful emotions point to something unresolved within them, while pleasant emotions are encouragements to keep 'going with the flow'. Childlike joy is the natural state for all humans; we only experience pain when we lose touch with this and take the external world too seriously. Emotional pain is simply the result of attaching too strongly to the interactions in an ever-changing world.

This notion was still difficult for Michael because he had been taught for so long that emotions were embarrassing, that being 'Spock-like' was preferred in our society. But he also realized that there was a terrible price to be paid for such beliefs, because emotions cannot be withheld and suppressed without great effort. Emotion is simply energy, and when that energy is trapped within the body, it does a great deal of personal and social damage...and in the end, it's released anyway.

3. Fear and love are the two basic forms of emotional energy

Remembering what Louise had said, Michael had come to understand that each emotional impulse has a source. On one side there was fear and doubt, which caused people to feel insecure, to judge each other and to try to control their surroundings. Fear and doubt were the sponsoring energies behind anger, hatred, violence, cruelty, war, and all things destructive. On the other side there was love and faith, which allowed people to trust in the process of life, accept what cannot be changed and forgive everyone unconditionally. Love and faith were the sponsoring energies behind compassion, kindness, generosity and peace.

And, Michael realized, fear and doubt don't feel good, while love and faith *do*. In this sense, our emotions are constantly telling us whether we are in a state of love or a state of fear. Fear stems from the basic belief that we are not OK, that we need to control our world lest it consume us. And that feels stressful and painful. Love, on the other hand, accepts the world as it is and works with others to do the most compassionate and kind thing in every situation. Love is easy, while fear is hard. The mistaken notion that 'life is supposed to be hard' is merely a reflection of the level of fear that pervades both individuals and societies.

4. Thoughts and projections create physical reality

Michael tapped his pen on his desk and looked up in the air. If emotion was the energy that resulted from an initial stimulus, like when someone does something that triggers 'happy' or 'sad' feelings, then the following thoughts are the justification of, or story behind, that emotion. And if thoughts have vibrations like everything else, then emotions and thoughts together are constantly interacting with the world

235

in which we all live. Feeling and thinking are the 'Ego Self' that Louise mentioned. If the human mind creates internal projections of the sensory input from the world and then projects those images back onto the world, then each person on the planet is determining, in part, how the world looks.

Michael struggled for a bit, and then nodded to himself. The way each person perceives the world is an exact reflection of his internal environment. So if we are constantly at war, it is because we have fearful, warlike thoughts. If we experience a world that is beautiful and at peace, we have thoughts consistent with that reality. Everything that results from human choices started first with a thought or an emotion, which means that as we think, we create.

Pausing for a moment, Michael saw that this was the basic premise behind the creation of the universe. If one of the fundamental laws of the universe was 'cause and effect', and thoughts have an effect on the physical world, then wouldn't it make sense that at least part of the creation of the world could have been by some conscious, creative *idea*?

5. Human beings are, by nature, social and connected

This was the easiest one for Michael to understand. Human brains and bodies are interconnected just like everything else in the universe, and they constantly resonate and 'loop' with each other. Almost everything humans do is social, or at least geared towards seeing the self as a part of a larger group. The most severe emotional pain anyone can feel is to be 'cast out', either by another person or a group. This fact makes social anxiety an extremely common experience, as exemplified by people's fear of public speaking, embarrassment and exclusion.

Michael also learned, however, that people are at their most powerful when they connect and resonate with each other. When individuals share with each other, come to agreement around a higher purpose, and choose to act cooperatively, they can do amazing things. Michael saw, through his own experience, how trying to keep himself separated and isolated had actually limited his abilities as a creative person….which is ironic given how was easy it was to listen, feel heard, and connect with those around him. It was now obvious to Michael that the isolation that destroys so many people, especially children, was an unnecessary act of self-abuse.

6. People are motivated by autonomy, meaning and purpose

Through his conversation with Joe the performance consultant Michael had come to accept that beyond a certain level of compensation money is not a motivator. Throughout his entire life Michael had believed that money and power were the primary drivers behind all human activity. But he realized he was wrong. Money and power are simply things that people think will bring them love. And Michael recognized this fact very personally. He had spent his entire life trying to make more money, get greater titles, and more 'direct reports'...but to what end? Michael now understood that what he was really searching for was acceptance, respect and love. Especially from his father.

In truth, someone who already feels loved and accepted needs only to earn enough to keep himself and his family safe. Beyond that money is nice but not necessary. Once someone feels safe, they are primarily motivated by the freedom to be who they are, work how they want, find the deeper meaning in what they do, and develop a purpose toward which they can strive. Essentially people want to learn, care, explore and create...all things that children do naturally. So in reality, Michael realized, people just want to return to the hopes and dreams that they abandoned in childhood. And what's wrong with that?

7. Leadership is the act of helping others unleash their energy

As Michael wrote this learning, he became aware that his job as a leader of this organization had nothing to do with getting work done. Certainly he had goals to hit and milestones to reach, but without everyone doing their best work, all of that would be impossible. Michael circled the word 'leadership' and knew that in reality his job was to somehow get other people to use their energy to do what they had all agreed to do. Or had they all agreed? Michael shook his head. In most cases, no, they hadn't explicitly agreed. In reality, goals were handed down and given out like pink slips. *Do this.*

Michael smiled as he saw that he had not really been a leader but more of a task manager. Handing out to-do's and then sitting back and hoping, or demanding, that they would get done. Total disengagement. Leadership was more than that. Leadership meant getting involved with people, understanding their lives, and helping them understand the larger purpose to which they were ascribing. Communication…especially listening…was the only way to gain the assent of those being led. People dedicate their attention and energy on *their* terms, not someone else's. Michael decided to revisit this learning later, but he could already tell that his management style was going to change.

8. The universe is conscious and ordered

This point came with a great deal of hesitation. Michael still wasn't sure if he bought into this concept entirely, but he did feel it was something to be considered. Most of his life had been lived under the assumption that the universe was random and chaotic, and that the only way to live was to strive to control everything as much as possible. And wasn't it true that the very premise of modern science was that things are both knowable and, with enough thought and energy, *controllable*? But Michael also knew that the attempt to control all things was exhausting and based in his own fear of not being good enough, or strong enough.

It seemed that the alternative was to have faith that the universe is opening and evolving with structure, purpose and…awareness? Could it be true that all things are happening according to a grand set of rules? And if so, is it safe to let go of the need to control and simply let things unfold according to…well, according to the *nature* of things? Michael sat and grimaced. The idea of surrendering control was almost too much to contemplate. In order to do this, Michael felt that he would also have to trust that everything was happening for the greater good as well, and he had trouble buying that.

But then again, what was the harm in it? Was it better to live a life of doubt coupled with futile attempts to control, or to live a life of faith where one could believe that everything was happening for a reason and trust that everything was going to be OK? Michael already knew the answer to this, but actually letting go was a challenge. In order to truly let go, Michael paused, he would have to believe that...

9. Love is at the base of all things, and the source of all energy

If life is to be lived in faith and joy and peace, then Michael would have to believe that the energy described by quantum physicists, the light at the ground of all matter, was not only conscious but *loving*. This would imply that there is some sort of conscious, aware God who has nothing but love for all he/she/it has created. So here was the rub. Michael felt like he would have to believe in God, to have faith in a source of all loving energy, in order to be the person he wanted to be.

This struggle, Michael realized, had consumed him most of his life. He had been brought up in a society that put Man first and celebrated Man's ability to achieve all the things to which he set his mind. God was 'over there', outside the realm of Man's doings. God was a fairy tale in the dead, mechanistic world espoused by modern science. But this notion no longer suited Michael, simply because it caused so much pain inside of him.

Then it occurred to Michael. What if both were true? What if Man was a very powerful creator who had the ability to alter the world *and* the world was a conscious, loving and ordered place? He had been proceeding under the assumption that it had to be one or the other...science or religion, fact or fantasy, logic or love. But this seemed far too limiting. And if Michael could indeed create the world he wanted, then he could add another point to his list of learnings.

10. Directed action and love are compatible

Michael realized, strangely, that he had been operating under the belief that taking directed, concerted action was incompatible with being a loving person. He remembered what Louise had said about being able to defend yourself physically while at the same time harboring only love for your attacker. Wasn't this the idea, that as humans we can choose to act, even in a harsh or violent way, but have love at the root of it all. The key, Michael nodded to himself, *was the feeling we held inside.*

It was quite possible, in this world, to be directed and to be caring. To believe that love was at the root of everything, and to also do our best to remember and *act* from that love. Michael recalled how Ayn Rand had suggested that being peaceful and loving was somehow akin to being lazy, to letting the world affect us. He now realized how mistaken she had been. It is quite possible to be John Gault, the achiever of great things, *and* proceed under the assumption that to be loving in all circumstances is for the highest good of all. It wouldn't even be necessary to believe in God if our actions all proceeded from a loving place, because in coming from love we actualize the nature of God anyway. God is Love and Love is God…and the rest is semantics.

Michael put his pen down and looked at his list. Indeed, he had learned a lot over the past six months. More importantly, things inside him had begun to shift. He felt less anxious and angry, and felt like he had more energy. There was a happiness beginning to bubble up inside of him that he had not felt since he was a child…or that time he meditated briefly in his back yard. He sat and tapped the pen on the desk.

"So what do *I* stand for now?" he asked out loud. It was all well and good to reflect on the learnings and knowledge he had gained, but what did this all mean for the way he would *be*?

He picked up another piece of paper and wrote across the top:
"My Values"

Starting another list, Michael wrote the first thing that came to mind:

1. Performance

Michael knew why this was at the top of his list. For most of Michael's childhood, his father had drilled into him the importance of doing his best, trying as hard as he could, and doing what he said he was going to do. Execution. Taking care of business. Getting things done.

This is what 'performance' meant to Michael.

There was also, Michael knew, the negative corollary to performance that had made his life quite stressful. This was the 'be better than others' or 'win at all costs' notion of performance that Michael wanted to release. He chose in that moment to define performance as being the best he could be, regardless of what anyone else thought. His notion of performance was noble rather than competitive. To be the best person he could possibly be in all circumstances.

2. Integrity

Pausing for a moment, Michael stared at the word and wondered what he meant. Certainly he meant honesty, which he felt was imbedded in the concept of integrity. But what did he mean when he thought of 'acting with integrity'? For Michael the word 'congruous' came to mind...to internally be 'in sync' with oneself. What appealed to Michael was the notion of doing the right thing according to his own beliefs. To be consistent with the things he held as deep truths.

The opposite of this was 'hypocrisy', which for Michael was the act of doing something that deep down he knew was inconsistent with his values. So, Integrity was, in a sense, a 'meta-value'...one that ensured that he was acting in concert with his soul. He paused for a moment and smiled. He liked the idea of acting with integrity. Walking the walk, not just talking the talk. Being.

Michael sat and stared out the window again. Just then, he smiled as he was reminded of his grandfather who had been a teacher and school administrator.

3. Growth

Michael's grandfather had been such a wonderful influence. He was an incredibly nurturing and loving person. Although Michael didn't have many memories of 'Grandpa H', he did remember his kindly face and deep, sonorous voice. Michael also remembered his grandfather's admonition to 'learn something new everyday'. How impactful those words had been, Michael thought. From that day forward, Michael had looked around and tried to learn all he could about his world, to pick up interesting bits of knowledge, no matter how arcane.

But at this point in his life this value had taken on an expanded meaning. No longer was book or 'worldly' knowledge enough. Michael saw that the deeper learnings centered more around wisdom and self-understanding. Learning was much more than rote memorization of information. It represented the growth of the self, the inexorable movement from *what is* to *what can be*. In this sense, Michael's life had been one grand learning experience. First learning about things in the world, then about life, then about himself, and now about his spirit. Everything Michael learned took him to the next level, to a better vantage point from which he could see a higher and more expanded version of himself.

4. Responsibility

As Michael wrote this word, he heard his father's stern voice saying, 'Good God, son, take responsibility for yourself'. For many years Michael had no idea what this meant. It usually only arose when Michael was defending himself or trying to explain what had happened. His father saw his defense as something bad…an attempt by his son to disavow his own actions or to blame others for his circumstance. But Michael knew that he was just scared. Scared of not receiving his father's love, which made him defend himself when he acted 'irresponsibly'.

In that moment Michael saw an opportunity to reframe this word as a positive value rather than a negative accusation. In this new version of 'responsibility', he saw an empowerment of the self, an opportunity for each person to choose a response to any circumstance. Michael knew that for him this meant becoming more aware of his responses and choices in each moment. It also meant accepting that his choices created his reality and that any negativity he felt was his own creation. Maybe this is what his father really meant…to take ownership of all situations. Michael liked this value, because it gave him a sense that although he could not control the external world, he could control his *internal* world, which was all that mattered anyway.

5. Decisiveness

As he wrote this word Michael thought of his father again. If there was anything Roy Benson embodied, it was decisiveness. His father did not question much, because he believed that to be equivocal about one's decisions was a sign of weak and muddled thinking. Michael agreed, but for different reasons. Michael increasingly believed that the thinking mind was useful only to a point, and then a course of action had to be taken with what information was at hand. To some extent this stemmed from a belief that he could not know everything and that he had to risk failure no matter what decision he took.

Michael knew he had not always embodied this value. His chattering mind wanted to blame people for the past and create anxiety around the future. Louise had been helpful in this, explaining that the thinking mind was afraid of the silence and certainty of 'the now' because it felt like its role was to defend, protect and explain. For Michael, decisiveness was the purposeful quieting of this mental noise to allow for thorough, reasoned decision-making. His decisions may not always be right, but he valued the ability to look at all the information and take action.

Looking over the list so far, Michael liked what he saw. But he also knew that these were values that were more or less instilled in him. These were largely things that he had been told by his parents, teachers and mentors. He liked them well enough, but he also felt that he wanted to expand beyond what he had been taught. He wanted to *grow*.

Given all he had learned, Michael decided that he wanted to cultivate a new set of values that represented the person he knew he could be. In some ways, he wanted to re-discover the person he had been as a child. As he thought about his 'younger self', one word popped into his head.

6. Joy

Michael sat and stared at the word. "Is that even a value?" he asked himself. But even if it wasn't, the word did have a certain appeal. Michael recalled himself as a young boy when he was so happy and excited about life. Joy seemed to be his natural state. And then life had happened. Painful experiences, betrayals, endless hours trying to be good enough for his teachers, parents, bosses. Joy had lost its role in his life, and he very much wanted to make a place for it again.

So, Michael decided he was going to make up his own rules. From now on joy, laughter and unexplained happiness were a value. He would value joy in all its forms, internal, external, random and planned. Play would be the active form of joy. Each day he wanted to find reasons to play and laugh, to rekindle the feeling of joy he felt when he woke up in the morning as a child. As he thought about this, a powerful wave of giddiness rose up in his throat. He wanted to run into the hallway and hug somebody.

But he would have to take this one step at a time, Michael thought, as he smiled to himself. It might scare people if he suddenly started acting in unexpected and unconventional ways!

7. Kindness

On a roll, Michael brought forth another memory from childhood. He remembered clearly how good it felt to both be kind and to be treated kindly. And he knew from his discussions with Louise that the corollary to kindness is 'compassion'. When he envisioned the world he wanted to create, he saw unlimited kindness and compassion for all people. This world had become far too harsh, and there was really no need for it. Kindness felt so much better than meanness, yet in the business world he felt so much pressure to be 'tough'. In his world kindness had somehow been conflated with 'softness'.

Michael decided he didn't want to continue thinking that way. From now on he would endeavor to be kind *and* caring in all situations, regardless of the circumstances. Even under attack he could choose to be both kind and decisive. He could show compassion while being powerful. Wasn't this the hallmark of all great leaders in history? Those who could be forceful while at the same time show a deep caring for those being led? Didn't it take more strength to be compassionate and kind in trying circumstances where most men would choose vitriol and anger?

Michael nodded to himself. He resolved that his leadership and way of being would be based in kindness.

8. Acceptance

As Michael wrote this down he thought about all the times he had been in resistance to events in his life. So much of the chaos in his mind had been generated by a perceived need to control, which was driven by the fact that he could not accept what was going on around him. He realized that if he was to be truly responsible for his reality, he had to accept that certain things simply *were*. Acceptance didn't mean he couldn't try to change things in his life, but instead meant that he could work on these things from a place of peace.

In the past there were so many things that Michael claimed he did not 'like' about his life, and had tried to fight these things. This ongoing battle had resulted in a constant tension within his heart, as if his life was meant to be one long fight to maintain wholeness against the chaotic centripetal forces trying to rip him apart. Michael now understood that the only answer left was to surrender any notion of control. To let go, and let things happen. His ego rebelled at this notion, but he also knew that the alternative was unsustainable.

This thought let Michael to quickly jot down the next value.

9. Faith

Michael's ego rebelled against the idea of acceptance because he knew deep down that in the past he simply had not had faith that things would turn out OK. But thinking back, Michael remembered a time when he was younger when he did have faith, when he accepted quickly and laughed easily, but that was quashed by the doubting stories he heard from the adults around him. So much of his life had been spent doubting that this world was essentially a good place. The hurt part of him was convinced that the world was a scary, mean place that had to be doubted lest he be taken for a fool.

Michael sincerely wanted to have faith. He wasn't sure if he could simply let go of all of his doubts, but he knew that in order to move forward without fear he would have to trust that this world and his life were part of something greater…something beautiful. There was purpose in everything, Michael knew. But this belief was doubted by his thinking mind, because this part of him was afraid of the alternative. This would be a work in process, but Michael was determined to hold it as a value.

Pausing, Michael saw that this made 9 values. He liked each one, but he felt that something was missing. And besides, he liked the idea of a round number of ten. Closing his eyes, one word appeared.

10. Love

Love. Michael wasn't exactly sure what he meant by this, because his thinking mind was chattering that love is too complicated, it meant too many things. Romantic love, filial love, fatherly love? But deep down Michael felt what he could not mentally construct. Love, for him, was the deep feeling of gratitude and goodwill for and toward all people and all things. It was the warm sensation when he watched a sunset, the lightness he felt after he laughed, and the peacefulness inside when he knew he was true to himself. Love was a state of being, not a thought. When his mind slowed and his body calmed, he could sense the love coursing through him. It was life itself.

Michael had no idea how he was going to bring this state into his life, but he knew that he valued it above all things. When Louise had spoken about love being the source of all things and the consciousness behind the material universe, Michael intuitively understood. As a child Michael could have easily identified this force, but now it happened only when he was relaxed and at peace. Michael realized that love had always been present in his life, but he had simply closed himself off to the current. He had denied what was inside of him, and he wanted to change this.

Sitting back in his chair, Michael became aware of the choices he had made in the past and those that faced him right now. Was he willing to let go of doubt, fear, and anger? He was willing, but would he make that choice today? He felt a flash of anger about the past, about the stories that he had unknowingly taken as truth. Michael felt the pull to judge himself as deeply flawed, but he also knew that this judgment presumed an imperfection that was a lie in and of itself.

Could he forgive his family for their patterns? Could he forgive his peers for their flaws? *Could he forgive himself for his choices?* If he was truly going to let go of his fear and anger, he was going to have to accept that everyone, including himself, was doing the best that they could do. Michael was going to have to forgive everyone for everything, unconditionally.

This was a tall order, Michael knew. But he also knew that creating a new self – a happier, more loving self – required it. There was no room for judgment in this new value system. There was only room for those thoughts that affirmed the wholeness and goodness of all things. Michael wasn't sure how he was going to do it, but he wanted to try. And this, he smiled, was something he could celebrate about himself: his courage.

Chapter Twenty-Two

Michael let his list of values sit on his desk for a few days. As he looked at them from time to time, he became aware that values were by themselves not terribly effective unless they were put into practice. 'Walking the walk' as his father would say. Picking up the sheet of paper, he decided he needed to express some sort of intention, some statement that said he was going to commit to putting these things into practice.

Pulling out another sheet of paper, Michael wrote across the top: "My Intentions"

He wrote: "It is my intention to live the values that I have established for myself. I intend to perform to my highest ability, act with integrity, grow a little bit every day, take responsibility for my thoughts and actions, and to be decisive in my approach to all things. I also intend to bring joy into my life through smiles and laughter, be kind to all whom I encounter, accept all situations with equanimity, have faith that everything is happening as it should, and to love everyone and everything unconditionally."

Putting the pen down, Michael looked at what he had written. For the first time in his life he felt clear about what he wanted. He smiled at the peace and knowingness he felt inside. These intentions incorporated both sides of Michael's values: the *doing-ness* that he felt was important to make progress and the *being-ness* that was crucial to his happiness. Yin and Yang. Michael knew this was the whole that had eluded him for so long.

Another idea came to him. Why not set a statement of intent that he can share with everyone around him? A statement of how he wanted to be with everyone in his life? His father had done something like that, but it was reflective of a different time. Michael smiled again as he remembered his father's 'you agree to do x, y and z and I agree to pay you'. Classic Roy Benson. Although Michael wanted to add more 'love' to the message, he thought his father was on track in terms of personal responsibility and integrity.

Grabbing another piece of paper, Michael wrote an agreement for himself and his team:

I, a valued member of my team, agree to do my best to perform to my highest ability, help other team-members achieve and grow, respect everyone whom I encounter, and be the best, most caring, and most loving person that I can possibly be.

I, Michael Benson, agree to support you, believe in you, care about you and be honest with you at all times.

We both agree that we want to hear the truth from each other. We agree that we will be open and honest, say the difficult things, but always be respectful. We value each other deeply and want the best for everyone we encounter. We intend to unleash our highest energy to do great things in the world.

As Michael put signature lines at the bottom of the page he felt a rush of goose-bumps run down his back. This document had meaning. More importantly it had *heart*. This was truth. Michael understood very clearly that this was a new way of operating, a way that took the performance aspects of planning, goal setting and compensation, and added a human dimension. In some ways it added a *spiritual* dimension. This was something he could live with and for. This way of operating resonated deeply.

Michael's logical mind immediately began to think of how to implement this. Sure he could get everyone to sign it, but how was he going to display these newfound intentions? If he didn't make a concerted effort to walk this talk, then it would just be another piece of paper like every other 'vision document' his company had prepared over the last 10 years. Michael needed to systematically identify all of the opportunities to be different and make a conscious effort to bring this new way of being into those situations.

Michael put yet another clean sheet of paper in front of him and began to write down each process or work activity in which he was involved. As he wrote, he immediately began to see patterns. The first pattern he noticed was that most of his work activities involved people. In fact, upwards of 90% of the things he did every day were some kind of social interaction. This made sense to Michael because he had always believed that a business was primarily a *social enterprise*. Businesses, like any other organizations, were simply groups of people coming together to achieve a shared purpose. So it was no surprise that a manager or leader would spend most of his or her time with people.

The other pattern Michael noticed was in the type of activities in which he was involved, in aggregate what he would call 'management'. As far as he could tell there were three main areas. First were 'personnel processes', or those that involved bringing people into and moving them out of the organization. These were hiring, training and firing activities. Second was what he saw as 'communication processes', where information was exchanged on an ongoing basis. Things like meetings, emails, conversations, reviews and presentations. And last were 'bureaucratic processes', or those tasks that he and every manager generally hated to do. Plans, reports, budget reviews, etc.

As Michael looked at his list, he noticed that there was another dimension to this. All of these activities involved other people, all of whom needed to be considered. First there was his team. For lack of a better term he called this 'downward management'. Then there was, of course, 'upward management' and 'customer management'. On top of that there was the management of functions such as 'project management', 'crisis management', and 'sales management'.

Michael sighed as he looked at his list. He knew there were more, but this seemed like a pretty good start. He placed each of these items on a grid, and then thought about how he would implement his values in each one of the processes and management situations. Michael looked at the top of the list where it said 'hiring' and realized that he would have an opportunity to take his values for a spin in about fifteen minutes. He had an interview with a new candidate.

Getting up to grab a cup of coffee, Michael thought about how his approach to the interview might change. He wanted to keep the procedural aspects of his interview process because he liked how his company screened for talent. Only the best candidates made it in the door after being screened by HR. These people had talent, and that often made it hard for Michael to choose. But he also knew that with his new values he could look for an added dimension...one that ensured that the people coming in the door *cared* about what they did, and that they would be kind, loving and joyful people to work with.

As he walked in the conference room and greeted the new candidate, Michael felt completely different. In the past he would have seen this person with an impatient, object-oriented view. He would have looked at the person as an 'it' who had to prove that they belonged with his company. But now he had a very different feeling. Michael saw this person as a unique soul with potential to do something great in this world. He saw unlimited energy within the person, and was grateful that she had come into his presence. His demeanor was very serene and loving.

Almost immediately he saw that his approach had an effect on the candidate. She relaxed and matched Michael's smile. She did seem nervous, but not nearly as nervous as he had somewhat sadistically encouraged in past candidates.

As he began to ask questions, Michael focused all of his energy on being *present* with her. He became genuinely interested in her outlook and her reasoning for her decisions. He listened with a complete lack of judgment as she described her choices and her world view. Michael truly began to *empathize* with her, to see what her life was like. As he connected to this person, he began to see very clearly that she would not fit well within his new value system. It wasn't a specific thought that cued Michael to this fact, but instead a general feeling. Something was not *right*.

Following his gut, Michael asked increasingly open-ended questions about her belief system and her values. When she answered, he became fascinated with her outlook. In a totally non-judgmental way, he came to experience her world from her perspective and could tell that she had quite a bit of anger and a strong victim mentality. The words she chose and the examples she used told Michael that she was extremely competent, but very likely a management challenge. He knew this wasn't going to work out.

As he finished the interview he made it a point to express his gratitude for her presence that day. He expressed how he knew that interviews were challenging and nerve racking, and that he was thankful that she took the time to come in and talk. She seemed relieved at Michael's kindness, and said she was very impressed at how easy he was to talk to. And for some reason Michael could tell that she *knew* that she was not right for the company. There was an unspoken conversation going on, and both of them understood that things were not going to move forward.

But she didn't seem angry, Michael noted. Rather, she seemed relieved. She even said that she loved the company and hoped someday to be lucky enough to work there. The entire conversation was a wonderful process, and actually energizing to Michael. He met a nice person, make a clear decision, and felt like they both came away feeling good about the situation.

Sitting back down at his desk Michael realized that implementing these values might not be as hard as he thought. These were basic human desires, ideas that resonated with most people. Who didn't want to experience joy, kindness and faith? Even if everyone didn't believed in the larger existential or spiritual context, didn't we all want to be treated kindly and experience joy? And wasn't it nice to give those things?

Michael suddenly felt wonderfully relieved and happy. Over the following weeks he used his list to look for opportunities to apply his new way of being. One of the first things he did was to set up, and for the first time *keep*, regular meetings with all of his direct reports. And he resolved to change the tenor of his meetings as well. Each time he spoke with someone he became extremely present and focused on trying to understand the perspective of each person.

In the past Michael's meetings would have involved going over goals, to-do's and problems, all the while pushing and cajoling his team members to do more, faster and better. The meetings were usually wrought with tension and often resulted in frustration on both sides. In his new style, however, Michael found himself spending most of the time listening and trying to understand what was happening in each person's world.

At first it was a bit tiring. Michael found himself wanting to interject and help solve the problem. Resisting that urge was exhausting. Each person was so *different*. Some people were held back by their insecurities, while others were overcompensating through an inflated ego. Michael did his best not to judge anyone, but instead simply listened, clarified what he heard, and then asked how he could be of service. And to his great surprise virtually every one of his reports found a way to move themselves closer to their goals. Michael's involvement changed from *pushing* for progress to - progress.

As Michael began to relax into his meetings, he also became more aware of persistent issues with people who didn't seem to be responding to his new approach. The more he listened to these people, the more he became aware that they fundamentally did not enjoy what they were doing. They seemed to be fighting a part of themselves, and that was reflected in their performance. Normally Michael would have pushed and

254

struggled to gain the performance he wanted, but this time he simply reflected back what he was hearing and seeing.

This approach had a strange effect. Some people responded by admitting that they were not doing as well as they could, with almost no prompting from Michael. It appeared that they already knew that they were not performing to their ability, which made it easier for Michael to help them get back on track. Others, who were having challenges greater than Michael could address, seemed to 'self-select' out of the organization. After a number of meetings, both Michael and the employee came to the realization that he or she did not belong there, and for the most part the transition was very pleasant and easy. Michael found that as long as he listened and created a safe environment for people to express themselves, he could say or suggest just about anything. He was building trust, which allowed for transparent and direct communication.

After one meeting, Michael sat back and reflected how simple it seemed. Listen for understanding, build trust, care, support, be kind, and communicate openly. Doing these things had almost instantly resolved the conflicts and emotional overhead that he had previously experienced. It was not as if he was ignoring his goals either…he was actually achieving them faster and with more ease than he had ever experienced.

Given his success with his one-on-one meetings, Michael resolved to expand his approach to group meetings. In his first meetings he spoke with his team and told them that from that point forward, each meeting would start with a clear intention to come to conclusion on a particular topic or decision. Then the meeting format would include an open discussion in which every person was offered a chance to speak, and that the rules would be to 1) listen to understand what each person was saying, 2) respect each person's right to speak, and 3) be open to learning.

At first, Michael got what he was expecting: strange stares from everyone in the room. But as the meeting got going and Michael persistently interjected to remind each person of the ground rules, the tone of the conversation changed. People began to truly listen to each other. When Michael sensed that there was tension, or saw that something was not being explicitly expressed, he would call the issue out on the table and ask each person to comment. This clearly made people feel awkward and uncomfortable, but the release of tension and the 'saying of the unsaid' resulted in a much more productive conversation.

Michael noted again after one particular meeting that the topics of the gathering had not changed, but the tone was much more positive and open….which in turn made the time much more productive. In the past Michael had noticed how he would leave meetings frustrated and angry, and assumed that everyone had felt the same way. But now he left meetings feeling happy, even if the result was not what he had wanted. People were communicating and discussing much more openly, and that was having a positive effect on their willingness to compromise, cooperate and produce.

So successful were these interactions that Michael worked with his team to create and roll out a whole series of new programs and cultural norms. Some of these included:

- A mandatory 3 month trial period for all new employees so that the group could experience the person before making a decision on whether or not to bring them in permanently.

- An on-boarding process that indoctrinated new employees around not only company operations, but also communication values and cultural history. Michael got deeply involved in working with new employees to ensure that they felt welcomed and understood, while at the same time conveying the purpose and meaning of working for the company.

- A standing rule against gossip, ongoing email conflicts or talking about anyone who was not in the room. Michael was particularly insistent that if there was a conflict or misunderstanding of any kind, it was to be brought to light *face to face*. Michael had seen first hand the inefficiency and 'emotional overhead' that had resulted from people talking about each other and sniping behind the scenes. His organization would be known for openly and safely relieving any emotional stress.

• An open meeting each month with no agenda except to ask questions, speak openly and communicate freely. Michael promised to answer any questions, no matter how difficult, and to allow anyone who wished to speak to say anything they wanted. No restrictions. Completely open sharing.

• A free-day each month during which people could work on anything they wanted related to making the company better. Ideas could cross organizational boundaries or involve other teams. No restrictions. At the end of the day people could, if they chose, to present their ideas to the larger group and get feedback.

• A 'love a customer' day, in which everyone in the company who had customer contact would reach out to that customer and 1) express gratitude to them, 2) get to know them, and 3) find one thing that the company could do better to serve them.

• An ongoing training regimen that focused on communication skills, specifically 'empathetic listening'. In each of these sessions employees learned to become present and listen deeply to each other's perspectives. These sessions were to become some of the most powerful organizational work Michael had ever done.

• A values review where each employee got to choose what they wanted the organization and company to represent. When everyone had expressed their preference, Michael got the group together to discuss the common values across a number of dimensions.

• Discussions instead of presentations. Rather than people standing in front of a room talking 'at' the attendees, there would be an emphasis on two-way dialogue. The person leading the discussion was encouraged to facilitate a discussion that allowed everyone to speak and be heard. To support this Michael arranged for communication and facilitation training.

• In order to keep himself honest, Michael implemented a 'direct feedback' process in which he openly encouraged people to tell him what they thought about him, the company, their work, anything. This was the toughest for Michael because the feedback was not always 'good'. He had to prepare himself to listen with empathy to everything people said, without judgment or recrimination.

As he began these programs Michael also started to read much more. He realized that in some cases he was out of his element…his short courses in organizational behavior were proving insufficient. He read books about conscious business practices, motivation, leadership, anything he could get his hands on. And while he learned valuable techniques and processes, he also saw that they all proceeded from one fundamental proposition: that being a loving, caring and aware manager made for good business.

In a moment alone in his office Michael reflected on this idea. All of the technical aspects of business that he had learned in business school – the process orientation, financial planning, operations management – all of these things were merely tactical activities that ensured the basic input and output functions of an organization. The real juice, Michael now understood, was in helping people feel good about themselves, getting them to communicate with each other, and constantly working to ensure that the entire organization is working together towards a common purpose. Everything else was merely window dressing.

Love. "Who would have thought?" Michael said out loud as he shook his head. It would've seemed ridiculous to him a year ago. But now he felt like it was the only answer. Love was indeed the basis of all things. This wasn't something that Michael could point to externally… he certainly had not yet seen any evidence in tangible, financial terms. But he did feel differently inside, and he felt like that mattered a great deal.

There was a certain *knowing* to all this. Michael had worked with different motivation and human dynamics programs and processes for most of his career, but none of them created the shift within himself that had occurred over the past six months. It wasn't so much the *things* he was doing, but the way he was doing them. There was something different in the way he held himself. A different *presence*.

Michael smiled as he thought about it. He was becoming a different person. He went from being an angry and frustrated manager to being a leader who genuinely cared about the people with whom he shared his day. For the first time in his career Michael felt relaxed with and within himself. He felt totally comfortable expressing his feelings and beliefs, and knew he was acting with integrity at all times. In a strange way Michael had reverted back to his real self, and it felt good.

At the end of one particularly good day Michael grabbed his laptop and decided to spend some quality time with his family. His new regimen had not only taken a great deal of work off his plate, it had also given him more energy at the end of the day. With this energy Michael intended to bring more love into his family as well, which he hoped would have the same effect.

Michael smiled to himself again. If he could create a happier family, a happier work environment, and a happier self then wouldn't all this be worth it?

Chapter Twenty-Three

Michael was looking forward to meeting with Louise again. They had not spoken since the week before his father had passed away, and so much had happened since then. There were so many things he wanted to share with her, and this time they were not all frustrated, angry stories.

As he sat down in front of her, he reflected on the growth he had achieved over the past 6 months. Louise had been instrumental in his progress and a supporting force in his life. He did not know how to thank her.

She looked at him quizzically as if reading his mind. "Michael, you look different. More peaceful. How has everything been since your father passed away?" She knew that Roy Benson had passed because Michael had cancelled their meetings during his father's final stages.

Michael hesitated before answering. "Louise, I simply don't know how to begin. So much has happened in my life…yet even more has happened inside of me. I have become aware of so many things, and I feel so entirely different that I can't really put into words what I want to say."

Louise smiled and nodded softly. Michael felt like she understood completely.

He continued. "Well, I guess I can say some things for sure. First, my back doesn't hurt anymore. I don't know why, because I haven't been doing anything different physically. The pain just, well, went away.

I woke up one morning and noticed it wasn't there."

"Second, I don't feel as angry anymore. I know I probably didn't come across as angry before, but I know that I was suppressing a great deal of frustration with my life and my world. That just seems to have gone away. Instead I feel a sense of peace most of the time. It's not that I don't have flashes occasionally…I do. But they come and go quickly. It's easier to be serene in difficult situations."

"Third, I feel…how can I put this? I feel more connected to people. I don't know if this makes sense, but in the past I always felt like I had a wall between myself and everyone else. Like I was trying to keep myself isolated. But now I actually want to get to know people, to understand them."

Michael shook his head and continued, "I had the most incredible conversation the other day. I went in to talk to my boss, Armand, about a challenge we were having with a particular production process. Now normally this would have been difficult, to say the least. Armand would have gone on the attack, and I would have defended, and the whole thing would have been incredibly stressful for me. But this time…"

Michael looked up at Louise and smiled, "…this time I simply went in with a different intention. I resolved to simply listen and to be as present as possible. I wanted to understand his perspective and just get an idea of how I could best be of service. And the most incredible thing happened."

Louise was beaming as she listened.

"Armand started in the usual way," Michael nodded, "with anger and frustration at our inability to fix the problem. But instead of my defending myself as I normally would, I simply sat and listened. When he paused, I merely acknowledged that he was frustrated and said that I understood. He vented for a bit longer but then, well, he ran out of things to say. His frustration lost steam and he quieted down."

"But the strangest part was where the conversation went next. He started to tell me all sorts of things about his life, both current and past.

I learned how he grew up, the internal struggles he faced, the pain of his family life. I have never, ever heard Armand Lacoste speak of anything except work, and yet here he was baring his soul to me. Louise, I was stunned. Even more, I was deeply touched. This man was clearly very lonely, and very sad. Work was the only thing he felt he could control, and when he couldn't, he got angry and frustrated. It was so clear, and so *human*."

Tears formed in Louise's eyes. "What you're sharing touches me deeply Michael. We all share the joys and pains of being human. This is true empathy – it's a part of our loving nature."

Michael fought back tears himself. "I think I really understood in that moment, Louise. We are all so much more alike than we are different. We all simply want to be loved, accepted, and understood. We fight to avoid being vulnerable, to need anyone or anything, but we can't avoid our own nature. We are connected beings, all looking for the communion that will make us whole."

"And at the same time," Louise interjected, "we are already whole and perfect as we are. We are all experiencing what we need to experience to grow. It is one of the great conundrums of the human mind, to understand that we are complete as we are but also *more* with others. I don't know if we will logically ever be able to truly understand this, but we can feel it in our hearts. We can know it without understanding it."

"Yes," Michael agreed, "and I think that's what I have been experiencing. *A knowing*. When I'm with people - listening to them, helping them, understanding them – I feel like I am completely on-point. I feel like I'm acting in the highest version of myself. All of the concerns that used to consume me fade into the background.

"And people respond!" Michael continued with mock surprise. "More and more people want to spend time with me, talk to me, and not just at work. It's like I have a magnetic field around me, an attractive energy. If I have a problem or a need, the right people just seem to appear! It gives me such a sense of gratitude to know that so many people care."

"That's because *you* care." Louise pointed at him. "You are reaping what you sow. When you love, you get love in return. It is a fundamental law of the universe. Every action has an equal reaction."

"Yes!" Michael exclaimed. "It also works to change angry situations as well. When I went home the other day, my wife was clearly in a... let's say 'angry state'," Michael laughed. "In the past I would have gone into my shell and just avoided her until it blew over. But this time I did something different…inspired I think by my conversation with Armand. This time I went to her, gently hugged her, and told her I loved her. And my God, Louise, she melted in my arms. She sobbed and hugged me and poured out all of her worries and concerns and everything that she had been angry about. Then she apologized to *me*. I think I'm still in shock at the change in our interaction!"

Louise laughed softly. "This is the power of love, Michael. It has the power to change everything. For thousands of years various religions and spiritual traditions have tried to tell us this in a hundred different ways, but we still somehow choose to live under the mistaken notion that anger and separation are the way to interact with each other. And so we suffer as we create our own living hell. It's all so simple, isn't it?"

"But what keeps us from doing what seems so natural?" Michael asked. " I mean, when my kids were little, and when I was little for that matter, we would naturally hug each other and apologize and forgive. Love came so easy. What happened – why can't we just do this now as adults?"

Louise frowned for a moment and looked down. "Well, Michael, it's purely social inertia. Thousands of years of war and fighting and telling negative stories about each other. We talk about 'them' being 'evil' and we focus on all the differences between each other. We teach our kids that 'that boy is bad' and 'that girl does things incorrectly'. We project onto each other our own collective insecurities, and so create a world of separation and hatred."

She continued. "But there's something happening here, Michael, and you are part of it. Whereas in the past only a small number of people spoke the truth about love, now we are seeing larger and larger numbers of people coming to this conclusion. Two thousand years ago there were only a handful of people on the planet who understood what true, unconditional, spiritual love meant. Today there are tens of thousands of average people like you who have gathered the courage to step out and try to be different. To try to love in a world that laughs at such sentimentality."

Michael knew exactly what she was talking about. He felt that there were very few people with whom he could discuss this openly. He nodded and said, "Yes, it may be difficult to discuss, but I think the key is *showing* them. I can see that by simply *being* a loving person, feeling that love inside of me, I am affecting the way people are with each other. In just these short few weeks, I have seen a huge difference in the way people are responding to me. I think it may be a matter of being, not talking."

Louise got uncharacteristically excited. "Yes, Michael! And this is how the world will become a better place. As more people in organizations, especially leaders like yourself, become loving and aware, we are going to see massive, incalculable benefits. Some may be tangible, like more productivity and higher standards of living, while others will be felt, such as increased personal peace and a deeper sense of wellbeing. This is how human beings are evolving, Michael, and you are an integral part of that. You are at the vanguard."

Michael sat for a moment, stunned at the implications. Never in a million years did he see himself as anything but an average guy struggling to figure out his purpose in this world. But upon reflection, he could see that Louise was right.

"You know, Louise, I think you're a very prescient woman." He reached out and touched her hand. "I'm reminded of a business school class where we discussed the most recent thinking in motivation and organizational behavior. We went back and looked at the history of organizations and the various methods leaders employed to get people to produce. At first, management styles were very authoritarian. Then came the complex hierarchy and more worker involvement. Now we are talking about intrinsic motivation and personal purpose. If everything is truly heading toward a connected and loving world, and I believe it is, then the next logical step will be to bring these fundamental values into the workplace. I believe it might be the next frontier in human productivity."

Louise sat quietly for a moment and smiled. "The beauty is, Michael, that it is all happening on purpose. This is the natural unfolding of the universe. We are moving toward love in a step-by-step, unstoppable process."

"Yes," Michael acknowledged. "And I guess I don't need to worry about my role in all of this except to do my best to grow into the most loving, caring and kind person I can be. Can it be as simple as all that?"

Louise didn't answer but simply looked deeply into Michael's eyes.

"I think I already know the answer to that," Michael smiled. "That's the purpose I've been seeking, the purpose of life."

Epilogue

For six months Michael steadfastly held to his intentions and values, and the results were nothing short of astounding. As he reflected on his progress, he saw that in every way his life had become more meaningful, successful and peaceful.

Perhaps the most dramatic improvements, at least externally, revolved around his business life. Prior to his father's passing Michael's career was something of a merry-go-round. He took each new position with hope and excitement, only to find himself in a pressure-packed, political, and sometimes absurdly challenging performance environment. But now the situation was almost entirely different.

For the first time in his life Michael enjoyed coming into work in the morning. His relationships with his co-workers, direct reports and, most surprisingly, Armand, had become closer than he ever could have imagined. Michael increasingly saw these people as a second family, and enjoyed his time with them immensely. Of course he didn't personally like every person with whom he worked, but he found that even with those with whom he did not 'connect', he had a cordial and open working relationship.

With this closeness came a cooperation and coordination that Michael had never before experienced. The human system that made up his organization became flawless in execution…notably without a tremendous amount of process overhead. Because each person was open, honest and respectful, conflicts were resolved quickly and without undue acrimony. Emotional exchanges did occur, but the individuals involved were patient and able to express themselves without fear of retribution or judgment.

His group had truly become a team, one that cared about each other and wanted each individual to be successful in their own way. Everyone had something to add, yet people understood that someone had to lead and make decisions. At the end of the day not everyone liked every decision, but they trusted that everyone cared about the same things and would try to do the best for the organization as a whole.

The results were obvious. Sales had increased by 20% over a six-month period. Michael had made a special effort to work with the salespeople to ensure their listening and empathy skills were constantly improving. He did this not so much with formal training, although this was certainly a part of it. Most of his work was done through *modeling*...by being empathetic and a good listener. Michael found that *being* a certain way had much more of an impact than trying to tell others how to be.

Customer retention increased as well. Whereas in previous years they could expect to lose anywhere from 5-10% of their customers each year, Michael's organization had not lost a single customer in the past 6 months and had developed a communication regimen that ensured deep visibility into customer intentions. Previous to this regimen Michael was regularly ambushed by customer unhappiness. Now, he felt that he knew each customer so well, and communicated so often, that he intuitively began to sense there was a problem sometimes before the customers themselves. And he found that when there was a service problem the customers were much more forgiving because, as one said the other day, 'We really like working with you guys'. This was one of the greatest compliments Michael had ever received from a customer.

For Michael the most important improvements were certainly around team dynamics, sales and customer retention, but he also noticed many secondary benefits. Strangely, sick days began to decrease. Michael wasn't certain what was causing this, but he suspected that it had something to do with the changed atmosphere in his organization. When everyone was together, it was simply more *fun* than before. People laughed and smiled, something he had not seen previously. There was a palpable lightness to the group, even when things were not going as planned.

There was also a consequent increase in the acceptance rate of candidates, and the retention rates of existing employees. Michael laughed to himself when he realized that people now really wanted to work for his company, and when they got here they were extremely loyal. There had been a number of times when very highly qualified candidates said that they were taking a pay cut to be with Michael's group because they sensed that it was a happier, more meaningful place to be.

Unintentionally Michael had created somewhat of a 'cult following' within the company. Many people expressed an interest in working for Michael's group because they had heard that he really cared about his team members and had created some kind of magical 'performance engine'. Michael smiled to himself when he thought of how simple it had been, and how easy it would be for everyone to do this.

Love works, Michael thought to himself. He had always been cynical and skeptical of anything that spoke of 'love' outside of a romantic relationship. But now he was a solid convert. Just by taking on new values and exercising leadership, which really meant being a kinder and nicer person, Michael had effected change throughout his entire organization. People were kinder to each other, more creative, more joyful, and much, much more productive. Even when there seemed to be a 'cultural outlier', someone who had trouble sharing or connecting with others, the community had a way of healing that rift. Either the person left of their own volition, or they began to change to fit the warmth and connectedness of the group. A self-correcting system!

Perhaps the most surprising thing for Michael was the changed nature of his relationship with Armand. As Michael had become more present and caring, Armand had become more open and supportive.

Michael felt that Armand was beginning to see him as a confidant, someone he could turn to in challenging times. Armand had even begun to suggest that Michael would make a good replacement for him, and confided that he had brought the idea up with the Board of Directors. Michael couldn't help but to note the irony of this turn of events. He had gone from pariah to 'heir apparent' in 6 months!

Michael sat looking out his window. Not only was his organization performing much better, but his management life had become so much easier as well. Gone were the days of having to cajole and push and demand performance. Each of his direct reports had begun to take leadership roles that he never would have imagined, and they were all beginning to develop their own teams in the way Michael had tried to model. Although each had a different style, all of them approached leadership in a loving, caring and compassionate way, and each was experiencing the benefits of this new way of being.

Largely Michael's job had become one of listening, teaching and value setting. He now spent most of his time taking the pulse of the organization, creating a meaningful value system and communicating the larger purpose of their efforts. All within a loving, warm context. Michael laughed as he realized that he was being paid to simply be a good human being. Certainly his talent for organization and detail came into play, but this was now only a small part of his job. Most of his management life was now a wonderful web of relationships that fulfilled him as much as it did the shareholders. He was finally aware of what it meant to 'profit broadly'.

Michael shook his head to think that some companies had ethical issues so large they could bring down the organization. It was so unnecessary. Michael couldn't imagine anything like that happening in an organization where people truly cared about each other. Trashing the environment? Misleading shareholders? Stealing from one another? Unthinkable. Even the idea of talking badly about a co-worker had become unimaginable. Michael realized that this is what a healthy, integrated culture was all about: Shared values that respect everyone and everything connected to that culture. A true community.

In this sense Michael realized that he had re-defined profit to be something much larger than financial gain. He now saw profit as *maximizing love*, which included personal happiness, kindness to all, *and* monetary benefits. In fact, the very concept of love had changed in Michael's mind. In the past he had seen it as an emotional state, a bliss that one felt toward certain people. But now he saw that it represented something much greater, something with much more power.

Michael increasingly saw love as a force, a currency of the universe that flowed through all life. Love, to Michael, became the positive, giving energy that was the font of all creation. He saw that nothing lasting could be created without this energy. Nature was a perfect example. All of man's physical creations, if left untended, would return to nature within a couple hundred years. Buildings would be consumed by the natural life force that has existed on this planet for millennia. Michael realized that his life force, this 'creative constant' is love made physical. So in order for man to create anything lasting he must do so with love… otherwise it is but a mirage in the sands of time.

Michael thought of his family. This was something created out of love, and because its foundation was consistent with that force it was ever lasting, ever renewing. Certainly things would change, people would pass on, but the loving feeling that existed between family members was persistent. This is the power of family. Michael's experience over the past 6 months had given him a new appreciation for the potential of this powerful human system. With the love of family, anything can be created.

Michael reflected on how quickly his family life had changed for the better. Whereas in the recent past he had seen his family as a burden, something to be put on his to-do list, now he saw them as a source of energy. And as he shifted his mindset, so too did his experience with his loved ones shift. His children responded with affection and excitement when he came home. His wife smiled at him much more, and looked at him with the eyes of someone in love. Wasn't this how it was supposed to be? Sadly, Michael had spent his whole life believing that money would somehow buy this happiness…when in fact it was so much simpler than that. He had been consumed by the idea that he had to 'create' happiness, when in reality it was something that every human being was granted at birth. Happiness was the feeling that manifested when love was present. Nothing more and nothing less.

And wasn't this what he was trying to create at work? A family of individuals who worked together for mutual benefit? Michael paused. He realized right then that for thousands of years human beings have been forming groups for this very purpose: To experience the feeling of love, happiness and a sense of fulfillment that comes when people work with and for each other. Isn't this the unstated purpose of every group, society and country? This is why forgiveness is so important, because to forgive is to let go of the anger that separates us and get back to the business of loving each other. There is no other imperative more powerful than this human drive. All others are merely illusions of a fearful mind.

Michael once again looked around his office, watching his co-workers pass by his door on their way to helping each other succeed. He felt an intense compassion for these people. Every one of them was navigating this life the best they could, learning to connect and love the best they could. He wondered how many of them knew how close it was, how the love they were seeking was right inside their hearts. Michael marveled at the sheer potential of it all.

"If we only understood our own power," Michael said to himself.

If each person on the planet could learn to apply the loving energy that existed within their souls, then there would never be another war, no reason for hatred, and certainly no more fear. The physical universe held so much energetic potential that the very idea of 'lack' seemed silly. The challenge faced by the human race was to figure out a way to encourage the expression of this energy, and Michael was now convinced that this could only be accomplished through the leadership of average people living by the examples laid down by countless saints and sages.

When doubt crept in, as it often did, Michael reminded himself of what he had learned long ago about the power of ideas: One individual living a life of love, compassion and forgiveness can have the power of a thousand people expressing hate.

Michael smiled as it occurred to him. "Love is leverageable". Love creates, maintains and heals. It is the ultimate business resource: An unending flow of energy that has the potential to create unlimited positive outcomes. That's what he felt like he was doing at work, using his own potential to create successful outcomes for everyone and everything he knew. And it was working.

His Dad popped into his mind. What would Roy Benson have thought of all this? Michael knew that in his last days his father had seen in a flash everything Michael had spent weeks trying to understand. He knew his Dad would be proud, and it made him feel warm inside.

Smiling, Michael got up from his desk and looked around his office. His work life had taken on a new meaning, and he intended to live it to its full potential.

"Its *showtime*," he joked to himself as he walked out into the hall.

About the Author

K.C. Hildreth is a consultant and coach who teaches people and groups how to live fully into their potential. For 30 years K.C. has founded businesses, coached individuals, facilitated teams and advised leaders using a mix of science, psychology and spiritual concepts. Many of K.C.'s ideas and methods are drawn from his eclectic mix of self-exploration, deep educational training and real-world experience. K.C. lives with his wife in Los Angeles, CA and Park City, UT.

Made in the USA
Lexington, KY
30 January 2017